Albert Schweitzer

Albert Schweitzer

A Biography

NILS OLE OERMANN

OXFORD
UNIVERSITY PRESS

OXFORD
UNIVERSITY PRESS

Great Clarendon Street, Oxford, OX2 6DP,
United Kingdom

Oxford University Press is a department of the University of Oxford.
It furthers the University's objective of excellence in research, scholarship,
and education by publishing worldwide. Oxford is a registered trade mark of
Oxford University Press in the UK and in certain other countries

Published in the United States of America by Oxford University Press
198 Madison Avenue, New York, NY 10016, United States of America

British Library Cataloguing in Publication Data

Data available

Library of Congress Control Number: 2016941049

ISBN 978–0–19–878422–7

Printed in Great Britain by
Clays Ltd, St Ives plc

For Ole Jonas, Leo, and Carl Magnus

Contents

List of Plates

List of Plates

Abbreviations

AS–HB	Rhena Schweitzer Miller and Gustav Woytt (eds), *Albert Schweitzer–Helene Bresslau: Die Jahre vor Lambarene: Briefe 1902–1912* (Munich, 1992)
Barch	Bundesarchiv Berlin-Lichterfelde
BStU	Archive of the Federal Commissioner for the Records of the State Security Service of the former German Democratic Republic
GA	Albert Schweitzer Central Archive Gunsbach
GW	Albert Schweitzer, *Gesammelte Werke in fünf Bänden* (*Collected Works in Five Volumes*), ed. Rudolf Grabs (Munich, 1974)
HSB	Verena Mühlstein, *Helene Schweitzer Bresslau: Ein Leben für Lambarene* (*Helene Schweitzer Bresslau: A Life for Lambarene*) (Munich, 1998)
TPB	Albert Schweitzer, *Theologischer und philosophischer Briefwechsel 1900–1965* (*Theological and Philosophical Correspondence*), ed. Werner Zager in association with Erich Gräßer, assisted by Markus Aellig, Clemens Frey, Roland Wolf, and Dorothea Zager (Munich, 2006)

Timeline

14 Jan. 1875   Ludwig Philipp Albert Schweitzer born as the second of five children to the Pastor Louis Schweitzer and his wife Adele Schweitzer, née Schillinger, in Kaysersberg, Upper Alsace

1880–1885   Attends the village school in Gunsbach and the secondary school in Munster, Alsace

1883   First organ concert

1885–1893   Attends and graduates from the advanced secondary school in Mulhouse

1893   Studies theology and philosophy at the University of Strasbourg

1894–1895   Military service in Strasbourg

1896   Decides to 'serve others' after his thirtieth birthday

1898   First examination in theology

1898–1899   Spends time in Paris (studying the organ with Charles-Marie Widor, Isidore Philipp, and Marie Jaëll Trautmann) and Berlin (studies theology with Adolf von Harnack, among others)

1899   Awarded a doctoral degree in philosophy; his thesis is entitled *The Religious Philosophy of Kant from the Critique of Pure Reason to Religion within the Bounds of Mere Reason*

1899–1900   Trains as a pastor in Strasbourg

1900   Second theology examination and subsequent ordination. Awarded a doctoral degree (licentiate) in theology; his thesis is entitled *The Problem of the Last Supper Based on the Scientific Research of the Nineteenth Century*

1902   Habilitation degree and subsequent position of lecturer at the faculty of theology in Strasbourg; his habilitation thesis is entitled *The Secret of the Messiahship and Passion*

14 Jan. 1919	Birth of daughter Rhena
1920	The Treaty of Versailles makes Schweitzer a French citizen. First honorary doctorate from the University of Zurich in theology
1920–1923	Concert and lecture tours in Sweden and later throughout Europe
1921	Publication of *On the Edge of the Primeval Rainforest*
1923	Completes vol. i, *The Decay and Restoration of Civilisation* and vol ii, *Civilisation and Ethics*, of *Philosophy of Civilisation* and *Christianity and the Religions of the World*
April 1924	Writes memoirs *Memoirs of Childhood and Youth*
1924	Second departure for Lambarene, without Helene
1924–1927	Rebuilds hospital with funds procured during his travels
5 May 1925	Death of his father, Louis Schweitzer
27 Oct. 1926	Death of his father-in-law, Harry Bresslau
1925–1928	Publication of popular stories *More from the Primeval Forest* to fund the hospital
1927–1929	European concert and lecture tour to raise money for Lambarene
1928	Receives Goethe Prize of Frankfurt am Main. Honorary doctorate from the University of Prague in philosophy
1929	Appointed honorary member of the Prussian Academy of Sciences on the recommendation of Adolf von Harnack
1929–1931	Third stay in Lambarene. Helene forced to leave at Easter 1930 on grounds of ill health
1930	Declines chair at the theology faculty of the University of Leipzig. Publication of *The Mysticism of Paul the Apostle*
1931	Publication of his autobiography *Out of my Life and Thought*
1932	Honorary doctorates from the Universities of St Andrews in law, Oxford in theology, and

	Edinburgh in theology and music. Goethe Centennial Anniversary address in Frankfurt am Main.
Apr. 1933–Jan. 1934	Fourth stay in Lambarene
1934	Hibbert Lectures on philosophy of religion in Oxford and Edinburgh
Feb.–Aug. 1935	Fifth departure for Lambarene and return in the same year
1936	Recording of Bach's chorale preludes in Strasbourg
Feb. 1937–Jan. 1939	Sixth stay in Lambarene
1938	Publication of *African Stories*
Mid-1939–Oct. 1948	Seventh and longest stay in Lambarene. In August 1941 Helene travels to Lambarene via Angola and stays until 1946
1949	First and only trip to the USA, address in celebration of Goethe's 200th birthday on 8 July in Aspen, Colorado. Receives honorary doctorate from the University of Chicago in law
Oct. 1949–May 1951	Eighth stay in Lambarene, together with Helene until June 1950
1951	Building begins on the leprosy village *du village lumière* with the money raised during the trip through the USA
1951	Awarded Peace Prize of the German Book Trade
Dec. 1951–July 1952	Ninth stay in Lambarene
1952	Awarded Prince Karl Medal by the king of Sweden. Awarded the Paracelsus Medal for life's work as a doctor. Receives honorary doctorate from the University of Marburg in theology. Admitted into the Academy of Moral and Political Sciences in Paris
Dec. 1952– May 1954	Tenth stay in Lambarene
Oct. 1953	Awarded the 1952 Nobel Peace Prize in absentia. Received in person in 1954 and spoke on 'The Problem of Peace in the World Today'.

	Schweitzer uses prize money to complete construction of leprosy village
1954	Performs his last public Bach concert in Strasbourg
1955	Admitted into the civil class of the German order *Pour le Mérite.* Made honorary member of the American Academy of Arts and Sciences
Dec. 1954–July 1955	Eleventh stay in Lambarene, together with Helene
1955	Receives honorary doctorates from Cambridge and University of Capetown, both in law. Bestowed the Order of Merit by Queen Elizabeth II
Dec. 1955–July 1957	Twelfth stay in Lambarene; Helene departs May 1957
1 June 1957	Death of Helene Schweitzer Bresslau in Zurich
Dec. 1957	Thirteenth departure for Africa
April 1957	'Declaration of Conscience' broadcast on Radio Oslo
1958	Signs petition to the United Nations against nuclear testing along with 9,235 scientists
April 1958	Three speeches on the danger of nuclear testing, broadcast by Radio Oslo
1959	Last visit to Europe and, at the end of the year, fourteenth departure for Lambarene
1960	Receives honorary doctorate in medicine from the Humboldt University, East Germany
1961	Receives honorary doctorate in engineering from the Technical University Carolo Wilhelmina of Braunschweig
April 1963	Celebration of his golden jubilee in Africa
4 Sept. 1965	Albert Schweitzer dies in Lambarene of cardiac arrest. Buried next to his wife Helene

Introduction

'To show what really happened.' This is how Leopold von Ranke, the German historian (and a teacher of Albert Schweitzer's father-in-law) describes the task of a historian.[1] Whether historians can actually discover what really happened is doubtful. But they should try. Historians and, above all, biographers are neither investigative journalists nor hagiographers. Their task is at once more modest and more demanding: they must trace the course of a life and reveal the fundamental decisions, values, motivations, and role models of the individual whose life they are portraying. The life of Albert Schweitzer offers a challenge to the biographer in that he was a multifaceted personality who led a long life, and was romanticized by many. When in its 1960 Christmas issue the German magazine *Der Spiegel* declared that Schweitzer looked 'like a close relative of the dear Lord God himself',[2] the author was referring to more than his appearance. But who was Schweitzer behind this facade? Who was he 'really'? This is the question I will attempt to answer in this biography.

A new biography of Schweitzer is long overdue. Many of Schweitzer's private writings as well as new documents from the archives have been uncovered since the publication of earlier Schweitzer biographies, and they shed a new light on his life. My approach to the study of this complex personality will be guided by Albert Schweitzer's own 1905 biography of Johann Sebastian Bach, which received unanimous praise for its synthesis of his life, thought, and work. And it is these three aspects—life, thought, and work—that I will also use to explore the life of Albert Schweitzer.

Our first inclination might be to measure Schweitzer's actions by his own ethical standards, as his fame and influence were based on his moral credibility. Was Schweitzer able to live up to his own fundamental principle of 'Reverence for Life'? This question deserves an answer. And in answering it we must not hesitate to point out his shortcomings, not only in the service of truth but in the belief that a more nuanced portrait will do him more justice than any two-dimensional success story.

Schweitzer's life did not lead directly from the parsonage in Alsace to the University of Strasbourg, then on to his hospital in Lambarene, and end with the Nobel Peace Prize in Oslo. In every life there are twists and turns—and Schweitzer's life was no exception. These detours and setbacks, however, are barely discernible in Schweitzer's 1931 autobiography *Out of my Life and Thought*, where he presents his life as a massive, well-constructed edifice, the cornerstone of which was the principle of Reverence for Life, and the almost inevitable outcome of which was the Nobel Peace Prize. To date, biographers, journalists, and hagiographers have told and retold this story with relatively little critical modification. They have emphasized the modesty and moral authority of a universal genius, a man who travelled in a third-class railway compartment only because there was no longer a fourth-class one. Their Schweitzer was a man whose demeanour and charisma set him apart from other intellectual giants of his time. He was credited with 'the purposefulness of a master-builder in the planning of his own life and enormous strength in implementing decisions he had once made even if it took decades'.[3] Even Winston Churchill—otherwise not known for his exuberant praise—called him 'a genius of humanity'.[4] In its 1949 cover story *Time Magazine* labelled him 'one of the most extraordinary men of modern times'.[5] But not everything Schweitzer records in his autobiography corresponds with what is found in the archives and in his unpublished writings. And it is on the basis of these historical sources and more recent publications that I will attempt to sketch a more realistic picture of Albert Schweitzer.

Many authors writing about Albert Schweitzer have chosen to concentrate on one specific aspect of his life. There are books on Schweitzer as a physician, a theologian, and a philosopher.[6] In this book, as both a historian of Africa as well as a theologian, I will attempt to do justice to the whole man, to Schweitzer the theologian and the philosopher, the musician and the physician, the husband and the director of a hospital in tropical Africa, the author of popular bestsellers[7] as well as fundamental works on the philosophy of civilization. After all, it is how he applied his many talents, both intellectual and practical, in many different fields that makes Schweitzer such an exceptional figure. His theology determined his ethics, his time spent in Europe shaped his image of Africa, and his time in Africa finally altered him personally as well as his image of Europe.

It is difficult to say what is more remarkable in Schweitzer's life: the long periods of routine or his ability suddenly to change course. Why does someone with three doctoral degrees suddenly go to the depths of the jungle to build a hospital on stilts with a roof of corrugated iron? Without much fuss, Schweitzer repearedly came to surprising decisions: as a 30-year-old with a postdoctoral habilitation degree, he enrolled as a first-year student in medicine; as a theologian, he became a much sought-after expert on Goethe; his theological history of dogma was followed by a celebrated biography of Bach; and, as a New Testament scholar, Schweitzer became a philosopher of civilization; the accomplished organist became a master organ-builder; as a father and husband, he conducted a not entirely unproblematic long-distance relationship with his wife and daughter over several decades and two continents; and, finally, as a kindly doctor in an obscure African village, he travelled the world to meet the great and powerful.

Many questions about Schweitzer remain unanswered. How did his hospital, being but one among many hundreds of hospitals built in tropical African after the Second World War, become known around the world? How did his philosophy of civilization fit into the thought of his time? How did his study of medicine and science influence his thinking? Schweitzer wrote several tens of thousands of letters[8] and corresponded with leading politicians, intellectuals, and dignitaries of his time—from Einstein to Khrushchev to John F. Kennedy—but were his actions a result of political and strategic calculation? Was he in the end perhaps 'only' a man skilled at self-promotion, someone who was best at selling himself and his work? In 1960 *Der Spiegel* asked whether he was really 'a retiring and humble man' or a celebrity with a beard.[9]

Albert Schweitzer as a *homo politicus* has been largely overlooked. Little of his remarkable political correspondence—he wrote innumerable letters to public figures in both Europe and the United States during the Second World War and the cold war—has been researched and analysed, and a great amount still remains unpublished. At times these letters were openly critical of American policy on nuclear armament and the Vietnam War. They were interpreted as supporting the German Democratic Republic, and he was accused of being too close to communism. But Schweitzer never let himself be harnessed to a particular cause. He read his daily newspaper in a remote African jungle and set a high store by his political neutrality. He accepted both an honorary doctorate from the University of Chicago and one from the Humboldt University in East Berlin.

A comprehensive scholarly biography of Albert Schweitzer has yet to be written. This book endeavours to fill this gap. Yet it will ultimately be up to the reader to evaluate Albert Schweitzer's life and work in its entirety.

1

A Sense of Devotion

From the Parsonage to Theology (1875–1903)

A Pastor's Son in Alsace

In his speech introducing the winner of the Nobel Peace Prize in 1952, Gunnar Jahn, the chairman of the Nobel Committee, spoke extensively about the laureate's childhood and youth, believing that these moments 'distinguish his entire life and work'.[1] Jahn did not only refer to the origins of Albert Schweitzer's love of music, theology, medicine, or even Africa. He believed that Schweitzer's character and his passionate search for truth and knowledge through experience were products of his early years. In order to understand Albert Schweitzer, it will therefore be necessary to begin by examining his family as well as his childhood home, his *heimat*. He may have spent the greatest part of his life far from Europe, yet he always remained close to his Alsatian roots.

Ludwig Philipp Albert Schweitzer was born in Alsace on 14 January 1875 as the son of Louis and Adele (née Schillinger) Schweitzer. His father was pastor of the Lutheran community in Kaysersberg. The paternal side of Schweitzer's family had brought forth many schoolmasters and pastors, while on his mother's side it was the pastors who predominated. The newborn baby was christened Albert in memory of his mother's brother, who had died in 1872. Like Schweitzer in years to come, his uncle had been a curate at the church of St Nicholas in Strasbourg. At this time, Alsace, together with the neighbouring region of Lorraine, was part of the German Reich and a pawn in the growing conflict with France. After the Franco-Prussian War of 1870–1, this region fell to the Reich and would remain part of Germany until after the First World War. In July 1875, shortly after the birth of his son, Louis Schweitzer accepted the post of pastor to the Lutheran diaspora in Gunsbach in the Munster Valley, where he would remain until his death in 1925. Although Schweitzer was born in nearby Kaysersberg, his childhood memories are primarily of Gunsbach and later of his time as a student at Strasbourg. Yet he remained above all one thing: a native of Alsace. Both Germans and French celebrate this famous Alsatian as one of their own. When he was awarded the Nobel Peace Prize, both countries laid claim to their famous son: 'As the 'German scholar' was awarded the Nobel Peace Prize in 1952, France, which had interned him during the First World War, protested in Stockholm [Oslo] that Schweitzer was French. The doctor himself said on the subject: *homo sum* (I am a man).'[2]

Under international law Schweitzer was born a citizen of the German Reich and so was in possession of a German passport. Yet the 1920 Treaty of Versailles made him, as an Alsatian, a French citizen. But did he consider himself to be German or French? What was the political atmosphere in his father's parsonage? Schweitzer, like so many Alsatians and Lorrainians, was born a German 'by chance'.[3] Though his family was considered Francophile, he was not raised in a patriotic 'spirit of nationalism'. After the Franco-Prussian War, the majority of the Schweitzer family was 'politically oriented towards Paris',[4] and the family was unanimous in speaking out against the German annexation of Alsace in 1871. Louis Schweitzer's two brothers, Auguste and Charles (the latter Jean-Paul Sartre's grandfather), even moved to Paris. Louis Schweitzer, who remained with his family in Alsace, was said to have a 'rather chilly' relationship towards the new German immigrants.[5] As with many Alsatians, language was always an important political factor. Letters among Schweitzer's family members were written in French, while the family spoke the typical Alsatian German dialect, which Schweitzer, with his fairly high, almost singing voice, would retain even in Africa. Though Schweitzer was brought up with both languages, he considered German to be his mother tongue.[6] At school and university he was taught in German.

At his birth, however, it was far from certain that Schweitzer would live to attend the local primary school. Schweitzer, who would one day be grateful for his robust health, was born sickly and underweight.

Village talk had it that 'the wee lad will be the new pastor's first funeral'.[7] Yet, against all expectations, Schweitzer quickly gained strength. And indeed it was his physical strength that was to introduce him to the nature of ethical conflict. Schweitzer later recalled in his *Memoirs of Childhood and Youth* how, after he had beaten a schoolmate in a wrestling match, the boy complained: 'Yes, if I got to have broth twice a week, as you do, I would be as strong as you are!' This criticism of the advantages of his social rank was felt deeply by the young Schweitzer: 'The broth became nauseous to me; whenever I saw it steaming on the table, I could hear Gregor Nitschelm's voice.'[8] It especially bothered Schweitzer that his schoolfellows thought he was a spoiled child of the local gentry.[9] He wanted to be like the other children, an aspiration that was to create further moral dilemmas. Schweitzer later recalled an occasion when he and a friend were building slingshots to shoot at birds in the hills near Gunsbach. But, when the 8-year-old was out with his friends, the bells of the village church began to ring:

> I shooed the birds away, so that they flew where they were safe from my companion's catapult, and then I fled home. And ever since then, when the Passiontide bells ring out to the leafless trees and the sunshine, I reflect with a rush of grateful emotion how on that day their music drove deep into my heart the commandment: 'Thou shalt not kill.'[10]

These are the first expressions of what Schweitzer would later formulate as the principle of 'Reverence for Life'. We also see a love for animals that would later lead Schweitzer to keep pets and tamed wild animals in Lambarene as well as to avoid harming other creatures, such that he would be mocked as a 'saviour of worms' and would not only tolerate but encourage the daily trail of ants on his desk in Africa by feeding them a sugary syrup.

Music was also a crucial factor shaping Schweitzer's youth. His grandfather Johann Jakob Schillinger had been a well-known organ-builder, and three of his uncles were organists. It was, therefore, only natural for Albert at the age of 5 to be taught by his father to play on a piano his grandfather had built. By the age of 8 he was introduced to the organ, and by 9 he was standing in for the Gunsbach organist during church services.[11] His music teacher was the master organist Eugen Münch, who had left the Academy of Music in Berlin to take up a position at St Stephen's church in Mulhouse. He was so satisfied with his student's progress that after only one year of lessons the 16-year-old Albert Schweitzer was again able to substitute for his teacher as an organist at church services. What appeared to be the ability of a naturally gifted musician was in fact the result of hard work, and Schweitzer faced many setbacks. In the early stages of his training, Eugen Münch judged Albert's recital of set pieces as wooden: 'If a boy has no feeling, I certainly cannot give him any.'[12] It was this harsh and premature judgement, offered after Schweitzer had played a Mozart sonata he had not practised carefully enough, that spurred him on to do better in his next lesson. He was able to change his teacher's mind by mastering Felix Mendelssohn Bartholdy's 'Song without Words' in E major:

> My teacher said little, but putting his hands firmly on my shoulders, he moved me from the piano and himself played for me 'Song without Words', which was new to me. Next I was given a piece of music by Beethoven, and a few lessons later I was found worthy to begin with Bach. Then after a few more lessons I was told that after my confirmation I should be allowed to have lessons on the big and beautiful organ in St Stephen's. Thus a long cherished and hidden dream came to fulfilment.[13]

Schweitzer's teacher knew how to motivate young people, and this episode taught Schweitzer that motivation, while not sufficient in itself, is nevertheless essential if a person is to succeed. The extent of Schweitzer's regard for Münch can be seen in his dedication of his first publication to him.[14] It was also Münch who inspired his lifelong love of Bach, a love that would cause him to waver in deciding whether to pursue a career in music or in theology. Although he eventually chose theology, Schweitzer remained devoted to the organ and in 1893 went on to study with the renowned master organist Charles-Marie Widor in Paris.

It was not only Schweitzer's love of the organ, but also the roots of his liberal theology that stemmed from his home in the Gunsbach parsonage. His father, Louis Schweitzer, far from being a typical country clergyman with a modest education and little training in music, had studied theology in Strasbourg, and his grandfather, Johann Jakob Schillinger, had been an advocate of the ideals of the

Enlightenment.[15] The theological liberalism in his parents' Lutheran parsonage was indebted to rationalism and shaped Schweitzer both theologically and culturally. Even as a young boy he asked questions about the biblical stories that were taught in Sunday school. How, asked the 8-year-old boy, was it possible that Jesus' parents were considered poor when the magi had given them such generous gifts? And why did not the shepherds who had witnessed the saviour's birth become his first disciples? Questions such as these might have been discouraged by many pastors, but not by Louis Schweitzer. Albert was always encouraged to ask questions, something he would do his life long. He learned to find the courage to persist in asking apparently trivial questions, knowing that he might have to live with uncomfortable answers. Following a rainy summer, Albert observed that, although it had been raining for nearly forty days, there were no signs of a biblical flood in Gunsbach. His father explained to the little 7-year-old rationalist that in Noah's time the drops of rain were much larger, like 'buckets'. This made sense to Albert. When his teacher told the story of Noah and the flood and neglected to mention the size of the raindrops, he called out: 'Teacher [...] you must tell the story correctly. [...] You must say that in those days it didn't rain in drops, but it poured in buckets.'[16]

Schweitzer's long-standing scepticism about 'indisputable' ecclesiastical teachings and dogmas surely had its origin in his father's enlightened parsonage, where he was encouraged to be critical. This was anything but the normal state of affairs, as Schweitzer's memory of his confirmation class shows:

> On one point—on that I was quite clear—my ideas differed from his in spite of all the respect I showed him. He wanted to make us understand that in submission to faith all reasoning must be silenced. But I was convinced—and I am so still—that the fundamental principles of Christianity have to be proved true by reasoning, and by no other method.[17]

Here we also see the groundwork being laid for Schweitzer's later interest in the historical Jesus. Schweitzer would recall these two sides to his young self. On the one hand, he described himself as 'given to daydreaming',[18] an introverted and obsessive reader, and someone with an advanced ethical sense for his age. This sensitivity is highlighted by the episode with the bird hunt. On the other hand, Schweitzer recognized in himself a side that does not easily fit into the picture of the universal genius or of the kindly and patient doctor in the jungle. In his autobiography he admitted that, despite his natural reserve, he was subject to fits of explosive anger, a trait he believed he had inherited from his mother. This would account for the numerous fights he had with other boys. This impulsive behaviour outlasted his childhood and was to burden him all his life. He recollected a game of cards with his sister:

> When I was nine or ten years old I struck my sister Adela, because she was a very slack opponent in a game and through her indifference let me win a very easy victory. From that time onward I began to feel anxious about my passion for play, and gradually gave up all games. [...] I have had to struggle very hard against this passionate temper.[19]

From his time at St Thomas College in Strasbourg, there are also accounts from those who remember Schweitzer's loud outbursts.[20] And in Lambarene he could become ill-tempered when work did not go according to plan. In a personal interview for this biography, Claus Jacobi, editor of the German magazine *Der Spiegel*, confirmed the impression of other visitors that Schweitzer was firm and at times overbearing when he was dissatisfied with his African workers. Evidently Schweitzer was aware of this trait early in his life and tried to overcome it throughout his life. He was more or less successful. Occasionally he slapped the face of one of his African employees in Lambarene, but there is no record of more serious physical violence. The closing lines of Schweitzer's autobiography from the Sermon on the Mount—'Blessed are the meek'—should therefore be seen in the light of this character trait. He could be meek and mild, but evidently he could also be the opposite.

Schooling and Early Years

Schweitzer started school in Gunsbach in 1880. Learning to read and write was far from easy for him,[21] as he was never one to sit around indoors, and he wanted to be one of the village boys and be accepted by them. When, in an attempt not to stand out, he refused to wear gloves and leather shoes instead of the mittens and wooden clogs the poorer children wore, his father boxed his ears. When he refused to wear a new overcoat for fear that his friends should think him conceited, his father even locked him in the cellar.[22] Albert's rebellion was unsuccessful. He conformed to his parents' expectations and ate the despised broth while trying to fit in with his village friends, although only to the extent he could justify to himself—as on the bird hunt that morning.

Schweitzer had a high degree of empathy. At a wedding ceremony performed by his father,[23] he saw a young disabled woman. Schweitzer asked whether she was the bride. His question was met with a pitying smile, for only a child would think a disabled girl could be the bride. After this incident Albert vowed to marry the girl, if only because the world did not take her seriously and overlooked her prodearing qualities. What at first sounded like a child's quixotic pronouncement had a deeper source in young Albert. The desire to be different from others, to do and to change things, would be a driving force behind much of Schweitzer's actions. His reason for wanting to marry this young woman was not because she was disabled but because she had been rejected as a 'cripple', and in a church of all places.

Yet Albert Schweitzer was not always courageous as a schoolboy. In his autobiography he tells a story about a Jewish cattle-trader named Mausche, who came from the neighbouring village. The boys in Gunsbach had it in for him, simply because there were no Jews in their own village. One day, when Mausche was crossing the river with his donkey cart, he was followed by a crowd of hollering children, as was often the case. Schweitzer joined in and even admired those 'daring' boys who folded their shirts and jackets to look like a pig's ears and waved them directly in front of Mausche's face. Still, Schweitzer was able to observe and critically to assess what was happening:

In this way, we followed him out of the village as far as the bridge, but Mausche, with his freckles and his grey beard, drove on as unperturbed as his donkey, except that he several times turned round and looked at us with an embarrassed but good-natured smile. This smile overpowered me. From Mausche it was that I first learnt what it means to keep silent under persecution, and he thus gave me a most valuable lesson. [...] He had the reputation of being a usurer and a property-jobber, but I never tried to find out whether this was true or not. For me he has always been just 'Mausche' with the tolerant smile, the smile which even today compels me to be patient when I should like to rage and storm.[24]

No matter whether Schweitzer had already recognized that this was wrong when he witnessed the scene or only later when writing his childhood memoirs; most adults would probably not have admitted that they had humiliated another person like this, while Schweitzer openly reports what he saw and learned from the experience. Schweitzer also stood out from the rest of his classmates in his appearance. In an early class portrait from his school in Gunsbach, we immediately see the boy with a serious look on his face, the only one wearing a starched white collar—the pastor's son once teased by the village boys as a spoiled child of the local gentry.[25]

In 1884 the 9-year-old was sent to a secondary school in nearby Munster. He was 'shy and reserved'—again a legacy from his mother—and would often giggle when he felt insecure, which earned him the nickname 'Isaac' (meaning 'he laughs' in Hebrew), as well as numerous entries in the class book.[26] After transferring to the grammar school in Mulhouse, he earned mediocre marks. His parents were able to afford this school only with the help of the grandfather's half-brother, Louis Schweitzer, who lived in Mulhouse. He and his wife Sophie were childless, and they offered to take Albert in free of charge. As principal of the primary school in Mulhouse, he also interceded on behalf of his great-nephew, who had unsatisfactory marks, to secure Albert a place at the grammar school.[27] Since the secondary school in Munster did not teach Latin, there were some problems for a village boy going on to study at a grammar school in the bigger city. Schweitzer needed to make up for this lack of knowledge, and his early marks sowed doubt as to whether the money put into sending him to school had been altogether wisely spent. It is, of course, said of some great thinkers and politicians, such as Albert Einstein or Winston Churchill, that they did not do well in school, letting their later achievements shine all the brighter and their teachers appear all the more ignorant. However, in the case of Schweitzer, who always had difficulties coping with the regular workload at secondary school, it is slightly more complicated. Throughout his educational career, Schweitzer was motivated to study only subjects that interested him—such as history or later at university any topic related to the study of the historical Jesus. His performance in required subjects—whether his examination in Hebrew, the examinations for his ordination as a Lutheran pastor, or his doctoral examinations—all left as much to be desired as his schoolwork had. In other words, he was far from being a model student. He was simply not suited to learning the set curriculum. Aside from a 'quite good' grade in history, he left school on 18 June 1893 with an 'otherwise very mediocre leaving certificate'.[28]

Under the strict eye of his great-uncle, Schweitzer struggled with his schoolwork. Later he would conceal his difficulties by telling amusing anecdotes from his time at school. For example, he recalled how on the day of the final oral examination the candidates were expected to wear formal dress when meeting the school commissioner of Strasbourg, Dr Albrecht. While in possession of an old frock coat, Schweitzer was forced to borrow the trousers from his portly great-uncle. In order for the construction somehow to hold up, Schweitzer had to lengthen the braces with his shoelaces, which still left a generous gap between waistband and waistcoat, much to the amusement of those present—with the exception of the examiner Dr Albrecht. While Schweitzer's translation of Homer from the Greek was not impressive, he nevertheless did well in history by giving a thorough account of the differences between Greek and Roman forms of colonization.

In the light of the high number of students leaving German grammar schools after failing their final examinations, it is not unlikely that, had circumstances been less opportune, Schweitzer would never have passed his final examinations and been awarded his leaving certificate. A fear of failure must have been a steady companion for the schoolboy. In fact, his early marks were so bad that the headmaster even suggested Albert be taken out of school.[29] The turning point came in the fourth form when Schweitzer's class was given a new head teacher, Dr Wehmann, who immediately recognized that his poor academic performance was connected to his emotional inhibition and low self-esteem.[30] Only three months later Albert had already climbed several places in the class ranking. Dr Wehmann, a gifted and inspiring teacher, had managed to teach what 'no exhortations and no punishments can'. Throughout his university studies in Strasbourg, Schweitzer would call on Dr Wehmann regularly. After returning from Africa in 1919, he was met by the news that Wehmann, who had suffered from mental illness, had taken his own life. This was a

particularly harsh blow to Schweitzer, who was also psychologically
and physically unwell at the time.

In his last two years at school another teacher had a profound
influence on Schweitzer. Wilhelm Deecke, the school's headmaster
and teacher of ancient history, introduced him to Plato and ancient
philosophy. Schweitzer described him as 'a Stoic in modern dress'.[31]
And this was also how many people would describe Schweitzer when
it came to how he set and achieved his goals. During his time in
Mulhouse, Schweitzer felt he had learned 'a sense of duty'. What
separated Schweitzer from his teacher were their birthplaces and the
diverging mentalities of the Alsatian and the Hanseatic German.
'His somewhat stiff manner—he was a native of Lübeck—prevented
us at first from feeling at ease with him, but we soon got accustomed
to it.'[32]

Another experience from Schweitzer's youth left its mark on him.
His father's tales of far-off countries had awakened an enthusiasm in
him for missionary service, but it was on family visits to nearby
Colmar that this enthusiasm was focused on Africa. On the Champ
de Mars, Frédéric-Auguste Bartholdi, a local sculptor and the
designer of the Statue of Liberty, had created a monumental statue
in honour of Admiral Bruat in which the four continents were
depicted as figures in stone. It was the African sculpture that so
impressed Albert:

> It is a figure of Herculean proportions, but the face wears an expression
> of thoughtful sadness which I could not forget, and every time we went
> to Colmar I tried to find time to go and look at it. The countenance
> spoke to me of the misery of the Dark Continent, and even today
> I make a pilgrimage to it when I am in Colmar.[33]

The statue was destroyed in the Second World War, but the bust of
the African remains intact. As the German poet Hesse wrote, 'each
beginning bears a special magic,' and the visits to the 'sad Negro of
Colmar' were just such a beginning for Schweitzer. James Brabazon
describes Schweitzer's youth in Mulhouse as 'long, quiet years […]
undramatic but full of incident'.[34] Far away from Gunsbach, they
must have been dark years too for this shy boy fond of nature. Yet he
did not become embittered, but instead struggled, showing much
discipline, as he would again and again in his later life.[35]

One further important aspect of Schweitzer's mentality had its roots in his early years. Whether it was as a privileged child of the gentry and the son of the pastor in Gunsbach, as a schoolboy living with his relatives, or as a young and independent student of theology, Schweitzer felt a significant part of his motivation to work in Africa was due to his constant feeling of being both personally and materially indebted to others for his relatively carefree youth. While he did not go to Africa motivated by guilt alone, he did have the conviction that he had to return something of what seemed to him undeserved good fortune:

It struck me as incomprehensible that I should be allowed to lead such a happy life, while I saw so many people around me wrestle with care and suffering. Even at school I had felt stirred whenever I caught a glimpse of the miserable home surroundings of some of my school-fellows and compared them with the absolutely ideal conditions in which we children of the parsonage at Gunsbach lived. [...] Then one brilliant summer morning at Gunsbach, during the Whitsuntide holidays—it was in 1896—there came to me, as I awoke, the thought that I must not accept this happiness as a matter of course, but must give something in return for it. Proceeding to think the matter out at once with calm deliberation, while the birds were singing outside, I settled with myself before I got up that I would consider myself justified in living till I was thirty for science and art, in order to devote myself from that time forward to the direct service of humanity. Many a time already had I tried to settle what meaning lay hidden for me in the saying of Jesus, 'Whosoever would save his life shall lose it and whosoever shall lose his life for My sake and the Gospel's shall save it.' Now the answer was found. In addition to the outward, I now had inward happiness.[36]

Schweitzer did not consider the seven years he spent in Mulhouse to be part of this happiness, but, at least in retrospect, he would always describe his childhood as being generally 'happy'. His memories of Gunsbach always seem more light-hearted than those he had of Mulhouse. Meanwhile, as a young man Schweitzer increasingly felt that he needed to show his gratitude for having received so much that he did not deserve. This gratitude, he decided, was to be expressed by spending his life in serving humanity.

Schweitzer had a weakness for the newly fashionable sport of cycling, an activity that was to bring him closer to his future wife,

Helene Bresslau. For a schoolboy in Mulhouse a bike was an expensive purchase, but it also promised new freedom. Schweitzer earned the money by giving private lessons in mathematics.[37] Though he had little money himself, he bought a second bicycle for his younger brother Paul from his savings. 'Happiness is the only thing that multiplies when it is shared,' he would later write. Schweitzer may have been very frugal and worked hard for his money, but he was just as generous in spending it on others.

A Student of Theology, Philosophy, and Music

After Schweitzer had graduated from school, he used the time before beginning his studies in Strasbourg in the winter semester of 1893–4 for a journey devoted to music and culture. Although he was already a gifted organist, his uncle, a businessman in Paris, gave him the opportunity to receive individual instruction from the famous organist Charles-Marie Widor, who had taken over the organ course at the Conservatoire in Paris from César Franck in 1890. Schweiter's relationship with this teacher would grow steadily closer, ending only with Widor's death in 1937, and make Schweitzer one of the great organists and organ scholars of his time. Thanks to the instruction he received from Widor, Schweitzer was to advance from a talented organist to a celebrated interpreter of Bach's organ music. This was not only to be intellectually as well as musically a source of lifelong satisfaction; it also helped him finance his work in Africa.

Life in metropolitan Paris was a liberating experience for Schweitzer. In the late summer of 1893 his uncles Charles and Auguste—one a businessman, the other a teacher—introduced him to Parisian society. He was remembered for dancing all night. This is in keeping with a quote from Schweitzer when he was over 80 years old. Asked whether he disapproved of dancing, his pithy answer was: 'He's a fool who doesn't dance.'[38] From Lambarene, too, there are accounts of dances, which Schweitzer, though he did not take part in them himself, nevertheless gladly permitted.[39] Throughout his life Schweitzer was neither puritanical, nor a teetotaller. He was also not—as many believed—a vegetarian, although it is true that in Lambarene he preferred to eat fish, vegetables, and soya beans, while eating less and less meat as he grew older.[40]

The late summer of 1893 in Paris saw not only Schweitzer's first steps on the dance floor, but also his first closer contact with women. Since Schweitzer did not mention these encounters, much less relationships, in his memoirs, most of his biographers have depicted him as a modern asexual saint. In fact, from his student days it was evident that he had an effect on women. It is difficult to assess how far these relationships went, as, unlike those of many of his fellow students, they did not develop into open love affairs. In Paris, Schweitzer felt attracted especially to older women. In his autobiography, as was customary at the time, he only casually mentioned his frequent visits to his new acquaintance Adèle Herrenschmidt.[41] Whether his relationships with women such as the highly gifted musician Fanny Reinach, the countess Melanie de Pourtalès, or Adèle Herrenschmidt were of a wholly platonic character—those of a young man who admired these women and appreciated their advice—or whether, as suggested by James Brabazon, these relationships were occasionally of a romantic nature, must ultimately remain unanswered. In any case, these relationships left no lasting traces in his life.[42] The one exception came later. After a rather prolonged relationship, Helene Bresslau became Schweitzer's wife.

More important than his female acquaintances at this time was his relationship to Charles-Marie Widor. And this late summer of 1893 was to become an important one for Schweitzer, as the reserved and unsure schoolboy became a self-confident master student in the first discipline he was to take up—namely, music. It was from Widor—who would not tolerate mediocrity—that Schweitzer acquired his unwavering pursuit of excellence. Theology and philosophy, two further disciplines in which Schweitzer would also excel, were to follow.

Schweitzer began studying Protestant theology and philosophy at the Kaiser Wilhelm University of Strasbourg in late October 1893. The university was founded in 1872, a product of the nationalist politics of the times—Alsace-Lorraine had been annexed by Germany following the Franco-Prussian War—and as a result its faculty members were relatively young. In particular, the theology department with lecturers such as Karl Budde, Ernst Lucius, Emil Mayer, and Schweitzer's later mentor Heinrich Julius Holtzmann was less orthodox than many other faculties of theology in Germany. Before Schweitzer began attending lectures in philosophy and music theory along with the standard courses in theology, he spent his first semester learning Hebrew. This four-month course was a challenge for Schweitzer, who was not apt at learning languages; in fact, he was never able to achieve more than a reading knowledge of English. However, after 'just barely' passing his exams in Hebrew, instead of setting the language aside, he did the exact opposite: 'Later, spurred on again by the desire to master what did not come easily to me, I acquired a sound knowledge of that language.'[43] Early in his studies Schweitzer made the impression of being a determined and ambitious young man with a very wide range of talents. Soon he no longer felt challenged by his course in theology. Yet after only one semester he was forced to interrupt his studies.

On 1 April 1894 Schweitzer was enlisted to serve one year of compulsory military service in Strasbourg. Unlike most recruits, whose anecdotes about their service tend to revolve around the food and night marches, Schweitzer wrote in his memoirs that during a manœuvre in the area of Hochfelden in the autumn of 1894 he had used his free time to study for an examination in New Testament studies. Schweitzer's account of his time in the military was not exaggerated, even though a recruit with a New Testament in Greek stowed away in his backpack would surely have been a rarity. He recalled that 'the kindness of my captain—Krull by name—made it possible for me during routine operations to be at the university by eleven o'clock almost every day, and so to attend Windelband's lectures'.[44]

Following his military service, Schweitzer chose an unorthodox way to organize his studies. It had become clear that the subject he was most interested in was the life of Jesus, and he soon began concentrating on it, 'often to the neglect of my other subjects'.[45] He devoted himself more to personal interests than the university curriculum. Owing to the relatively unstructured curriculum of the theology degree, this approach worked well. Many other students chose a more systematic approach, working their way first through the exegetic subjects and arriving at philosophy and history only very late in their degree programme, but Schweitzer let himself be guided by his 'intuition' and chose his main areas of interest early on. In Jesus studies, his interest lay in the life of the historic Jesus and eschatology.

In philosophy, he was primarily interested in Kant's philosophy of religion; in Bach, it was the connection between music, theology, and personality; and in psychology, it was the psychiatric assessment of the life of Jesus. From this broad spectrum of subjects, Schweitzer always chose specific topics of general interest to his contemporaries but still left some scope for further work, allowing him to make his mark in academia. It might be mentioned here that his praise of the university should give present-day education policymakers food for thought: 'I was so grateful that the German university treats its students as adults and does not keep them on their toes by constantly examining them as is the case in other countries, but instead offers them opportunities for independent scientific work!'[46]

Studying theology, philosophy, and music theory—all in less than four years—must have involved hard work and efficient preparation. And the varying degrees of success he met with in his exams suggest that this was indeed the case. Moreover, it does not come as a surprise that he did not find the traditional university examinations easy, in contrast to researching and writing on topics he had chosen himself. All in all, Schweitzer worked extremely efficiently. An example is his choice of the Last Supper as a topic for his thesis, a subject he was familiar with from his first theology examination in the autumn of 1897. This saved him the trouble of searching for new literature.

As did all students at this time, Schweitzer wrote his final thesis in a mere eight weeks. The topic that had been assigned to him was 'Schleiermacher's Teaching on the Last Supper Compared with the View of It Found in the New Testament and the Reformers' Confession of Faith'.[47] This work, coupled with his earlier interest in historical Jesus studies, also served as the topic for his doctoral thesis.

Similarly, Schweitzer saw and made good use of these synergy effects in nearly all his final exam papers. On closer inspection, they have much more in common than might appear at first glance. A work on the reason for and meaning of Jesus' suffering, for example, is divided into two parts by Schweitzer—the first part to become his doctoral thesis, the second his postdoctoral habilitation thesis, which would qualify him for a professorship. The latter was also enriched by problems relating to the Last Supper, well known to him from his first examination in 1898. He took a similar approach in choosing a topic for his doctoral thesis in medicine thirteen years later. He used his knowledge of the historical Jesus as a basis to follow his interest in psychiatry, a burgeoning new field in medicine, in his doctoral thesis. *The Psychiatric Study of Jesus: An Account and Critique* (Tübingen, 1913) was immediately submitted for publication at the renowned theological publishers J. C. B. Mohr. All this is legitimate and helps to explain his productivity in both Strasbourg and Lambarene: efficiency paired with an eye for the right topic at the right time.

Kant and the Study of Philosophy

After his examinations in theology on 2 May 1898, Albert Schweitzer concentrated on writing the thesis for his doctoral degree in philosophy. His topic was the religious philosophy of Kant and had been suggested to him by his professor, Theobald Ziegler, on a rainy day during a walk they took together under Ziegler's umbrella. Schweitzer set himself the task of exploring the structure and genesis of Kant's philosophy of religion. It made for a complex undertaking, as Kant's philosophy of religion is difficult to integrate systematically into his broader thinking. In the summer of 1898 the young student was busy working on his study of Kant in Strasbourg, in his lodgings at Fischmarkt No. 36, and—although he was probably unaware of the fact at the time—in the very house that had been home to Johann Wolfgang Goethe over a hundred years before.[48] For the winter semester 1898–9 Schweitzer moved to Paris, to the rue de la Sorbonne No. 20, with the intention of putting his thoughts in writing in the shortest time possible. A task that would take many others years was completed by Schweitzer in six months, writing mostly at night, with barely any references to the secondary literature available in the university libraries of Paris.[49] This unorthodox approach shows again that Schweitzer had neither the depth nor the breadth required of a university philosopher. Rather, he took advantage of the time after his theology exam to live in Paris for a while, work on his philosophy thesis, and play the organ with a master of the art. Financially, this sojourn was made possible by a Goll scholarship, which had the sole condition that at the end of six years the recipient return to Strasbourg with a doctoral degree in theology. After less than ten months, in

March 1899, Schweitzer had finished his thesis in philosophy and had it published by J. C. B. Mohr in Tübingen under the title *The Religious Philosophy of Kant from the Critique of Pure Reason to Religion within the Bounds of Mere Reason*.

Schweitzer's ambition in this work was to trace the development of Kant's philosophy of religion exclusively in the light of his own writings. He aimed above all at disproving the supposed unity of Kant's concept of religion. Once again, Schweitzer's first impression proved trustworthy: Kant's concept of religion is indeed not of one piece, but had been changed repeatedly over the course of the philosopher's life. Schweitzer insisted that his thesis was none the worse for playing the organ with Charles-Marie Widor or the piano with Isidore Philippe, for practising new and experimental techniques in playing the piano with Marie Jaëll Trautmann, a famous pupil of Liszt, or for spending time on art and socializing, and certainly not for visiting his Parisian patronesses and his father's brothers.[50]

Biographers have praised Schweitzer's 325-page manuscript as a formidable philosophical work, one that is still 'highly valued'.[51] A closer inspection, however, prompts a more sober evaluation. Schweitzer's writing on Kant's philosophy of religion is both spirited and eloquent. His main criticism was that Kant's concept of religion remained essentially lifeless and thus fell short of his more substantial writings on reason and ethics. Schweitzer argued that in the end Kant's concept of religion led to an inconsistency within his own philosophy. He attempted to demonstrate that the contradictory premisses it contained made it impossible, even for Kant, to devise a coherent philosophy of religion that was both critical and ethically motivated.[52]

By identifying Kant's approaches towards the philosophy of religion, Schweitzer ultimately illustrated the opposition 'in the philosophy of religion of German Idealism and the deep moral religion of Kantian moral absolutism'.[53] Schweitzer was praised for his analysis of Kant's writing by Ernst Troeltsch. On the occasion of the hundredth anniversary of Kant's death, Troeltsch had composed a monumental study of Kant's philosophy of religion and noted in reference to Schweitzer's book—as Schweitzer himself would later recall with satisfaction—that, for him, Schweitzer's work was the last word on the

Kantian philosophy of religion. 'So be a little proud of your friend!' the proud student wrote to Helene Bresslau.[54]

What Schweitzer's thesis lacked in terms of methodology was a precise philosophical analysis of the concepts of religion and freedom in Kant's work. This would normally have required a thorough study of sources as well as a discussion of secondary works on the topic. The research that such a task would require, however, could hardly have been completed in a matter of months. As a result, Schweitzer postulated more in his thesis than he was able to support, and he made no secret of it:

> To investigate the literature on Kant's philosophy of religion in the Bibliothèque Nationale proved to be impractical on account of the cumbersome regulations of the reading room. I therefore resolved without further ado to write the thesis without troubling about the literature, and to see what results I could get by burying myself in the Kantian writings themselves.[55]

Schweitzer did see a problem in Kant's work that has often been noted—namely, that his critical philosophy of religion and ethics are little connected and are treated separately. The questions on resurrection and eternal life that are so central for Christian theology are ignored in Kant's *Critique of Pure Reason*. When Schweitzer talks of a lifeless philosophy of religion detached from any religious experience, what he means is that, while Kant recognizes the religious dimension of philosophical ethics, it is a major inconsistency that he is unable to bring this in line with the demands of a critical idealism and his own concept of freedom. This is because in Kantianism, strictly speaking, no form of Christian metaphysics has a contribution to make to a universal postulate of reason and moral law. Furthermore, Schweitzer was irritated by the fact that, for Kant, who explicitly claimed to be concerned with 'religious thinking', the postulate of immortality played no role at all.[56] Regarding Schweitzer's criticism, however, an academic philosopher would immediately ask whether the systematic inconsistencies identified in Kant's work by Schweitzer are in fact genuine philosophical problems or whether they are not instead the unsound criticism by a theologian of how Kant engages with religious questions. In the light of this, it is hardly surprising that, despite current interest in Schweitzer's concepts of life, environment, and nature, he has never been accepted by philosophers as one of their own.

This observation touches on a fundamental problem of Schweitzer's self-understanding. Although he was aware that he was not and had never wanted to be a philosopher in the classical sense, he did want his life to be appreciated, not only in terms of theology, but above all through his philosophy. This concern is what lies behind a letter he wrote to his East German biographer Rudolf Grabs, a man he held in high esteem, on his decision to accentuate Schweitzer as a philosopher of civilization:

> Dear Friend. And now as to the biography! It surpasses even the previous books. I have read it several times and was deeply moved, and I always have it within reach while working at my desk. The approach is the only right one: the philosophical perspective. This is hardly expressed in any of the other works on my person. With you, however, it is plausible and gives the portrayal an inner coherence.[57]

If Schweitzer was not a university philosopher, was he then a practical philosopher of civilization and an ethicist? Or was he, as a theologian, more a philosopher of religion, even though his first doctoral degree was in philosophy and not in theology? Schweitzer himself rendered such speculations null and void, for he avowed that his principle of Reverence for Life was not intended to be a grounded system of philosophy or ethics, but instead was meant as a practical philosophy for the common man. It was, in fact, a world view. In his correspondence with one of his students of theology, Fritz Buri, he openly acknowledged that over long periods he had seen himself as a mere 'amateur philosopher':

> You have psychoanalysed me and freed me of the complex I was only an amateur philosopher. I believed I had to think of myself as one, as I only knew what a border station was (I know well how one's heart beats at such passport control and customs stations), but never caught on to what a border situation was and never managed to understand what the cipher code being deciphered is about, nor about bracketing (wait, that's Husserl), nor about the existence one ought to know so much about, nor the illumination of existence, and the like, about categories of which one ought to know what belongs in which drawer. There I was in the border situation of the poor old black woman whom

the missionary, in the time when such people first came here, met weeping. And on asking why she despaired thus, she answered: 'Oh, I can just never become a Christian and never get to heaven because I am too old and stupid to learn reading and writing.' For the missionaries taught reading and writing so that the people might read the Bible. And in the examination preceding the baptism, they had to demonstrate their skills in reading and writing. I was like this old woman regarding philosophy, of whom I tell this true story, and we even have the same age. How the missionary guided her out of her border situation, I do not know. But I do know how you did it with me. A nice job you did. 'Not to worry,' you said, 'it's not the words that count but the thoughts! And should you never learn to read in the books of the existentialists, you may nevertheless (not disregarding, of course, the required modesty) count yourself among the philosophers as the existentialists do. For you too roam around border situations, and you too concern yourself with the illumination of existence and with the deciphering of cipher codes, only you do it subconsciously. And all the while, you silly fellow, you manage almost better than they do. As a sleepwalker you walk the roofs that they in daylight have trouble to slide along.' So I was caught in a micromania which you conjured and analysed me out of. [...] Forgive me for talking in such exuberant manner of the release your talk brought me. I am a little ecstatic that you have made my philosophy respectable once more.[58]

Schweitzer was obviously painfully aware that his doctoral thesis in philosophy would not make him a fully-fledged academic philosopher. After some months in Paris he must also have recognized that his study of Kant—unlike *The Quest of the Historical Jesus* or the biography of Bach that would follow—would never become a major work, at least among academics. It hardly comes as a surprise then that he would keep a lifelong critical distance from the practice of academic philosophy, and decades later would criticize it as removed from the world, a 'scholarly imitation of philosophy':

It still played, indeed, some sort of role in schools and universities, but it no longer had any message for the larger world. In spite of all its learning, it had become a stranger to the world, and the problems of life that occupied men and the age had no part in its activities. [...] From this impotence came the aversion to all generally intelligible philosophising, which is so characteristic of it. Popular philosophy was for it only an overview—prepared for the use of the masses, simplified, and thus inferior—of the findings of the individual sciences that it had sifted and put together to make a world view.[59]

Schweitzer felt academic philosophy lacked that fundamental something that can be measured only by whether its discussions and results are ultimately appreciated by the general public. Still, early on in life he decided to earn a doctorate in this same 'imitative discipline'. Throughout his life Schweitzer saw himself as a practical philosopher and would later call his Reverence for Life principle a 'world view' rather than an ethical theory, for in Lambarene he had affected a clean break with the speculative philosophy of his time in Paris and Berlin.

After hearing some lectures at the Sorbonne University in Paris and after handing in his hastily written thesis to his philosophy supervisors Theobald Ziegler and Wilhelm Windelband,[60] Schweitzer spent the summer of 1899 in Berlin, where the door to what was to become his philosophy of civilization first opened. With his usual efficiency he prepared himself for the defence of his thesis awaiting him in Strasbourg by reading 'the chief works of ancient and modern philosophy'. A doctorate in theology required comprehensive examinations covering the breadth of philosophy. It is hardly surprising that the results gained by a student of theology who had worked intensively on his thesis for barely a year would not live up to his professors' expectations. Despite weaknesses in the defence of his thesis, Schweitzer was awarded a doctoral degree in philosophy in July 1899.[61]

The summer of 1899, which he spent in Berlin, was crucial to many developments in Schweitzer's life beyond the boundaries of academic philosophy. Most of his time in the capital city was spent building an intellectual network. He was introduced to the renowned theologian Adolf von Harnack and attended his lectures. Harnack, like Schweitzer, sharply distinguished between the history of Jesus and the early Christians, on the one side, and the ecclesiastical history of dogma, on the other. It was Harnack who, thirty years later on 7 March 1929, would recommend that Schweitzer should be appointed an honorary member of the Prussian Academy of Sciences, one of the highest academic honours awarded in Germany at this time. The reasons in

favour of his membership were stated in the letter of appointment
signed by Harnack:

> We recommend *Schweitzer* not as a corresponding member, although
> this honour would also be due to him, but as an *honorary member*, in
> order to express that this versatile man is not being considered for
> the Academy in only one respect, but that he is of importance to
> both classes of the Academy and that the Academy is doing itself an
> honour in including this Alsatian scholar, a connoisseur of art, an artist,
> and a physician, who has none to match him, among its honorary
> members.[62]

Four months later Schweitzer commented on his appointment in a
letter to Max Planck:

> And now I belong to this Academy, which I [...] got to know so well
> then [visiting the Curtius house in 1899], as is hardly ever possible in
> youth to form such a close relationship. [...] That I may now read the
> session reports in the jungle is a delightful prospect.[63]

Schweitzer expressed the close connection he felt with Adolf von
Harnack in a letter of condolence to the theologian's family written
in 1930, only one year after Schweitzer's appointment to the Prussian
Academy of Sciences: 'Ever since 1899 when I came to Berlin to
attend his lectures, and where he was kind enough to invite me to
his home, I was devoted to him with love and admiration.'[64]

In the summer of 1899 Schweitzer attended a course of lectures
offered by Georg Simmel in Berlin and met prominent intellectuals of
his time, such as the theologians Otto Pfleiderer and Julius Kaftan as
well as the philosopher Friedrich Paulsen. As we have already seen,
Schweitzer felt he could always pinpoint the turning points in his life.
For his future work on the philosophy of civilization, this key moment
was found in a visit to the famous salon of Clara Curtius, the widow of
Ernst Curtius, a brilliant Hellenist scholar, archaeologist, and tutor of
Emperor Frederick II. This salon was frequented by the intellectual
elite of Berlin, including many members of the Prussian Academy of
Sciences. Schweitzer had been asked to join this circle on account of
his acquaintance with the stepson of Clara Curtius, the district superintendent of Colmar, Friedrich Curtius, who had recommended
him.[65] A central concept for his future philosophy of civilization was
brought up during one of these evenings in the summer of 1899:

Suddenly one of them—I forget which it was—came out with: 'Why, we are all of us just nothing but Epigoni!' It struck me like a flash of lightning, because it put into words what I myself felt. [...] When at the end of the [nineteenth] century men began to review every field of human activity in order to determine and evaluate their achievements, this was done with an optimism that was incomprehensible to me. Everywhere it was assumed that not only had we made progress in inventions and knowledge but also that in the intellectual and ethical spheres we lived and moved at a height we had never before achieved and from which we should never fall. My own impression was that in our mental and spiritual life we were not only below the level of past generations but were in many respects only living on their achievements. [...] And now—here was someone giving expression to what I myself had silently and half unconsciously objected to in our era! After that evening at Professor Curtius's house, I was always, along with my other work, inwardly occupied with another book, which I entitled *Wir Epigoni*, or 'We Inheritors of the Past'.[66]

As was later the case with his decision to study medicine and his choice of Lambarene as the place for his life's work, or with his moment of sudden understanding of the Reverence for Life during a boat ride on the Ogowe River, Schweitzer felt he had identified the central impulse for his future philosophy of civilization and ethics in this one casual remark in a conversation: 'Why, we are all of us just nothing but Epigoni.'[67] In Greek mythology, the term 'Epigoni'—literally, 'those born afterwards'—refers to the sons of the heroes in 'The Seven against Thebes'. Towards the end of the nineteenth century, many felt that they belonged to a generation of imitators, even freeloaders, living off the intellectual achievements of the past. The term Epigoni expresses then the oppressive feeling that since Greek antiquity—at the latest since the Renaissance—culture and philosophy had produced nothing of original value. It is an expression of intellectual and cultural decline. In his philosophy of civilization, Schweitzer attempted to show the Epigoni of his time the reasons for their decline and so help them once again become life-affirming and optimistic individuals. 'At the beginning of the summer of 1915, I awoke from a sort of stupor. Why only a criticism of civilisation? Why content myself with analysing ourselves as Epigoni? Why not go on to something constructive?'[68]

Schweitzer had a clear notion of what was to become the core of his concept of civilization:

> We may take the essential element in civilisation to be the ethical perfection of the individual as well as of society. But at the same time, every spiritual or intellectual and every material step forward has a significance for civilisation. The will to civilisation is then the universal will to progress which is conscious of the ethical as the highest value of all.[69]

Written in Lambarene, Schweitzer's critique of civilization 'We Inheritors of the Past' has its roots not in a university lecture hall but in a salon of intellectuals in Berlin. At the moment when he was preparing for an examination in the academic discipline of philosophy, Schweitzer stumbled on the key that would seal his final farewell to any form of academic philosophy. He was well aware that his doctoral degree in philosophy would not be followed by an academic career in philosophy.

Curate, Doctoral Student, and Outsider

At the turn of the century, Schweitzer made two decisions: one was of more personal importance, the other had academic consequences. On 31 November 1899 he gave up smoking, a habit he had indulged in frequently. He would not smoke again for the rest of his life.[70] Later in Lambarene he would be highly displeased by smoking on the hospital premises, and even his grown daughter Rhena only dared smoke a cigarette there in secret.[71] What seems like a trivial footnote in fact reveals of one of Schweitzer's personality traits. If, as Thomas Alva Edison noted, 'genius is one percent inspiration, ninety-nine percent perspiration',[72] then Schweitzer was indeed a perfect model of an exacting genius who worked hard for his success. Those who would like to depict him as a 'genius in the wilderness' to whom everything came easily cannot do justice to his personality.[73] Schweitzer approached his day's work—which often lasted well into the night—with visionary precision in his choice of topics paired with a realistic notion of what was manageable.

This combination led to the second of his significant decisions. Following his interlude in Paris, Schweitzer decided to give up philosophy in favour of theology. He did not, however, give up philosophizing, something he would continue to do all his life, but only the option of pursuing an academic career in philosophy. Instead, he chose a more conventional career path in theology, combining a doctoral degree in theology with practical training as a pastor. The Goll scholarship that he had secured before studying philosophy allowed him to follow his academic interests as a doctoral candidate at the University of Strasbourg for the coming years. At the same time he fulfilled his regular responsibilities as a curate, as most theologians do after their first theology examination, albeit usually full-time. Schweitzer held the usual services and taught the confirmation classes at St Nicholas in Strasbourg while continuing his studies in theology. Once again, Schweitzer organized his life so that he could work both intensively and efficiently.

Schweitzer remained loyal to the University of Strasbourg both as a doctoral student and later as a student of medicine. The town was familiar to him, and it allowed him to combine his many activities. As a lecturer he remained principal of the College of St Thomas of Strasbourg, a college for students of theology, and continued to live there as a student of medicine, in close vicinity to the medical faculty and only a stone's throw away from his church, St Nicholas. Thanks to his robust health, Schweitzer could get by with very little sleep, even in his old age, and four to six hours usually sufficed. In order to stay awake during his long nights studying and reading in Strasbourg, he would place his feet in a tub of cold water under his desk.[74] He soberly commented on his study habits around the year 1900: 'This is how my life passed during the years that were decisive for my creative work. I worked much and hard, with unbroken concentration, but without haste.'[75]

His decision around 1899–1900 to become a pastor expressed his attachment to the Lutheran church, even though in future he would often criticize the church's positions on a number of issues and the theological teachings on which they were based. In St Nicholas Schweitzer chose one of the most liberal congregations in Strasbourg for his post as curate. Much connected him with the parish: his mother's brother and his namesake, Albert Schillinger, a Francophile and liberal Lutheran pastor, had preached there during the tumultuous years of the Franco-Prussian War of 1870–1. One of Schweitzer's mentors at St Nicholas was Pastor Gerold, an old friend of Schillinger's, a fact that enormously simplified the organization of his practical training as a pastor. He considered having these two pastors overseeing his training as a stroke of luck:

> Mr Knittel represented orthodoxy softened by pietism; Mr Gerold was a liberal. But they fulfilled the duties of their office together in a truly brotherly temper. Everything was carried out in a spirit of harmony. It was thus a really ideal work that went on in this unpretentious church which stood opposite St Thomas.[76]

Owing to his controversial views on the historical Jesus, the young theologian was never permitted to preach in St Thomas of Strasbourg, nor was he allowed to play the Silbermann organ in St Pierre's of Strasbourg,[77] and even in St Nicholas he was not wholly accepted. After hearing his sermons, some parishioners complained about the new curate. In his autobiography Schweitzer plays down this criticism, putting it down to the brevity of his sermons. But a future university lecturer of theology—and especially one as liberal as Albert Schweitzer—must have met resistance from some of the more orthodox and pietist in his congregation. Schweitzer persevered and, at least in terms of length, followed the advice of his mentor and family friend Gerold and preached for at least twenty minutes.[78]

As a curate, Schweitzer earned 100 German marks per month; food and board at the college were free of charge. In addition, he had a doctoral scholarship amounting to 1,200 German marks per annum, which permitted a comfortable if frugal life.

From 1902 onwards Schweitzer gave many concerts, especially in Germany and France but also throughout much of Europe. He counted Cosima Wagner among his friends. The queen of Romania, Carmen Sylva, read his work on Bach and invited him to visit. Yet in all these years his home remained in Alsace, where he continued to perform his pastoral duties at St Nicholas even while he was a university lecturer or a student of medicine.

Unlike his practical training as a pastor, Schweitzer's second theology examination did not go smoothly, and he almost failed this more practical exam, which would have been rather embarrassing for a prospective holder of a doctorate in theology. Owing to the work on his thesis in theology, also to be defended in that year of 1900, Schweitzer had evidently failed to prepare sufficiently for the practical theological subjects that drew heavily on everyday church life. The situation threatened to escalate when Schweitzer was unable to name Karl Johann Philipp Spitta as the composer of the famous hymn *Psalter and Harp* and, to make matters worse, attempted to defend his ignorance by claiming the song was 'too insignificant'.[79] Unfortunately, this unflattering judgement was given in the presence of Spitta's son, Professor Friedrich Spitta, who held the professorship for New Testament and Practical Theology in Strasbourg and was on the examination committee. That Schweitzer passed his second exam despite this faux pas was chiefly thanks to the examiner Pastor Will, whom he had impressed in the subject History of Dogma and who interceded on his behalf. In 1900 he was also able to complete his thesis in theology.

What kind of theologian was Albert Schweitzer, who as a young man and against the odds had managed to submit a pioneering work on the historical Jesus? While many academic theologians still read Albert Schweitzer in questions of eschatology—the teaching of the last things and the end of all time—he knew that his eschatological interpretation of the life and death of Jesus was not something that would inspire Christians and fill church pews. While he was writing his thesis, his father once asked him what he was working on, and Schweitzer replied that he was writing 'a work on eschatology'. The sombre reply of his father was: 'My son, I pity you. Nobody will ever understand a word of your work.'[80] Yet the problem was not that he would not be understood; on the contrary. But it was not Schweitzer's writings on eschatology that would have the greatest impact on theology; it was his theological and historical work on a question that had intrigued New Testament Studies for more than a hundred years: who was the historical Jesus of Nazareth?

In *The Quest of the Historical Jesus: A Critical Study of its Progress from Reimarus to Wrede*, published in 1906, Schweitzer produced a comprehensive and detailed survey of the scholarship on this subject, and one that was also very well written. The explosive force of this treatise lay in its conclusion that Jesus was not the son of God, but a human being

who shared the prevailing Judaic ideas of the time about the end of
the world. When the kingdom of God was not forthcoming, Jesus
sacrificed himself in the imminent eschatological expectation that this
kingdom would soon follow his death. The disappointment of the
early Christians when this did not happen was overcome only by
Paul's transformation of the message of the kingdom of God: it is
in Christ, and so in a life in Christ, that, beyond the bounds of
time, the kingdom of God can be brought about in us. Schweitzer
called Paul's interpretation of the historic Jesus 'consequent eschatology' to express that Paul saw all of Jesus' pronouncements as well
as his entire life in terms of his expectations of the approaching
kingdom of God.[81]

Albert Schweitzer, and before him Johannes Weiß in his work
Jesus's Proclamation of the Kingdom of God (1892), saw himself as a New
Testament scholar working in a historical perspective. Their eschatological interpretation of the death of Jesus was at odds with the
historical and theological thinking of the liberal theology from which
they came.[82] This tension was mainly due to Schweitzer's emphasis on
the break rather than the continuity between this world and the next
and his portrayal of Jesus of Nazareth as a human being rather than
the son of God. Jesus may have seen himself as the latter, but, from
a historical perspective, argued Schweitzer, it was a man and not a
god who died. Schweitzer did not describe a kingdom of God
growing out of continuity with this world, but rather a 'kingdom
of God within ourselves', which can have an ethical import in this
world only through us and in us.[83] The historical life of Jesus only
has a meaning for us today as an ethical role model. Jesus wanted to
participate in God's kingdom by overcoming the world while being
a part of it. This was the motivation for Jesus and his actions.[84]
Schweitzer emphasized that, for Paul and the early Christians, their
imminent expectation of Christ's return could not, of course, be
kept up indefinitely. For his own times Paul concluded that humankind had to come to terms with this reality without resigning itself to
it. This approach would enable humankind to shape and change
the present.

For Schweitzer, as already for Adolf von Harnack, whose lectures
he had attended in Berlin, the Christology of the early church was
hardly more than a theological reworking of the Church Fathers,

where individual hopes of a direct relationship with God were projected onto Jesus. Schweitzer and Weiß argued the exact opposite: Jesus, as a representative of the Judaism of his day, is by no means close to the Christians of today, but is instead a distant figure. Lessening this distance by coping with the disappointed expectation of Christ's return was another instance of the 'crisis management' of the early church's theology.[85] The mystic Paul had been the first to achieve this in theological terms. Ethically, Schweitzer's conclusion is that in the longing for a just life it is not the historical Jesus who will provide guidance but only the Jesus who has been resurrected within humankind itself. It is above all the ethical spirit of Jesus that will encourage humanity to set out for new shores and change the world for the better. The members of his habilitation exam committee were apparently bothered by the fact that the resurrection of Jesus was seemingly no longer an event that could be historically understood. Schweitzer reworked his thesis as *The Quest of the Historical Jesus* and completed it shortly before setting off for Lambarene. It offers the reader a feeling for the magnitude of its criticism of the church and its theological force. The amended conclusion reads:

> The study of the Life of Jesus has had a curious history. It set out in quest of the historical Jesus, believing that when it had found Him it could bring Him straight into our time as a Teacher and Saviour. It loosed the bands by which He had been riveted for centuries to the stony rocks of ecclesiastical doctrine, and rejoiced to see life and movement coming into the figure once more, and the historical Jesus advancing, as it seemed, to meet it. But He does not stay; He passes by our time and returns to His own. What surprised and dismayed the theology of the last forty years was that, despite all forced and arbitrary interpretations, it could not keep Him in our time, but had to let Him go.[86] Fundamentally, our relationship with Jesus is of a mystic nature. No historical person can be placed into the present alive by means of historical contemplations or by considerations of their authoritative significance. Only by recognizing a common desire are we brought together and can we achieve a relationship with this historical person [...] and find ourselves in him. [...] Only in this way does Jesus create community amongst us.[87]

This fundamental questioning of established ecclesiastical teaching must have been immediately noticed by everyone who read Schweitzer's

habilitation thesis. In this light, it is hardly surprising that theologians
such as Helmut Groos or Martin Lönnebo accused him of losing the
personal God of Christianity in his theology and replacing it with Jesus
as an ethical role model. Lönnebo writes: 'The most difficult problem
in his theology lies in finally determining the object which is his
consolation.'[88] Groos adds:

> The God of Schweitzer's thinking is not the Christian God. Nor is he,
> on the other hand, the 'God of Philosophers', who requires a higher
> degree of trust in the metaphysical abilities of humankind than
> Schweitzer has. Tellingly, it is easier to say what Schweitzer's God is
> not rather than what he is: a very derived, barely defined torso-like
> thing which remains when one thinks it necessary to do without most
> traits of the traditional image of God without taking it to the logical
> conclusion and making a clean sweep of it.[89]

Though Schweitzer's position on the historical Jesus was not in fact
new, it was articulated more incisively and elegantly and was historically better argued than earlier formulations had been. Like the New
Testament scholar Johannes Weiß, Schweitzer also argued that Jesus
had not initially seen himself as the messiah. But, through the death of
Jesus, his ethics of love was extended to embrace all humanity, an
understanding Schweitzer would later express in his principle of
Reverence for Life. It is often overlooked that this principle involves
a highly controversial theological judgement regarding the historical
influence of Jesus. The impact and radical consequences of Schweitzer's research and work on the historical Jesus were seen by the editors
of the magazine *Der Spiegel* and somewhat exaggerated in their
reporting. The main tenor of their article on Schweitzer in the 1960
Christmas issue was that Schweitzer had been idealized by the public
and was consequently misunderstood on a theological, ethical, and
personal level:

> In Germany alone, his complete works have sold over a million copies.
> But Professor Yushi Uchimura of Tokyo University reports that in
> Japan, too, Albert Schweitzer is revered as 'the saint of the jungle'
> [...] This world-wide wafting of incense has been impregnated with just
> as extensive misunderstandings on the part of the public, especially of
> Schweitzer's disciples. [...] The theologian Albert Schweitzer counts as
> an exemplary Christian and has attacked more of the church's dogmas
> than any German theologian since Martin Luther.[90]

Although the article did not specify exactly which of the 'church's dogmas' Schweitzer had questioned, the observation is accurate. In Jesus of Nazareth Schweitzer saw a man of his time and not the all-knowing resurrected son of a fatherly God-figure in whose hands he had placed his death.

An outlook that makes do without God as a father figure and without Jesus as the messiah rising again on the third day did not remain without effect on Schweitzer's own piety. In a letter to Helene in the year 1906 he wrote:

> When I prayed last night, the prayer of the last days to gain strength for the coming winter, I asked myself again and again: What is God? Something infinite in which we rest! But it is not a personality; it becomes a personality only in us! The world spirit that in man comes to the consciousness of itself. Prayer: to feel the stirring of the highest being in us, to give ourselves to the divine within us and thus find peace. I wonder whether I can ever express this more clearly? [...] I am so happy to get out of all the theological clamour and to find myself alone, to think the thoughts I want to think—not as I would lecture on them, but as I want to live them quietly and simply [...] If I had to tell anybody what my religion consists of, I would not be able to do so...but you sense it, and you know it.[91]

God as an impersonal 'it', as a 'highest being' that is 'within us'— Schweitzer's at once authentic and apparently pantheistic piety here recalls Goethe's. Only the ethics that follows for Schweitzer is wholly different from that of the poet he regarded so highly: Schweitzer was not religious in an abstractly intellectual or cultural sense, but instead understood himself in a very elemental, even mystical, sense as pious. Nor was religion for him a 'feeling', as it was for the late Romantics. Instead, religion for Schweitzer was something deeply powerful that released a fundamental impulse for ethical action in all of humanity. In this sense, to be a follower of Jesus is something practical and liberating and not a dogmatic system the church should have monopoly over. Surprisingly, this position of Schweitzer never resulted in his being heavily criticized by his own church, in whose name he preached all his life and taught theology for many years.

Despite his theological proximity to the Unitarians, Christian free-thinkers, and the League for Free Christianity, Schweitzer always considered himself a member of the Lutheran church: 'It is important that the church keeps in her lap those who do not take part, a leaven that she cannot get rid of.'[92] At the same time he managed to engage prominent church leaders, such as Otto Dibelius, Heinrich Grüber, and Martin Niemöller, as patrons for Lambarene. Despite his controversial theological opinions, he never stood outside his church. Indeed, he was venerated as a modern-day saint in the United States in the 1950s, where he was pronounced 'the greatest soul in Christendom'.[93] However, when Melvin Arnold, editor of the Beacon Press, wrote just these words in the guest book in Lambarene, Schweitzer immediately crossed them out.

Theologians frequently accused Schweitzer of having reduced God to an ethical idea instead of understanding him as a personal presence.[94] Nevertheless, for a long time the church took the easier way of making Schweitzer into a modern-day saint while ignoring his theological position. Such prominent academic journals as *Zeitschrift für Evangelische Ethik* (*Journal for Protestant Ethics*) or *Evangelische Theologie* (*Protestant Theology*), for example, did not publish an obituary or appreciation of his ethics in 1965, the year of his death, nor in the following years. This is further evidence that Schweitzer had never become part of this academic theological community. Instead, he was all the more popular among German pastors in the 1960s, who would often begin their Sunday sermon with an anecdote about Schweitzer in Africa. One might be opposed to Schweitzer's interpretation of the life of Jesus, but who could object to a hospital in Africa?

Theologian or Mystic?

When reading Schweitzer's doctoral and habilitation theses in theology, one should bear in mind his role as an outsider. What induced him to examine the roots of the historical Last Supper for his thesis? And how does this topic relate to his later work on the historical Jesus? Early in his studies it could already be seen that his main interest was clearly not in theological systems and their doctrinal foundation. Instead, he detected two topics in the theological debates of his time that appeared to him as pressing as they seemed promising. Especially in his field of specialization, New Testament studies, the subject he always returned to was the quest for the historical Jesus. Schweitzer was little satisfied with its treatment by his theological teachers; indeed, he felt it had not been given the necessary priority.

In choosing his topic for both doctoral and habilitation theses, Schweitzer was led not only by personal curiosity—as his autobiography suggests—but also, as was often the case, by a strategic pragmatism. He could combine his two major academic theses into one work in two volumes. As a topic for his first theology examination in 1898, the board of examiners had assigned him the problem of the Last Supper in its historical dimensions, and especially in its treatment by the celebrated early nineteenth-century theologian Friedrich Schleiermacher. He then decided for his doctoral thesis as well as his habilitation thesis to write about the Last Supper in its theological and historical context with special consideration given to the historical Jesus, on the one hand, and the emergence of early Christianity, on the other. The origin of the Last Supper served as the bracket holding the two parts together. He could, therefore, use the research he had done for his undergraduate examination as preparatory material and combine it with the larger question—which was also closely related to the Last Supper—about the historical Jesus. This was a question that had interested him since the very beginning of his studies. Theological interpretations of the Last Supper range from a simple last meal with a symbolic importance for later Christians to the central sacrament of the Christian faith. Schweitzer compiled a short and concise study of the history of the problem in two parts. The first part, consisting of sixty-two pages, was narrowly focused on the Last Supper and was enough for him to be awarded a doctoral degree in theology on 21 July 1900. Only two years later, for the 109-page second part on *The Messiahship and the Secret of the Passion,* he was awarded his postdoctoral habilitation degree in theology.[95]

These texts may appear short to us, but their length was not uncommon in Schweitzer's time. However, the topic of his habilitation thesis was extremely ambitious and controversial. While he was awarded his doctorate without any open conflict with the faculty, the process leading to the habilitation degree proved to be problematic. Indeed, when he came to defend his habilitation thesis, Schweitzer would no longer be able to avoid publicly rejecting central theses advocated by his teacher Holtzmann, thus placing himself in territory far beyond the prevailing doctrine of the day. This took no small amount of courage. When, years later, a critic, obviously impressed by the historical synopsis in *The Quest of the Historical Jesus*, wrote that Schweitzer had produced a 'monstrous field of corpses in the great battle about the Life of Jesus, the sole survivor of which was Schweitzer', then one can understand why it was only a matter of time before his polarizing position was openly opposed.[96]

When writing on the problem of the Last Supper in his thesis in 1900, Schweitzer had already come to a conclusion that was problematic for the church: he asserted that the celebration of the Eucharist in early Christianity was not a symbolic representation of the atoning death of Jesus. Instead, he argued, this interpretation was added only in the Catholic sacrifice of the Mass and later in the Protestant Eucharist as a representation of the forgiveness of sins. Jesus' words at the Last Supper, therefore, had by no means the sacramental meaning that was later attributed to them. Indeed, they had been not sacred words of institution, nor a symbol of anything, but only a prayer of thanksgiving.[97] This, he continued, would explain why the Last Supper was celebrated by early Christians as *Eucharistia*, which in Greek means 'thanksgiving', and that it was celebrated with a view to the coming of the kingdom of God. However, the early Christians certainly did not see it as a sacrament, which it became only under the Church Fathers and as which it was later institutionalized and dogmatized within the church.

Yet Schweitzer was not content with a historical criticism of Eucharistic practice. In his habilitation thesis he placed the life of Jesus in its historical context and summarized over one hundred years of research on the historical Jesus. Methodologically, Schweitzer stood in the so-called Tübingen tradition of historical–critical biblical scholarship founded by the nineteenth-century theologian Ferdinand Christian Baur. Schweitzer held Baur in high esteem throughout his life and even visited his grave when he was 80 years old.[98] In his criticism of the ecclesiastical words of institution, Schweitzer solved the problem of the Last Supper by strictly rejecting its sacramental character while highlighting the mystical character of the celebration. It was misleading to canonize a symbolical memorial meal whose exegetical basis was far from certain—given that Jesus' command to 'do this in remembrance of me' (Luke 12:19 and 1 Corinthians 11:24–5) was itself unhistorical. According to Schweitzer, the Eucharist could be understood only as the expression of a longing for the imminent second coming of Jesus, a longing that remained even after his resurrection. The celebration of the meal became an analogy for the communion with Jesus, not the other way round. Jesus himself never instituted a sacramental meal. Instead, the Last Supper was a messianic meal, an expression of the expectation of the coming of the kingdom of God. As had David Friedrich Strauss before him, Schweitzer emphasized the eschatological character of the Last Supper and thus bridged the path to his habilitation thesis on the historical Jesus.

It will hardly come as a surprise that a candidate for habilitation who has claimed in his doctoral thesis that, of all the works written about the Last Supper, only *his* solution—and, perhaps, that of Schleiermacher—stands up to historical scrutiny should be prepared for opposition.[99] As a curate at St Nicholas, meanwhile, Schweitzer left unaltered the practice of the Eucharist that he had criticized as an academic scholar. He reasoned that he had wanted only to analyse a problem and that his eschatological understanding specifically led to a personal ethics in which each person might bring the hopes and wishes of his or her own time to the table of the Lord. In the celebration of the Eucharist, argued Schweitzer, the power of God and his kingdom arises in our hearts. Christian ethics means that God's love takes hold of an individual and that through their ethical actions this person partakes in this love. These arguments become theologically problematic when Schweitzer questions not only the character of the Last Supper as a sacred commemorative meal, but also the central historical element of this meal: the person of the risen Jesus of Nazareth.

Schweitzer's opponents were his equals in scholarly debate. The New Testament scholar William Wrede published *The Messianic Secret* at the same time as Schweitzer's essay and became his chief rival interpreter. Wrede, who generally showed a more thorough and critical understanding of the authenticity of the Gospel of Mark, maintained that the historical Jesus had not understood himself as the messiah in eschatological terms.[100] Yet why did Schweitzer, even though he was Holtzmann's student, choose him to supervise his habilitation thesis when their positions were completely at odds?[101] The material Schweitzer drew on to support his claims comes predominantly from Jesus' words in the Gospel of Matthew: namely, 'the Sermon on the Mount' (Matthew 5–7), 'the commissioning of the twelve apostles' (Matthew 10), and 'John the Baptist sends messengers to Jesus' (Matthew 11), as well as 'the Son of Man will judge the nations' (Matthew 25). Critics accused Schweitzer of a methodological error in failing to prove the historical validity of these passages by a detailed textual analysis. Instead, he took for granted that these passages in Matthew were authentic and attributed the words in them to Jesus—just as he did the words on his suffering and resurrection. Schweitzer simply claimed that all the material—especially as related by Matthew—that fell between the dates of Jesus' life and works identified in the Gospel of Mark was authentic. He thus subsumed the sources he used under his understanding of eschatological history, and not the other way around. His teacher Heinrich Julius Holtzmann summed up the massive criticism of Schweitzer's methods in the following terms:

> The summary way that Schweitzer ignores the findings of contemporary biblical criticism resulting from the labour of many consists of his treating the Matthean passages not only as faithfully preserved in their present form, but delivered at precisely the time suggested by Matthew's ordering of them and therefore indisputable in terms of their content and chronology. He then singles out precisely those passages that previous criticism had identified as anticipatory interpolations from later contexts.[102]

This criticism was justified and might have cost him his habilitation. Schweitzer must have been aware of his precarious situation, and it seems all the more surprising that only two votes were cast against him. It was Holtzmann of all people who strongly championed his appointment—though he was well aware of how far his student had distanced himself from him. When Schweitzer recalled the episode decades later in his autobiography, this conflict sounds much less severe. He smoothed things over, to say the least:

> I learned later that protests against my habilitation had been lodged by two members of the faculty. They expressed disapproval of my method of historical investigation and a fear that I should confuse the students with my views. They were impotent, however, in the face of the authority of Holtzmann, who took my part.[103]

In any case, the procedure was not without its difficulties. The fact that much later, in his autobiography, Schweitzer attacked Professor

Friedrich Spitta, familiar to him from his first theology examination, permits one at least to conjecture who the identity of one of his adversaries might be.[104] The habilitation degree brought Schweitzer no closer to a professorial chair. He never pursued a conventional career as an academic, as he wrote to Helene Bresslau.[105] On 1 March 1902 Schweitzer delivered his habilitation lecture at the Theological Faculty at Strasbourg on the logos doctrine in the Gospel of John.[106]

Schweitzer's eloquent work on the life of Jesus was published in 1906 under the title *From Reimarus to Wrede: A Study of the Quest of the Historical Jesus* and was reissued in an amended edition in 1913 as *The Quest of the Historical Jesus*. Whatever its methodological problems, it has the lasting merit of presenting a complex field of research spanning a century with great expertise and style and demonstrating that all scholars who had attempted to find a 'historically objective' core of the life of Jesus had essentially created an image of Jesus that is a product of their own religious context.[107] Jesus was made, as circumstances required, an ethicist of the Golden Rule, a social revolutionary, or an enlightened rationalist. Consequently, any attempt at a historical reconstruction of the life of Jesus must ultimately fail.

The title *The Quest of the Historical Jesus* itself suggests Schweitzer's tendency to portray his own work as he wanted it to be seen by others. No serious New Testament exegist in the prevailing liberal Protestant tradition at this point in time would have still seriously attempted to write a biography of Jesus. Instead, they announced—almost unanimously—that the existing sources were complicated and did not allow a biographical reconstruction of Jesus' life.[108] Furthermore, Schweitzer's model of 'consequent eschatology' depended on an extreme alternative between 'eschatological or non-eschatological', and, in the interest of his own position, he did not acknowledge mediation models such as those advanced by Ernst Troeltsch or Paul Wernle. Nor is Schweitzer's accusation that other scholars had projected the interests of their times always objective. Instead, it is systematically motivated, as his own reconstruction of the Annunciation and the life of Jesus demonstrates.

Schweitzer's counterposition to the historical search for Jesus of Nazareth consisted of endowing the term 'kingdom of God' with meaning for the present day by ethicizing and individualizing it.

If mysticism seeks the unity of God and man beyond history, then
Schweitzer was at his core a mystic and remained one throughout his
life. Crucial to Schweitzer's ethics is the elementary connection
between the life and work of Jesus and our human life:

> It is said that the ultimate knowledge, in which an individual recognizes
> that their own being is part of universal being, is of a mystical kind. This
> means that it is no longer realized in ordinary thought, but that it is
> somehow experienced. [...] Therefore thinking things through to the
> end leads somewhere and somehow to a mysticism that is alive and
> logically necessary for all human beings.[109]

This is how Schweitzer would later interpret Bach's music—as
something composed by a musical mystic and 'comforter', who conveyed to the soul by means of notes and harmonies that its true place is
beyond time. For Schweitzer, mysticism was a life-affirming tran-
scendence of the mundane world. It was not only accessible to a select
group of spiritually gifted or practised men and women; instead,
'ethical mysticism', as Schweitzer understood it, admitted all who
realize that the moral act lies at the core of life.[110] 'Naturally, a mystic
lives in every human being, but he is left to wither and be destroyed.'[111] Later, Schweitzer discovered this form of mysticism in
the writings of St Paul, who had added an ethical dimension to the
concept of the kingdom of God:

> Paul is a mystic. What is mysticism? We are always in presence of
> mysticism when we find a human being looking upon the division
> transcended between the worldly and other-worldly, temporal and
> eternal, and experiences himself while still among the worldly and
> temporal as belonging to the other-worldly and eternal.[112] [...] The
> fundamental thought of Pauline mysticism is thus: I am in Christ; in
> him I know myself as a being that is raised above this sensuous, sinful,
> and transient world and already belongs to the transfigured world.[113]

In the light of this understanding of mysticism, it was natural for
Schweitzer to follow his *The Quest of the Historical Jesus* with a book on
Paul as the first mystical interpreter of the life of Jesus. This book was
originally intended as a chapter in his book *Paul and his Interpreters:
A Critical History*, which was published in 1911 although the first draft
of it dates back as far as 1906. Though Schweitzer had lectured on this
topic, he only managed to return to the study of Pauline theology

in 1927, and the book was not finished until 1930. The reception of *The Mysticism of Paul the Apostle* was very positive. In it Schweitzer describes Paul as a Jew who, like Jesus, grew up in the Jewish community and lived in the expectation of the imminent coming of the kingdom of God. He portrayed Paul as someone influenced far more by Jewish apocalypticism than by Hellenism. For Schweitzer, the Hellenization of Christianity began after Paul, not with him.[114] Paul transferred Jesus' ethics of service into his time by means of the concept of the 'kingdom of God', which he severed from the expectation of the imminent coming by interpreting it ethically. Paul was thus the first theologian in Christianity who was able to reinterpret the frustrated expectations that the kingdom of God was at hand; it is in Christ and through a life in Christ that the kingdom of God may exist in us on an ethical plane beyond all time. One of Paul's main achievements was thus to make Christianity universalizable. Paul interpreted Christianity in the context of the religious horizon of Jesus' contemporaries, but went one crucial step further. The Christ described by Paul can become an ethical saviour beyond our own history by existing for all time as an ethical teacher within us—this, at least, was how Schweitzer saw it:

> Mysticism is not something foreign brought to the Gospel of Jesus. […] In Paul's doctrine of dying and rising again with Christ the words live again in which Jesus adjures His followers to suffer and die with Him, to save their lives by losing them with Him. […] In the same way the ethics of the Gospel of Jesus lives on in that of Paul.

The concept of the redemption of Christ means

> the ethics of the expectation of the Kingdom of God is transformed into an ethics of its preservation. It leaves behind its dependence on the eschatological expectation, and becomes bound up with the assurance that with Christ the fulfilment of the Kingdom has begun. In the only possible logical way, Paul rethinks the ethics of Jesus into the ethics of the Kingdom of God he brought, and in doing so it retains all the directness and force of the ethics of the Sermon of the Mount.[115]

The Mysticism of Paul the Apostle demonstrates even more than *The Quest of the Historical Jesus* how Schweitzer saw himself as theologian and ethicist. He was a person who understood the 'imitation of Christ' as

the practical implementation of Jesus' commandment of love. And it is
through this more practical rather than academic approach to ethics
that Jesus can be a Jew to Jews, a Greek to Greeks, and an African to
Africans. Schweitzer's book on Paul was a success. In 1930, the year of
its publication, the theological faculty of the University of Leipzig
offered Schweitzer a chair for New Testament Studies. The New
Testament scholar from Marburg, Rudolf Bultman, wrote to Schweitzer
concerning this option:

> You may well imagine that I am highly interested to hear how you
> decide on the matter of being offered a professorship in Leipzig! Should
> you accept the offer, then, admittedly, nothing can come of the plans of
> our eldest daughter [Antje, born in 1918, and at this point therefore
> barely 12 years old!] She is strongly impressed by your stories and has
> resolved to study medicine and then go to the Congo to help you.[116]

However, at this time the theological world was by no means open
to Albert Schweitzer, so that the publication of *From Reimarus to Wrede*
in 1906, which coincided with the beginning of his demanding studies
of medicine, appeared to be the end of his studies of theology. The
earliest reviews of his habilitation thesis expressed objections to the
book that were more forceful than Schweitzer's memoirs suggest. In
1902 the renowned *Theologische Rundschau*, for one, criticized in no
uncertain terms Schweitzer's work on the historical Jesus.[117] The
criticism went beyond the usual battles between rival schools of
thought. While Heinrich Weinel praised the work of Schweitzer's
teacher in Strasbourg, Heinrich Julius Holtzmann,[118] his verdict of
Schweitzer's habilitation thesis is only seemingly good-natured:

> But for all that, this book reveals—although nearly everything is
> wrong, or twisted, or exaggerated—not only that its author is blessed
> with an active fantasy and highly temperamental but also that he
> also possesses a highly gifted intellect. Only his gifts reside more in
> the area of systematizing logic than in historical perceptiveness,
> and the former qualities prevail to such a powerful extent that they
> rob him of the peace of mind to form a judgement and of the view
> for what is possible; also for what it is possible to know. He has
> dedicated his book to J. J. Holtzmann; one may wish that the gifted
> student may still learn much of his esteemed teacher's prudence and
> thoroughness.[119]

With such a review in the *Theologische Rundschau*, Schweitzer must have been aware that it was hardly likely he would be offered a professorship at any time soon. In his correspondence with Helene, Schweitzer makes it clear that the tension with the theological faculty persisted after his habilitation in 1902. He reported that during his time as principal of St Thomas the faculty tried to prevent him from tutoring exam candidates, with the exception of helping them revise their Greek and Hebrew. The reason, once again, was Schweitzer's position on theological issues: 'It's no good: the faculty fears that I will influence the students. And in my dreams I saw myself as an educator of Alsatian pastors!'[120] Schweitzer decided to be pragmatic and continued teaching only the classical languages to his students. He had challenged the experts, endangered his habilitation, lost his mentor, and had not heightened his prospect of receiving a professorship. Yet Schweitzer was not deterred, above all because he had no intention of becoming a professor of theology. Eventually he decided to take up the study of medicine. But this long programme of study needed to be financed. At this point, another project proved surprisingly successful as well as lucrative: Schweitzer's biography of Johann Sebastian Bach.

2

Saving the Whole

*From Theology to Bach and then to Medicine
(1903–1912)*

Bach, or the Art of Playing the Organ

Over the next few years Schweitzer was able to secure his livelihood
through his virtuosity in playing the organ as well as from his knowledge of Bach's works gained as cantor at St Thomas. Indeed, he
repeatedly claimed that it was Johann Sebastian Bach who had
financed his studies of medicine. His organ teacher from Paris,
Charles-Marie Widor, had taken him on as a new master student
from Eugen Münch after he had graduated from school in Mulhouse.
Widor was also instrumental in organizing large concerts for Schweitzer and promoting his biography of Bach, just as he would later
sharply criticize the 30-year-old Schweitzer on hearing of his plans
to study medicine. But how was Schweitzer as an organist in this
period between 1903 and 1905 also able to write an excellent study
of Bach's life and music? According to Klaus Eidam, it was 'a pioneering standard work in the literature on Bach […] for a long time'.[1]
Adolf von Harnack believed 'that it is far ahead of anything that has
previously been written about Bach and is, both in historical as well as
in musical terms, *the* Bach biography'.[2]

The key to this work lies in Schweitzer's theology. Schweitzer
saw himself as a theological mystic who sought the unity of God and
the human soul. Bach, Schweitzer believed, offers his listeners a
special, timeless access to their inner selves, to their present lives,
and to religion. Just as the mystic seeks unity with Christ, Bach's
music prepares the way for this unity. That is why Schweitzer
chose not to present Bach as a technically perfect composer or as

'guardian [...] of the grail of pure music', but rather as a 'poet and painter in sound'.[3] He concluded that music was Bach's way of expressing existential and religious experiences through his own 'language of sound':

> But it can only do this if the person who uses the language of sound possesses the mysterious faculty of rendering thoughts with a clarity and purposefulness surpassing its own natural power of expression. In this respect Bach is the greatest among the great. His music is poetic and pictorial because its themes are born of a poetic and pictorial imagination.[4]

Bach's music awakens sounds and images already existing in the listener and brings them to life in a unique way. The existential importance of this kind of music for Schweitzer explains his lifelong love of the organ, which can especially be seen as he lay dying in Lambarene and chose to listen to Bach and Beethoven on the gramophone. The last piece of music he heard was the Andante from Beethoven's Fifth Symphony, and his last words were 'How beautiful'.[5] It was the same piece of music that he had often played as a duet with Helene during their first years in Lambarene and again on the pedal piano before his internment in 1917 during the war. For Schweitzer, the music of Bach was far more than an aesthetic pleasure: it opened up new horizons. In his biography of Bach he thus placed a greater emphasis on the work rather than on the life of the famous composer. Yet he was able to interpret Bach's work on a mystical, ethical, and aesthetic level only because, as a theologian and musician, he was able fully to appreciate Bach's thinking and work.

> To give his true biography is to exhibit the nature and the unfolding of German art, which then comes to completion in him and is exhausted in him, to comprehend it in all its strivings and failures. This genius was not an individual, but a collective soul. Centuries and generations have laboured at this work, before the grandeur of which we halt in veneration. To anyone who has gone through the history of this epoch and knows what the end of it was, it is the history of that culminating spirit, as it was before it objectivated itself in a single personality.[6]

Schweitzer was strongly encouraged to write this biography by Widor, who had helped make Bach better known in France at that time by including his works in his organ course. In order to explore this new terrain and pass on this knowledge to his young French students, Widor needed a German-speaking student to help him interpret Bach's chorales, which demand an intimate understanding of their texts. Initially, Widor had encouraged Schweitzer to write only a short study focusing not on Bach as a person, but on the importance of Bach's thinking and personality for his understanding of music.

Schweitzer studied—in contrast to earlier scholars—Bach's work not only in musical terms but also as a spiritual and religious experience. Indeed, he counted Bach as the 'fifth evangelist'.[7] But how was it possible for him to unleash such a sudden and unexpected Bach renaissance with a single biography? Some twenty-five years earlier, Philipp Spitta (1841–94), a scholar of the history of music and secretary at the Royal Academy of Arts in Berlin (not to be confused with Karl Johann Spitta, whose hymns, to the irritation of his examiners, Schweitzer had labelled as 'unimportant' during his examination in theology), had produced a comprehensive two-volume work on Bach. It had been hailed by critics as 'the most impressive achievement in music history of the nineteenth century'.[8] There was apparently little left to be said about Bach. And then Schweitzer's *Jean-Sébastian Bach, le musicien-poète* appeared.[9]

Schweitzer had already come into contact with Bach through his teacher Eugen Münch, who before taking up the position as organist at St Stephen's in Mulhouse had discovered his own passion for Bach at the Academy of Music in Berlin. Münch soon encouraged his young pupil to play Bach[10] on an organ built by Johann Andreas Silbermann in 1765—the very Silbermann who was to play such an important role in Schweitzer's later essays on organ-building. The musician who most influenced Schweitzer's playing of the organ was his maternal grandfather, Pastor Schillinger, who was an acknowledged authority on organs and their construction. There had also been a Silbermann organ, dating from 1736, in his church. From personal experience, Schweitzer had great misgivings about the new organs being built in the late nineteenth century. In the autumn of 1896 he was travelling home from his first trip to Bayreuth when he decided to add Stuttgart to his itinerary. He was eager to inspect the new organ in the Liederhalle concert hall, which had been praised in the newspapers. After a closer inspection, however, Schweitzer came to the conclusion that this new type of organ had no musical or tonal advantages. This first impression was strengthened when he was later able to compare many organs, both old and new, and regularly exchanged views with organists and organ-builders alike.[11]

The French organ tradition, by contrast, seemed perfectly suited to Schweitzer and his interest in Bach. The most prominent representative of this tradition was the Breslau organist Adolf Friedrich Hesse (1809–63), who, in turn, had had a profound influence on Schweitzer's teacher Widor. Hesse ranked among the top organists and organ composers in the second half of the nineteenth century, and his interpretation of Bach's music in Paris was to prove very influential among French organists.[12] Hesse's public appearances in Paris, as well as his love for French organs, made a lasting impression on Schweitzer. It was the old French organs built in the Silbermann tradition, rather than the modern German ones, that made it possible for Schweitzer to play Bach's music in the way he felt it was intended to be played.[13]

Schweitzer made no attempt to hide either his decided preference for Silbermann organs or his dislike of the conventional organs of his time:

> Even today I have sometimes to look on helpless while I see noble old organs rebuilt and enlarged till not a scrap of their original beauty is left, just because they are not strong enough to suit present-day ideals; yes, and see them even broken up, and replaced at heavy cost by plebeian products of the factory![14]

The preservation of the old Silbermann organs was very important to Schweitzer because he considered them to be the archetype of the perfect organ. That the old organ of St William's in Strasbourg was replaced by a new model at the end of the nineteenth century caused him profound dismay. The organ of St Thomas, which had allowed him to understand the quality of the Silbermann organs, was the first that Schweitzer, with much effort and persuasion, had managed to save in 1907.

As an 'offshoot of his work on Bach', Schweitzer presented his views on this topic in a 1906 pamphlet: 'The Art of Organ-Building and Organ-Playing in Germany and France'. It was greeted with ridicule.[15] 'At first the only result was that some organists even gave up their former friendly associations with me. There was no lack of sarcastic letters. A well-known Berlin organ virtuoso said that I was ready for the lunatic asylum.'[16]

Such criticism did not overly bother Schweitzer: 'But my Allemanian stubbornness was not moved by this. It was something exceedingly strange to be the voice of the preacher in the desert. But my trust in the victory of truth did not leave me.'[17] In his efforts to preserve the legacy of Bach and Silbermann, Schweitzer was even accused of being too French. He clarified this relationship:

> German and French talents are destined to stimulate each other. In the art of organ-playing especially, just as we Germans can learn a limitless amount in technique and form from the French, they on the other hand can be shielded by the spirit of German art from impoverishment in their pure and perfect forms. By the interpenetration of both spiritual tendencies, new life will arise on both sides.[18]

In 1909 Schweitzer's efforts appeared fruitful: Guido Adler, professor of music studies in Vienna, asked Schweitzer to read a paper on the building of organs at the Third Congress of the International Society of Music. Schweitzer then sent, with Adler's agreement, detailed questionnaires in French and German to organ-builders and organists all over Europe, asking them to describe the problems they saw in the construction of organs. Schweitzer could hardly have imagined the answers he received, and then duly evaluated. Many respondents were personally insulting. Schweitzer was accused of wanting to 'encroach on the freedom of the organ builder' and 'tar all organs with the same brush'. Some saw their expertise questioned, while others feared that their livelihood was at stake. Nevertheless, Schweitzer recalled several positive responses: 'Along with the uncooperative and suspicious answers there arrived, however, an imposing number of others that went to the heart of the matter, and expressed the opinion that a discussion of organ-building was to be desired.'[19] At the congress in Vienna in 1909 Schweitzer read a paper on 'The Reform of our Organ Construction Based on a Survey of Organists and Organ-Builders in German and Romance Countries'. Schweitzer seemed to have made a point: his and two other papers at the conference were the basis for the publication 'International Regulations for Organ-Building', which 'swept

away the blind admiration for purely technical achievements, and
called for the production of carefully built instruments of fine tone'.[20]
This manual, which was printed in two languages and distributed
throughout Europe, was to set the standards for the construction of
organs. Schweitzer clearly took pleasure in this development:

> In the years that followed it came to be perceived more and more
> clearly that the really good organ must combine the beautiful sound of
> the old organs with the technical advantages of the new. Twenty-two
> years after its first appearance it was possible for my pamphlet on
> organ-building to be reprinted without alteration as the now accepted
> programme of reform, with an Appendix on the present state of the
> organ-building industry to make it a sort of jubilee edition.[21] [...]
> Letters running into hundreds have I written to bishops, deans, presi-
> dents of consistories, mayors, incumbents, church committees, church
> elders, organ-builders, and organists, to try to convince them [...] that
> they ought to restore their fine old organs instead of replacing them by
> new ones [...] And how often did these many letters, these many
> journeys, and these many conversations prove ultimately in vain,
> because the people concerned decided finally for the factory organ,
> the specification of which looked so fine upon paper! The hardest
> struggles were for the preservation of the old organs. What eloquence
> I had to employ to obtain the rescinding of death sentences which had
> already been passed on beautiful old organs! What numbers of organ-
> ists received the news that the organs[,] which on account of their age
> and their ruinous condition they prized so little, were beautiful instru-
> ments and must be preserved, with the same incredulous laughter with
> which Sarah received the news that she was to have descendants! [22]

Schweitzer was mocked for such efforts, even by his acquaintances:
'In Africa he saves old blacks, in Europe old organs.'[23]

The publication of the essay on 'The Art of Organ-Building and
Organ-Playing in Germany and France' led to the construction of
organs with mixture stops as they were built in Bach's time in such
renowned churches as St Reinold's in Dortmund or St Michael's in
Hamburg.

Schweitzer, together with Widor, explained not only how to understand Bach as a person but also how to play the music he composed.[24]
This meant reducing the intensity and embellishments that had
characterized interpretations of Bach's music since the late Romantic

period. After completing his habilitation thesis in 1902, he was looking
for a new project. And, instead of the theological history of dogma
he had planned to write, he turned to a biography of Bach. With
Widor's assistance, Schweitzer completed this project between 1903
and 1905 alongside his duties as university lecturer, pastor, and
organist. In his introduction to the German edition, Widor, who
was the author of several compositions for the organ, wrote how
impressed he was with his student's understanding of Bach's chorale
preludes:

> One day around 1899, when we were going through the chorale
> preludes, I confessed to him that a good deal of these compositions
> was enigmatic to me. […] 'Naturally,' said my pupil, 'many things in
> the chorales must seem obscure to you, for the reason that they are only
> explicable by the texts pertaining to them.' I showed him the move-
> ments that had puzzled me the most; he translated the poems into
> French for me from memory. The mysteries were all solved. During the
> next few afternoons we played through the whole of the chorale
> preludes. While Schweitzer—for he was the pupil—explained them
> to me one after the other, I made the acquaintance of a Bach of whose
> existence I had previously had only the dimmest suspicion.[25]

As the only narrative work on Bach published up to this point had
been in French, and there had been no introduction to the art of Bach,
Widor initially encouraged Schweitzer to write an essay introducing
organists and students of the Paris Conservatory to the chorale preludes. The essay should also discuss the 'essence of the chorale and
German church music',[26] for Widor believed that many French
musicians 'knew too little of them to enter thoroughly into the spirit
of Bach's music'.[27] Schweitzer saw this as an opportunity to put into
writing his thoughts and experiences from his time as organist of the
Bach choir at St William's in Strasbourg. Schweitzer understood that
it had 'become clear that this would expand into a book on Bach.
With courage I resigned myself to my fate.'[28] The start of this project
was propitious, as he managed to procure a set of Bach's works
from a woman in Paris for only 200 German marks.[29] This was a
bargain indeed, for complete sets of Bach were rare and expensive.
Schweitzer's achievement was to produce not a new portrait of the life
of Bach, but a new interpretation of his music. While Philipp Spitta

conceived of Bach's art as simply music, Schweitzer recognized in it above all the drive to convey in sound what was poetic and pictorial.[30]

Spitta's work was largely biographical and placed Bach's music in its historical context, while for Schweitzer Bach's life history was of only secondary interest. Instead, Schweitzer focused more on his works, dividing his material into types of music and analysing the organ works, clavier works, chamber and orchestral works, followed by chapters on 'Poetic and Painterly Music', 'Word and Sound in Bach', then discussions of the chorales, the motets, the songs, the oratorios, and the masses, before ending with a study of the 'Performance of Cantatas and Passions'. Spitta also interpreted Bach's music, and even surpassed Schweitzer in this respect, but the main difference between the two works is in how academic their treatment of their subject was. Schweitzer concluded that previous interpretations of Bach's work—such as Spitta's—had not done justice to his music:

> However, my design was not to produce new historical material about Bach and his music. As a musician, I wanted to talk to other musicians about Bach's music. The main subject of my work, therefore, should be, so I resolved, what in most books hitherto had been much too slightly treated, namely an explanation of the real nature of Bach's music, and a discussion of the correct method of rendering it. My work accordingly sets forth what is biographical and historical as introductory rather than as the main subject.[31]

Schweitzer thought that Bach's genius could be best grasped through his cantatas, which had been increasingly neglected during the nineteenth century. Moreover, a new understanding of Bach could be gained only from a combined aesthetic and religious perspective. It was Schweitzer's goal to 'stimulate music lovers to develop their own thoughts about the essence and spirit of Bach's works of art and the best way to perform them'.[32] He showed that Bach had taken an idea, often an image, from the text and portrayed this in music.

At this time scholars of music were split between advocates of 'absolute music' and those of 'pictorial music', to which Schweitzer also belonged.[33] In the chorale preludes, cantatas, and passions, Schweitzer saw characteristic pictures, poetic ideas, and motives:

> If the text speaks of drifting mists, of boisterous winds, of roaring rivers, of waves that ebb and flow, of leaves falling from the tree, of bells that

ring for the dying, of the confident faith which walks with firm steps, or the weak faith that falters insecure, of the proud who will be abased, and the humble who will be exalted, of Satan rising in rebellion, of angels poised on the clouds of heaven, then one sees and hears all this in his music.[34]

Rather than limiting himself to an academic interpretation of Bach's works, Schweitzer also gave practical advice on how musicians should interpret organ and piano music. The time seemed right: Schweitzer opposed a modern subjective reading of Bach and went so far as to ridicule the then prevailing late Romantic interpretations of his music. Indeed, his criticism launched an academic dispute at the centre of which was a discussion about symbolism in Bach's work: 'One recognized the deep relationship of Bach with the Lutheranism of his time; one investigated the symbolism of his tonal language.'[35] For Schweitzer, on the other hand, the work of Bach, as all truly sublime expressions of religion, did not only belong to a single denomination, but instead was part of the religious consciousness of all humanity. This, he argued, was an indication of the mystical appeal of Bach, over which no one church held a monopoly.

Since every church is also a sacred place, the cantata as sacred music transforms the room in which it is played into a space of religious worship.[36] The playing of cantatas should generate 'reflection and devotion' within the musician, without the necessity of drawing on liturgical or ecclesiastical elements. Schweitzer saw that because Bach's work had been mainly written for the church it no longer appealed to the spirit of the time, and had been neglected. The broad public had turned to the opera. Schweitzer went against this trend by emphasizing the ethical and mystical components of Bach's music in his biography while distancing it from a purely ecclesiastical space.

His work on Bach was by no means something Schweitzer did his spare time. The following excerpts from letters to Helene show how much of his energy between 1903 and 1904 was invested in it:

25 March 1904
2 o'clock in the morning. It is late at night: I reviewed and reworked the first half of a chapter of my Bach.[37]

29 May 1904
I have worked without pause copying the Bach manuscript; almost two hundred pages are complete and have been copied; they will

go to Paris before the end of the week. How wonderful when I have gotten rid of that job so I can devote myself to the third section of *The Last Supper*.[38]

13 [11] July 1904
One hundred completely finished pages of Bach are in Paris. They are negotiating with the publishers. [...] I am somewhat tired, as looking over the manuscript is very strenuous. But I am happy nevertheless. In six weeks the entire thing will be at the printer's.[39]

10 April 1905
Everything is coming together wonderfully! Now that Bach is complete, my poor head is beginning to rest and with my thirty years I feel once again as I did when I was eighteen years old.[40]

After completing the biography, Schweitzer confessed to Gustav von Lüpke that he had largely neglected his other responsibilities so as not to disappoint his friends in Paris.[41] The biography was ready for print in French in 1905, and the German edition followed in 1908. It was twice as long and published in two volumes, 'although my studies of medicine, the preparation of my lectures, my preaching, and my concert tours prevented me from busying myself with it continuously. I often had to lay it aside for weeks.'[42] After completing *The Quest of the Historical Jesus* in the late summer of 1906, Schweitzer was urged by Helene and his publishers to begin work on the German edition of his Bach biography. He soon realized that he could not translate his own work and instead resolved to 'make a new and better German [edition]'. The French book had 455 pages, and the German edition became, 'to the dismay of the astonished publishers, one of 844'.[43] The success of the German edition, however, was even greater than that of the French, and had the additional advantage of taking care of any of Schweitzer's remaining financial worries. In 1911 an English edition was published, also in two volumes.

Schweitzer explained that the greater length of the German edition was due in part to his being more comfortable writing in German than in French. Nobody speaks two languages equally well.[44] He described his relationship to the French and German languages as follows:

The difference between the two languages, as I feel it, I can best describe by saying that in French I seem to be strolling along the well-kept paths in a fine park, but in German to be wandering at will in a magnificent forest. Into literary German there flows continually new life from the dialects with which it has kept in touch. French has lost this ever-fresh contact with the soil. [...] In French I became accustomed to being careful about the rhythmical arrangement of the sentence and to striving for simplicity of expression, and now these things have become equally a necessity to me in German. And now through my work on the French *Bach* it became clear to me what literary style corresponded to my nature.[45]

Schweitzer composed the first lines of the German version of the Bach biography in the summer of 1906 while staying in Bayreuth, the holy grail of German nineteenth-century music. He attended a performance of Wagner's *Tristan*:

For weeks I had been trying in vain to get to work. In the mood of exaltation in which I returned from the Festival Hill, I succeeded. While the babel of voices surged up from the Bierhalle below into my stuffy room, I began to write, and it was long after sunrise that I laid down my pen. From that time onwards I felt such joy in the work that I had it ready in two years.[46]

The response to Schweitzer's biography of Bach was generally so positive because, as he asserted, he had a particularly keen sense for the spirit of the times:

The ideas which I put forward about the nature of Bach's music and the appropriate way of rendering it found recognition because they appeared just at the right time. By the interest aroused on the publication towards the end of the last century of the complete edition of his works it was brought home to the musical world that Bach was something other than the representative of an academic, and classical, music. Over the traditional method of rendering it they were similarly at a loss, and now they began to seek for a method which corresponded to the Master's style. But this new knowledge had as yet been neither formulated nor provided with a foundation. And so my book made public for the first time views which musicians specially concerned with Bach carried in their minds. Thus I gained many a friend.[47]

In 1905, the year the French edition of his Bach biography was published, Schweitzer showed he was also talented at networking among musicians. He met Cosima Wagner and her children, Siegfried

and Eva, at a Bach concert in Heidelberg and was afterwards often
invited to Wagner's residence in Bayreuth, 'Wahnfried'. Schweitzer
admired the music of Richard Wagner, although as a 'poetic' composer
he constructed his work entirely differently from Bach. Wagner, as
Schweitzer saw it, wanted emotionally to transfer his own images,
feelings, and associations to the listener through his music, while
Bach, who 'painted' with his music, let his listeners develop their own
colours and associations from his musical pictures.

The Wagner family would not let go of Schweitzer. When Cosima
travelled to Strasbourg some time later to visit her daughter Eva, she met
Schweitzer again. She asked her acquaintance, the local church historian
Johannes Ficker, to recommend a student of art history as a guide to the
city. Schweitzer asked permission to join the tour, and so the two were
able to get to know each other better. Cosima Wagner was delighted with
Schweitzer's research on Bach.[48] What the Wagner family and many of
his other readers appreciated above all was that Schweitzer had not only
written about Bach and his works, but that he had redefined Bach and his
work in terms of both intellectual history and theology. Schweitzer felt
drawn to the Wagner family because of his interest in Richard Wagner's
music, which he had admired since his boyhood:

> Together with my veneration for Bach went the same feeling for Richard
> Wagner. When I was a schoolboy at Mulhouse at the age of 16, I was
> allowed for the first time to go to the theatre, and I heard there Wagner's
> *Tannhäuser*. This music overpowered me to such an extent that it was days
> before I was capable of giving proper attention to the lessons in school. In
> Strasbourg, where the operatic performances conducted by Otto Lohse
> were of outstanding excellence, I had the opportunity of becoming
> thoroughly familiar with the whole of Wagner's works, except, of course,
> *Parsifal*, which at that time could only be performed at Bayreuth. It was a
> great experience for me to be present in Bayreuth in 1896, at the
> memorable first repetition of the Tetralogy since the original perform-
> ances in 1876. Parisian friends had given me the tickets. To balance the
> cost of the journey I had to content myself with one meal a day.[49]

Albert Schweitzer and Cosima Wagner maintained a friendly relationship over the following years. In his autobiography *Out of my Life and
Thought*, he recalled taking care of her after the First World War:

> During the Armistice period and the two following years I was to
> the Customs officials at the Rhine Bridge a well-known personality,

because I frequently went over to Kehl with a rucksack full of provisions
in order to send some from there to starving friends in Germany.
I made a special point of helping in this way Frau Cosima Wagner.[50]

Schweitzer kept up a lively correspondence with Richard Wagner's
descendants well into the 1950s. He wrote to Wolfgang, Siegfried
Wagner's son, concerning his father: 'Your father and I loved one
another. He is one of those people of whom I have the fondest
memories. Yet I believe we hardly ever wrote to each other. When
we were together, we enjoyed ourselves. It was enough for us to think
about each other.'[51]

Schweitzer considered the works of both Bach and Wagner to be
performative music, yet in very different ways. Language is a symbol
in music, and musicians are on a continuum between poets and
painters. Wagner is at one end and Bach at the other: 'He [Bach] is
the most consistent representative of pictorial music, a complete
antipode to Wagner. These two are the poles between which all
"characteristic" music revolves.'[52] Wagner believed that by connect-
ing word and sound together music had above all a poetic character.
This was the basis of Schweitzer's view of music. The degree to which
Wagner's music influenced Schweitzer in his interpretation of Bach
can be seen in how often Schweitzer spoke of Wagner in his public
talks on Bach.

Despite Schweitzer's early fondness for the music of Wagner—it
is not an exaggeration to call him a 'connoisseur and admirer of
Wagner'[53]—he remained both musically as well as emotionally
attached to Johann Sebastian Bach. In a survey by the magazine
Die Musik, he explained:

What is Bach to me? A comforter. He gives me the faith that in art as in
life what is truly true cannot be ignored and cannot be suppressed, it
does not need human help, but will assert itself by its own strength
when its time has come. This faith is what we need in order to live. He
had it. […] That is why his works are so great, and why he is as great as
his works. They preach to us: be still, be serene. And that Bach remains
a mystery to us, that we know nothing about what he thought and felt
other than what we find in his music, that he cannot be profaned by
scholarly or psychological intrusiveness, is so good. What he was and
what he experienced is only found in the sound of his music. […] His
music is a phenomenon of what is incomprehensibly real, just as the

world itself is. He does not try to find form for content; both develop together. He works as a creator. Every fugue is a world. His works are what is true. Neither education nor knowledge is needed to understand him, but only the unspoilt sense for what is true; and whoever is moved by him is able to understand in his art only what is true.[54]

Shortly before departing for Lambarene for the first time, Schweitzer, together with his teacher Widor, began work on an edition of Bach's organ pieces, including instructions on how to play and interpret them. The project had been initiated when Widor was approached by the US publisher Rudolph Ernst Schirmer.[55] When Widor died in 1937, before all of Bach's works had been published in the United States, a new co-editor was needed to complete this project. Schweitzer found this person in his former student and friend Edouard Nied-Berger.[56]

Another new development was the establishment of the Bach Foundation in Paris in 1905 by Gustave Bret, a former pupil of César Franck. From the start, Schweitzer was 'the most enthusiastic member'.[57] The Bach Society performed Bach's works throughout Europe, with Schweitzer accompanying their tours from Paris to Barcelona as organist until 1913. These regular concert tours financed his degree in medicine.[58] Even the fee for the state examination in medicine was paid for by his interpretation of Widor's *Symphonia sacra* at the 1911 French Music Festival in Munich.[59] It was only after he had completed the Bach biography that he devoted himself entirely to his studies of medicine.

Reaching a Decision

In Schweitzer's own recollections, the transition from being a biographer of Bach to a student of medicine was surprisingly smooth. Biographers have generally followed this own account of how, after four years as a university lecturer, his decision to begin studying medicine was the result of a resolution he had made in 1896 to devote his life to art and academia until his thirtieth birthday, after which he would serve humanity.[60] It was this very resolution that in 1905 he began to put into action—so he claimed later—by beginning his degree in medicine.[61] In a letter to the Director of Music Gustav von Lüpke, Schweitzer identified the exact day of his decision. It was

14 January 1905, and he was working on *The Quest of the Historical Jesus*, when he decided to take up medicine instead of pursuing an academic career in theology. He then reported this change of heart to the members of the theology faculty.[62] Biographers, such as the journalist Harald Steffahn, have assumed that Schweitzer's taking up of medicine and his subsequent work in Africa were part of a consistent plan, that he would make decisions that would determine 'the course of his life […] with such equanimity as if it were a matter of choosing a lecture'.[63]

In fact, these decisions appear to have been much less straightforward, as the correspondence with his future wife, Helene Bresslau, shows.[64] It was Helene who, a year before Schweitzer, first devoted herself to medicine by taking up nursing while he was still pursuing his idea of taking in orphans. This plan of his finally came to nothing when it was opposed by the local authorities. The biographical sequence of 'postdoctoral degree in theology, rejection of an academic career as theology professor, student of medicine, and jungle doctor in Lambarene' never existed as such. It was Schweitzer who created this impression by deciding to study medicine after receiving an invitation from the Congo mission in 1904, thus making good his resolution of 1896. Many of Schweitzer's biographers, such as Boris M. Nossik, have taken this account at face value. Nossik, too, portrays the event that was to shape Schweitzer's life so profoundly as a single decision, which Schweitzer made very calmly and which 'for a person who is caught up in traditional "rational thinking" [is] not so easy to understand'.[65]

In fact, Schweitzer's decision to become a doctor was fraught with inner turmoil. The years between 1902 and 1905 were a time when he was coming to terms with himself and his plans. After his habilitation in March 1902, Schweitzer took up a post in the faculty of theology and in 1903 gave lectures on the Synoptic Gospels and the Apostle Paul. He remained pastor at St Nicholas and even became principal of the *Collegium Wilhelmitanum* at the St Thomas Foundation, where he helped theology students prepare for their exams. In the autumn of 1902, he began writing his book on the art of Bach's music for the students of the Paris Conservatory.

University lecturer, assistant pastor, director of studies, Bach biographer—this sounds like a workload that would be unmanageable even for such a gifted and hard-working person as Albert Schweitzer. It would seem to leave little time left for further activities, much less pursuing a degree in medicine. This decision in 1905 to study medicine, his third degree, has led some to portray Schweitzer as a genius of 'superhuman strength'.[66] The Strasbourg historian Friedrich Meinecke wrote about him in his memoirs in 1943:

> I do not like overuse the word 'genius' [...] but I must apply it to one of the then youngest lecturers at the University of Strasbourg, one of the few native Alsatians among them. On first meeting him in my study, I was immediately captured by his pleasant appearance, his radiant features, his confident movements. That, I was told, is a lecturer in theology, who is not treated well by his professors as he has a somewhat restless nature. For he is not only carrying out his studies on early Christianity but lighting his candle at both ends, playing the organ exquisitely and working on a volume about Bach. My wife and I then gratefully listened to him giving a moving organ recital in the small St William's church on the Schiffleutstaden. A number of his younger friends praised him enthusiastically, yet even here one became somewhat confused on hearing that he had turned his back on theology and had taken up medicine as a third subject in order to go one day as doctor to the negroes. That was Albert Schweitzer, whose name is spoken with respect today wherever there is talk of the highest ethical standard embodied in a spirit of sacrifice in an individual life and of the most profound questions concerning Western civilization.[67]

Indeed, Albert Schweitzer was a paragon of efficiency. With his rooms and library at St Thomas, he could manage all of his responsibilities quickly and conveniently. He preached only on Sundays at St Nicholas, and his confirmation class was held only once a week during school time; most of his classes at the university were also located nearby. His lodgings in St Thomas were on the other side of the river from St Nicholas and the faculty of medicine. He tutored students during the semester, which was certainly not a full-time occupation and meant his rooms were rent-free. His work as a lecturer took no more than three hours per week during the semester, although his lectures on the theology of Saint Paul would have involved, as for any new university teacher, much work.[68] Evidently Schweitzer still had enough time in 1903 and 1904 to work on the Bach biography and give numerous organ concerts.[69] These two sources of income would allow him to continue his studies of medicine after his term as principal of St Thomas had ended in 1906. He was thus able to pursue a number of different activities at the same time to secure his livelihood, but he was not bound to any single position that would require his continual presence.

A look at Schweitzer's correspondence with Helene Bresslau confirms that between 1902 and October 1905 he spent much time thinking about how to implement his resolution of 1896. He often wrote about his motives for taking up medicine: he could not imagine an existence as an academic confined to an office, and instead desired to be able to serve humankind directly, 'namely, as a doctor, that I might be able to work without having to talk'.[70] To be independent, to act instead of just talk—this was what made the study of medicine for him, a master of language, so attractive. The magazine advertising for missionary doctors, the *Journal des missions evangélique*, was therefore much less the *momentum mirabile* portrayed in his autobiography, and rather the spark to go ahead with a long-held plan: 'The plan that I was now putting into practice had been in my mind for a long time. Its origin went back to my days as a student.'[71] And once again Schweitzer was able to put an exact date to his decision:

> One morning in the autumn of 1904 I found on my writing table in the College one of the green-covered magazines in which the Paris Missionary Society reported every month on its activities. [...] My eye caught the title of an article: 'Les besoins de la Mission du Congo'. It [...] contained a complaint that the Mission did not have enough workers to carry out its work in Gabon, the northern province of the Congo Colony. [...] The conclusion ran: 'Men and women who can reply to the Master's call with a simple: Lord, I am coming. These are the people whom the church needs.' The article finished, I quietly began to work. My search was over.[72]

The event described here reads like a typical report of a conversion experience, as found in the biographies of nearly every missionary at the time.[73] These reports would typically tell of a religious experience— often at a particular time—that was felt to shape the person's life and provide spiritual motivation from that moment on. Schweitzer's depiction of events suggests he also felt a moment of conversion at the hand of God, an experience without which he would never have found his way to equatorial Africa. However, we may assume that, as a man with a talent for planning, Schweitzer was not one to take such a serious decision hastily and begin studying medicine after perusing a missionary pamphlet. This view is supported by his actions after reading the Congo Mission magazine in the autumn of 1904 up until his pre-clinical semester in October 1905.

First of all, he completed his Bach biography in early 1905, and in May he began planning his resignation as principal of the St Thomas Foundation, an office that had given him financial independence. A letter to Helene Bresslau suggests that Schweitzer's decision of 1896 was not as compelling as he would have it seem in retrospect. Before 1904 he had seriously considered devoting his life to the training of pastors in Alsace and living as a director of studies, pastor, and teacher of theology. These comments, made shortly after enrolling as a medical student, relate to such a plan:

And in my dreams I saw myself as an educator of Alsatian pastors! I am giving up this dream bit by bit.—I had the feeling […] like a ship before its launch that trembles slightly as a bolt under the keel is knocked out and that knows, a few bolts more and then—I will not tip over, but glide freely and smoothly into the sea. […] Sometimes I feel as if events were coming thick and fast. Yet inwardly I am so calm, I cannot remember ever before having been so calm. It was moving: some weeks ago, Pastor Knittel told me: I will stay one more year. You will be unanimously declared my successor, and then in a few years you will be curate of St Thomas College.—He meant so well. O yes, that would be just the thing to ruin me! Imagine me as curate of St Thomas, member of the foundation board ... I would suffocate. […] I cannot understand any more how I ever could think that I was made to spend my life being a principal of the college. Alas—had I but found children! But the others would have thwarted this plan too.[74]

This letter to Helene Bresslau makes three things clear. First, that, even long after 1896, Schweitzer still toyed with the idea of a regular career in theology. Secondly, that even those close to Schweitzer—for example, his mentor Pastor Knittel—were under the impression that Schweitzer would follow an ecclesiastical rather than an academic career. Otherwise he would not have offered him his post after retirement. Thirdly, however, it also becomes clear that 1905, the year he decided to take up medicine, was the real crux in Schweitzer's life. In March 1903 he still described his election as principal of St Thomas College as 'a great turning point in my life' and as a duty, even if his adversaries in the faculty of theology thought the uncomfortably liberal lecturer had been 'sidelined in this way'.[75] Taking up medicine two years later must have seemed like an act of liberation from an increasingly stressful environment in academia and the church. Letters to Helene Bresslau offer a deeper insight into his decision-making process in retrospect: 'I just couldn't see the path yet. And now I am leaving peacefully, thoughtful, smiling [...] Out into life as fate ordained.'[76] Schweitzer knew, even on the day of his habilitation, that he would not become a professor of theology so soon. Yet after 1903 he no longer pursued this goal:

> I feel as if this whole life is an immense dream: people around me do not understand me any more [...] and especially why I don't care about my 'career' as professor! As if that would be my goal, the career of a professor!—No, I want to '*live*', live my life—you understand me![77]

These lines are addressed to the 'loyal comrade' of Schweitzer's memoirs, his future wife Helene Bresslau. She was at this point presumably the only person who knew of his plans to go to Africa. At first Schweitzer had wanted to take in orphaned children, but from 1904 onwards his thoughts went towards Africa, and he took up the study of medicine in order to learn enough about nursing for work in a remote missionary station. Schweitzer's decision to become a physician ripened only at a later date. A letter from 1905 indicates that at first he was not thinking about taking years to finish a complete medical degree. Instead, his original idea had been to resign his office as college principal by March 1906 in order to complete another history of dogma by September. Afterwards, he wrote:

> I would like to have six months in which to acquire some general skills necessary for the mission and especially to be able to do a bit of medicine. In this regard I am fortunate, for some of my colleagues from the faculty of medicine I am on friendly terms with will gladly let me into their clinics and teach me the elementary skills I need. I will already begin my studies in the following winter [1905]. Don't you

agree that knowing something about medicine is a necessity? […] That would take us to the spring of 1907.[78]

At this point, Schweitzer was thinking only about learning some nursing skills over a period of three semesters to serve him as a missionary, and not about becoming a doctor. It seems all the more surprising that in his autobiography *Out of my Life and Thought* Schweitzer refers to several letters that he dropped into a letter box in the avenue de la Grande Armée in Paris on 13 October 1905, 'in which I told my parents and some of my closest acquaintances that I would enrol at the beginning of the winter term [1905] as a student of medicine in order to go later on to equatorial Africa as a doctor'.[79] Here, too, Schweitzer smooths over in retrospect the path towards his decision as well as the conflicts that followed. He did indeed send the letter to several acquaintances, but not, as he claimed, to his parents, knowing how little understanding they—and especially his mother—would have for such a resolution. Instead, he wanted to tell his mother in person.[80] This plan, however, failed, as his parents had already been informed about their son's plans to study medicine and go to Africa before he returned from Paris. Presumably, someone who had received one of the letters had already talked to the Schweitzers. At any rate, an entry in the diary of Schweitzer's father shows that Schweitzer visited his parents after his return from Paris in order to tell them about his plans. Both, however, already knew about it and were hardly enthused at the prospect. As Schweitzer had expected, it was his mother in particular who was unable to come to terms with her son's turning away from a university career in theology.

There is also a revealing letter of 9 July 1905, in which Schweitzer officially offered his services to the Paris Evangelical Missionary Society. As is so often the case, he was much more restrained in his official correspondence and autobiography than in his private letters. He told the director of the mission he wanted to go to the Congo 'because I am especially attracted to this work'. In mid-1905 Schweitzer still gave his plan to train pastors as the major reason for entering the mission. Year by year, he recalled, the wish to become part of missionary work had grown in him:

I feel that in working together with the brothers of the Paris Missionary Society I would give everything I am capable of giving.[81] My plan to become a missionary is no sudden whim. I used to dream about it even in my childhood when I donated my pennies for the little African children. After completing my studies of theology and philosophy, I intended to devote myself to being a teacher and training pastors; but in the back of my mind I had always envisioned that I would not remain a lecturer and a principal at the college for ever. I have held this position for two years now, and my contract does not run out until 1910.[82]

Schweitzer also claimed, as he had done previously to Helene, that he would be able to live a life without scholarship, without art, and without intellectual work:

I felt true pride when I delivered my habilitation lecture at the age of twenty-seven. But all those things have failed to quench my thirst; I feel that this is not everything, that it is nothing. I have grown increasingly simpler, more and more childlike, and I have come to realise more and more clearly that the sole truth and the sole happiness consist in serving our Lord Jesus Christ wherever he needs us [...] That is why I ask you to accept me. I am focusing on the Congo because I am particularly drawn to working there. But if you need me somewhere else, I am likewise at your disposal.[83]

What is truly remarkable about this letter, however, is that for the first time Schweitzer recorded, in an official letter of application, his actual motivations for changing the course of his life so fundamentally. Schweitzer elaborated that he did not intend to complete a full medical degree and that he wanted to be prepared for whatever use the mission saw fit to put him to, whether missionary or medical work. He explained why he had never married and that the profession of pastor rather than university teacher would be his choice should his missionary plans fail:

I am completely independent. [...] I have never married so as to remain free for service in the mission and avoid being forced to change my plan against my better judgement. If I can endure the climate, I will marry; until then, I would not like to bind a woman's lot to my own so that I may be completely free to serve our Lord. If by chance I am not able to endure the climate or if I become an invalid due to the stress I would not become a burden to the mission, for I can always return to the pastorate in Alsace where I will be welcomed with open arms.[84] This is my plan [...] I will announce my resignation on 1 March [1906] and stay in office until September. Actually, I need some months to complete a work about the history of dogma.[85]

Schweitzer never did finish his history of dogma. This is hardly surprising, for it would have benefited only someone pursuing an academic career in theology, something Schweitzer was at this point no longer interested in. His real interest had shifted from questions of faith to ethics and the philosophy of civilization. This same letter also proves that Schweitzer had not originally planned to earn a medical degree, since that would require seven years of study, and, had that been his plan, he would hardly have offered to begin working for the mission in 1905. Part of the reason he decided to complete his studies of medicine with the state examinations and a doctoral degree was surely—alongside the practical reasons for completing his qualification—that his thirst for learning was such that he wanted to complete each degree programme he had begun. To the Paris Missionary Society, however, it certainly sounded rather different:

Afterwards, I would like to have six months in which to acquire some general skills needed for the mission and above all to study a bit of medicine. In this regard I have a good deal of support, as several colleagues from the faculty of medicine with whom I am closely connected will welcome me into their clinics and teach me the elementary things I need to know. I will already begin my studies next year. Don't you agree that medical knowledge is an absolute necessity? Coillard said it somewhere. Then we are in the spring of 1907. All this I explain to you […] to find out whether the Paris Mission will accept me or whether I should offer my services (reluctantly) to a German mission. But I do not want you to say anything of this and disclose my name to anyone until 1 March [1906], the day I will announce my resignation to the college and the university. […] Nevertheless, I would still like to know if you need or want me; that I should like to know before August [1905] in order to make the necessary plans. […] In October I am in Paris. I am half-Parisian, as I spend one or two months there every year. We can then talk about it in detail.[86]

In this letter to the Paris Missionary Society of 9 July 1905, Schweitzer presents himself as being very much a Francophile, and he briefly lists a number of advantages that make him suitable for missionary work: he has good networks in Alsace as well as in Paris; he is independent both personally and financially; he implies that he is less liberal than the mission might suspect; and finally he is flexible about where and how he will work in Africa. Schweitzer emphasized he was a bachelor, as did so many missionaries of the time in their letters of application. They wanted to appear unattached yet not unwilling to marry, since so-called 'missionary brides' would often follow their husbands-to-be after they had become familiar with their new environment.

Albert Schweitzer's conformance to the expectations of the Paris Missionary Society did not, however, lead him, as was expected of most other missionaries, to relate a conversion experience or some other defining religious experience in his life. Instead, this letter shows Schweitzer as a pragmatic realist. He was well aware of the dangers posed by missionary service, above all concerning his health and the possibility of becoming an invalid or even dying. At the same time this letter shows how Schweitzer anticipated misgivings and sought to forestall them. In this context he wrote to Helene on 9 July 1905, informing her that he had posted his letter of application for the Paris Missionary Society that very day:

My faithful comrade
My hand shakes a little: I just put the letter in the mailbox in which I tell the director of the Paris mission that I am ready and willing to leave in spring 1907. This is a peculiar day. I participated in an organ concert, and while I played, I asked myself: 'Will you ever be able to give this up?' [...] The letter has been written: clear, precise, without any sentiments, almost like a business letter. [...] I am happy. It is done. But I am afraid, not that I might regret anything. No. How could I live while I feel the obligation to go there? I go! But what will be my fate? How will my death be? What about my suffering? I go there to be with Jesus; He may do with me what He will. I will find Him, that I know. And to pray: 'Thy Kingdom come!' I want to find out what these words mean, that he said: 'Who loses his life for me and for my word, he will keep it.' If He only finds that I am worthy to serve Him.—And now, at this moment, nobody in the world except you has the right to know my thoughts. The others, including my mother, have had their share of my thoughts; the last one is for you.[87]

In this letter Schweitzer makes clear that, after his plan to work with children and orphans in Strasbourg had miscarried, he hoped to be sent abroad soon by the Paris Missionary Society to do missionary work. While in his letter to Helene he does not categorically exclude the possibility of completing his degree in medicine, he puts this decision in the hands of the Paris Missionary Society. So, after a meeting with the mission director in October 1905, he wrote to Helene from Paris:

> Well then: two years from now the Missionary Society will call me to the place where I am needed. If they have a vacancy before the time, I will go. I leave the seminary and begin my medical studies already this winter. If the society considers it useful to let me complete my medical studies, they will let me do so. This is the solution I like best because then we both feel more at ease. My religious views will then be a private matter. But if they need a missionary sooner, I will not finish my studies. Officially, the society knows that one week from today I will be available. You see, that is almost like a contract with a publisher. But I am for clear agreements. After our discussion, they had the send-off for several missionaries who return to the Congo. I sat, not knowing anyone, in a corner of the chapel. What an hour! I heard how these simple men took their leave; I was surrounded by women in black dresses, sad yet joyful, everywhere an animated atmosphere; the walls were decorated with pagan weapons [...] in the dim light of only a few gas lamps, my whole life passed in my thoughts, and I saw that everything had to come this way. And I was happy that I had been faithful to myself [...] and in the dark of the chapel, I saw you at the day of my departure [...] you were smiling. These men are simple and of great depth. No veneer.[88]

All of this reads as if Schweitzer were entering a religious order in the awareness that after being sent abroad he might not return to Europe alive. This version of events was noted some years later in a curriculum vitae that Schweitzer submitted with the application for his state examination in medicine. It is much more detached: 'On the friendly advice of some professors of medicine in this faculty, I have decided not to do some practical training in medicine, which would leave many gaps in my knowledge, but instead to take a proper degree in medicine.'[89]

The Study of Medicine

'On one of the closing days of October 1905 I set out in a thick fog to attend the first of a course of lectures on anatomy.'[90] And, although

Albert Schweitzer

each beginning does bear a special magic, as the poet Hermann Hesse writes, after this October there lay ahead for Schweitzer seven long years studying medicine. The first problem he faced was an administrative one: as a university lecturer with a habilitation degree from the University of Strasbourg, he was not permitted to enrol in another programme of study. And, as a guest auditor, he would not have been able to take the state examination in medicine—much less earn certificates or do any other kind of assessed work. However, after his colleagues had interceded on his behalf, the university administration finally granted Schweitzer a special permit to take examinations in medicine and, with the approval of his lecturers, visit lectures free of charge.

Taking up this new programme of study did not prevent Schweitzer, by now 30 years old, from continuing to preach in St Nicholas on Sundays and to give concerts for the Paris Bach Society in Paris and throughout Europe, from offering regular lectures at the faculty of theology, from writing a paper on organ-building, and finally, until the spring of 1906, from carrying out his duties as principal of St Thomas College. When Schweitzer stepped down from this last post, his friend Friedrich Curtius, then district superintendent of Colmar and president of the Lutheran Church of Alsace, gained permission for him to take four small rooms in St Thomas, and therefore remain close to the university as well as the university hospital. As a result, his move from one apartment to the other only involved Schweitzer's former students carrying his possessions, mainly a large collection of books, from one room into another. From early 1906 onwards, however, Schweitzer had to replace the salary he had received as principal of the college with earnings from organ concerts and royalties from his publications.

Despite all his extracurricular activities, Schweitzer proved to be just as dedicated a student of medicine as he had been of theology. And, with the start of the clinical semesters in the hospital and regular contact with patients, his enthusiasm for the subject soared. At times, Schweitzer complained about the dull learning by rote: 'All my interest in the subject matter could not help me over the fact that the memory of a man over thirty no longer has the same capacity as a twenty-year-old student.'[91] Besides, his need for sleep often got the better of him. As a result, many biographers have depicted

Schweitzer's decision to study medicine as one involving great sacrifice. They overlook, however, the personal pleasure he found in his studies, not only in learning practical medical skills, but also in his love of natural sciences. This made his studies of medicine satisfying in a different way from his work in philosophy or theology:

> But study of the natural sciences brought me even more than the increase of knowledge I had longed for. It was to me a spiritual experience. I had all along felt it to be physically a danger that in the so-called humanities with which I had been concerned hitherto, there is no truth which affirms itself as self-evident [...] How often does what is reckoned as progress consist in a skillfully argued opinion putting real insight out of action for a long time! [...] Now I was suddenly in another country. I was concerned with truths which embodied realities, and found myself among men who took it as a matter of course that they had to justify with facts every statement they made. It was an experience which I felt to be needed for my own intellectual development. Intoxicated as I was with the delight of dealing with realities which could be determined with exactitude, I was far from any inclination to undervalue the humanities as others in a similar position often did. On the contrary. Through my study of chemistry, physics, zoology, botany, and physiology I became more than ever conscious to what an extent truth in thought is established by facts. No doubt something subjective clings to the knowledge which results from a creative act of the mind. But at the same time such knowledge is on a higher plane than the knowledge based only on facts.[92]

When he writes about people 'who have lost their sense for what is real', Schweitzer was most probably expressing his clear frustration with theology and particularly with theologians. Schweitzer felt that his studies of medicine were liberating in both professional and personal terms; but only a person who has been under pressure can feel liberated, and Schweitzer had been caught up in grinding academic power struggles in the faculty of theology. At first he evaded these by taking up medicine; later he completely withdrew into his work in Lambarene. The decision to study medicine therefore not only opened the door to serving others in Africa, but also marked the end of an academic career—one that he was not pursuing as it would have offered him little fulfilment.

It is all the more surprising then to note how little Schweitzer related of his studies of medicine. Neither his autobiography nor his many letters to his 'loyal comrade' of these busy years between 1905 and 1912 reveal much of what must have occupied a considerable amount of his time. He writes in detail only about his decision to take up medicine in 1905 and the beginning of his studies, of the difficulties of the preliminary examination in May 1908, and of the easier clinical semesters. Unusually for a candidate about to take his preliminary examination, Schweitzer was correcting proofs of his Bach book for his publisher Breitkopf and Härtel less than a month before his examination. At the same time, he was preparing to write a book on Franz Schubert, an undertaking he then had to abandon owing to a lack of time, although his publishers in Paris had already announced the publication.[93] At an even closer date to his preliminary examination, Schweitzer was preaching, playing the organ, and even travelling to Santa Margherita Ligure, only to mention casually in a letter to Helene: 'I suddenly had a fright because of the date for the exam.'[94] That he, like other candidates, passed the exam only by dint of hard work and mindless cramming is evident from the daily routine he recorded for Helene during his holiday in Santa Margherita: 'I am leaving you again and returning to Ewald's lecture notes. Mornings: $9\frac{1}{2}$ to $12\frac{1}{4}$ physiology; 2–$4\frac{1}{4}$ anatomy; 8–10 physics and botany. That's how we live, that's how we live, that's how we live every day.'[95]

In his autobiography Schweitzer admitted that he nearly fell at the hurdle of the preliminary examination. At first he had attempted to learn the material for the exam by extensive reading of academic literature rather than by cramming from the standard lecture notebook: 'It was only in the last few weeks that I let myself be persuaded by my fellow students to join a cramming class, so that I got to know what sort of questions, according to the records kept by students, the professors usually set, together with the answers they preferred to hear.'[96]

Waldemar Augustiny's assertion that Schweitzer completed all his medical examinations in 'the shortest time possible'[97] is not correct for the preliminary examination. Yet, in the light of the writing and academic work that Schweitzer pursued alongside his studies of medicine, this is hardly surprising. Although he had predicted otherwise, Schweitzer passed his state examination in medicine with good marks. In retrospect his accounts of the following four years and the clinical semesters were confined to anecdotes. The more hands-on, patient-centred work in the clinic is considered by most students to be less strenuous, and it seemed to have been easier for Schweitzer as well. He completed his degree in medicine on 17 December 1910 with the final grade of 'excellent'. During a walk after his exam, Dr Madelung, who had taught him surgery, voiced his admiration for Schweitzer's achievements.[98] Schweitzer was justly proud of what he had achieved.

At the same time he lived a life as pastor and a member of Strasbourg's society. He officiated at the wedding of the future German president Theodor Heuss with Elly Knapp, perhaps the closest friend Helene Bresslau had in Strasbourg. Schweitzer was asked to perform the ceremony in St Nicholas, his own parish church, four weeks before his first examination in medicine. During the night before the wedding he had been on duty during a birth that was so protracted that on the following morning he walked straight from the delivery room into the church. The wedding guests noticed the distinct odour of antiseptic given off by the pastor.[99] It was not without pride that forty years later Schweitzer wrote of his memories to the first President: 'I go around the village and recount, "And I gave the sermon at the wedding of the President," which adds a further title to my reputation.'[100]

The frock coat Schweitzer wore to this wedding became an emblem of his frugality. He had had it made by a tailor in Gunsbach before travelling to Barcelona to give a Bach recital that was to be attended by the Spanish king. The anxious tailor did his best, and Schweitzer was so satisfied that he wore the coat not only in the presence of the Spanish king and at the wedding of Theodor Heuss, but also twenty years later when receiving the Goethe Prize, nearly half a century later when he was awarded the Nobel Peace Prize, as well as when he was decorated by Queen Elizabeth of Great Britain When asked about his continued use of the garment, Schweitzer answered: 'Of course, the thing will do service for another two hundred years.'[101]

Following his clinical examinations in 1911, Schweitzer had to complete a practical year at the hospital in Strasbourg in order to be awarded a licence to practise medicine. During this time, too, he continued work on *The Mysticism of Paul the Apostle*.

Schweitzer's study of medicine also broadened his theological interests. He lectured on the 'results of a critical history of theology and the natural sciences for the evaluation of religion' in the summer semester of 1911 and in the winter semester 1911–12. The last of these lectures he concluded with Goethe's words: 'In the beginning was the deed!'[102] Schweitzer intended these lectures to join together theology, the history of religion, and the natural sciences—and this was reflected in his third thesis, *The Psychiatric Study of Jesus: Exposition and Criticism*,[103] for which he was awarded a doctorate in medicine in December 1912. He simply lacked the time for a more elaborate experimental study—for example, in physiology or clinical studies. With this thesis in medicine, furthermore, he hoped to be able to refute earlier criticism of his theses on eschatology.

The main focus of this doctoral thesis was on psychiatry, an interest that was to stay with Schweitzer later in Lambarene and accompany his practical work. The main thesis of Schweitzer's theological work had been that, as a Jew, Jesus had shared the eschatological expectations of his contemporaries and that, after the redeemer had failed to appear, he had sensed his own calling as the messiah. Schweitzer's critics interpreted this as a claim that Jesus had been suffering from a delusional disorder and was therefore a pathological case. It was this claim that Schweitzer hoped to disprove, not only theologically but also using the most recent findings from psychiatry. However, the search for literature proved so extensive that at several points Schweitzer toyed with the idea of changing his topic.[104]

Schweitzer's examination of Jesus' supposed mental illness focused on paranoia. Psychiatrists such as Dr Georg Lomer (writing under the pseudonym of George de Loosten), William Hirsch, or Emil Rasmussen had claimed that Jesus suffered from hallucinations, paranoia, *dementia paralytica*, or a defective sense of self.[105] Such claims went at first unchallenged, not only because of the strong position of psychiatry as an academic discipline, but also because they could only be refuted by someone with expertise in medicine and theology. This gap between the two disciplines was closed by Schweitzer, who came to the perhaps predictable conclusion, in line with his theological research, that Jesus of Nazareth was not paranoid, but was instead a man whose messianic self-understanding could be explained by the expectation of the coming of the kingdom of God prevalent at the time. Schweitzer's thesis was barely acknowledged in the world of medicine and was to remain his only academic paper in medicine.

Schweitzer's third doctoral thesis was part of an old dispute with his theology teacher Heinrich Julius Holtzmann—almost as if he felt the need to set the record straight. This impression is confirmed in the foreword, in which he refers to his now deceased teacher and acknowledges that he had been motivated to write on this topic by Holtzmann's comment that Schweitzer's theological writings 'portrayed a Jesus whose world view looked like a complex set of delusions'.[106] Holtzmann and others had repeatedly accused Schweitzer of advancing an eschatological perspective depicting the world of Jesus as a world of fantasies. They argued that a man who saw the messianic expectation fulfilled in himself in this world must have been insane. Schweitzer therefore felt 'obliged' to follow *The Quest of the Historical Jesus* with this further work, because he had 'brought out the apocalyptic and, in modern terminology, the fantastical in the imagination of the Nazarene more clearly than any of the other researchers in this field had'.[107]

Schweitzer felt that in fact he had advocated the very opposite position to the one he was being accused of. Just as the contemporaries of Copernicus had been certain that the sun moved around the earth, Jesus of Nazareth, as a child of his time, had shared in the disappointed expectations that the kingdom of God was at hand.[108] But by no means did this make Jesus a paranoid fantasist. To prove this, Schweitzer not only repeated the theses he had established in his theological work, but also investigated the psychiatric studies that portrayed Jesus as mentally insane. The first thing that struck him was how all the authors made uncritical use of biblical passages to prove their claims. Their main source was usually the Gospel of John, which even Heinrich Julius Holtzmann would not have accepted as a primary historical source on the life of Jesus. Schweitzer came to the same conclusion in his psychiatric analysis as he did in his theological studies—namely, that these authors failed to see Jesus as a man of his time because they were insufficiently familiar with religious belief in Palestine at the time of Jesus. They presumed to make a psychiatric assessment without first understanding the historical and religious context. Schweitzer concluded that, while Jesus of Nazareth had been an exceptional personality, from a psychiatric perspective he had been entirely sane.

Although this conclusion was hardly original, Schweitzer needed one year longer than expected to complete his book because he had spent so much time reading current studies on the pathology of psychosis and hallucinations. The real achievement of this thesis lies in Schweitzer's observation—even if it was limited to only one case—of the great extent to which psychiatric constructs such as 'abnormality' or 'hallucination' are determined by culture. In view of Schweitzer's thesis in medicine, James Brabazon argues that Schweitzer's later criticisms of psychoanalytic methods were well founded.[109]

Schweitzer concluded his medical training with a course in tropical medicine, begun in Paris in early 1912 and completed with the awarding of his doctoral degree in late 1912. Schweitzer had now undergone twenty years of academic training, had three doctoral degrees and one postdoctoral habilitation degree. He was awarded an 'excellent' in his final degree in medicine, even if his thesis did not meet the same academic standards as his work in theology.

Schweitzer had done a third doctoral degree in order to withdraw from the world of his first two. Yet in the years he was studying medicine, he wrote surprisingly little about medicine and all the more about music, organ-building, and his thoughts on a philosophy of civilization. All this he recorded in the almost daily letters he wrote to the one person without whom Schweitzer might never have realized his vision of going to Africa: Helene Bresslau.

The Loyal Comrade

The influence of Helene Bresslau on Albert Schweitzer can be seen in photographs showing him sitting among the bags and crates destined for Lambarene. The pieces of luggage bore the initials 'ASB', which could also be found on the blankets and cutlery at the hospital in Lambarene. At a time when compound surnames were still uncommon between marriage partners, 'ASB' stood for 'Albert Schweitzer Bresslau' and symbolized the special bond between two people who spent much of their married life thousands of miles apart, and who would never be able to claim they had a normal marriage. It was not, however, until 1992, when their correspondence from the years between 1902 and 1913 was published, that the importance of Helene Schweitzer Bresslau to her husband was more clearly revealed.

These letters became the basis of an intimate biography of Helene Schweitzer by Verena Mühlstein published in 1998.[110]

After Helene's death, a portion of her correspondence was found by her daughter Rhena Schweitzer Miller, although her mother had left her under the impression that she had destroyed some of her own letters.[111] This would explain the fact that in their published private correspondence there are more letters from Schweitzer. Rhena believed her mother had suffered a typical 'woman's fate'[112] and argued that her mother's life in the shadow of such a 'great man' was far from easy. Besides the long time spent apart from her husband, Helene was troubled by several serious health conditions. These ranged from a serious back injury, the result of a skiing accident in the winter of 1907–8, to a bout of tuberculosis, which prevented her from travelling to Africa for several decades.

Helene Marianne Bresslau was born on 25 February 1879 in Berlin as the daughter of Caroline Bresslau (née Isay) and Harry Bresslau, a professor of history who had left the Jewish community in an attempt to become fully assimilated. Helene and her two brothers were baptized and raised as Protestants of the Augsburg Confession.[113] After receiving a full professorship at the University of Strasbourg, Harry Bresslau moved to Alsace with his family at Easter 1890. How unusual it was for unbaptized Jews to be made full professors is shown by the fact that only twenty-five Jews had been appointed to such positions in the German Reich by 1909.[114]

After Helene Bresslau had passed the examination allowing her to teach at upper secondary school for girls, she spent two years studying at the conservatory in Strasbourg. Following a trip to Italy in the winter of 1899–1900, she devoted herself to studying art history. Her interests were almost as wide-ranging as Schweitzer's.

The romantic attachment between Albert and Helene began in a highly conventional fashion: the carefully planned seating arrangement at the wedding of Lina Haas and Willibald Conrad in 1898 had Albert and Helene sitting next to each other. Helene was a friend of the bride, and Albert was invited through the acquaintance of his father with the district judge Richard Haas from Kaysersberg.[115] It was a conventional start to a relationship in that, at the age of 19, Helene was at a suitable age for marriage, as was Albert, a recently qualified theologian and 23 years old, and weddings were always welcome occasions for match-making. On the other hand, the two came from very different social backgrounds. Albert was the son of a liberal pastor from provincial Alsace, culturally and politically oriented towards Paris, and from a modest background. ·Helene was the daughter of a Jewish professor, a committed National Liberal from the capital and, as the son of a banker and brick manufacturer, a member of the Jewish bourgeoisie. Although a wedding between a university lecturer and the daughter of a professor would have been just about socially acceptable, it would not have been a common occurrence, especially if the groom was a theologian.

Albert and Helene's story does not appear to have been one of love at first sight. They did not meet again until three years later in 1901, and in the meantime Albert spoke of having formed acquaintances with other women, particularly in Paris. While Helene's brothers studied medicine, natural sciences, and mathematics, she completed her teaching examination and then attended lectures in art history, a subject considered suitable for a daughter from a wealthy family. But this stereotype does not do justice to her at all. Her dedication to nursing was far from an ordinary occupation for the daughter of a professor. Verena Mühlstein, her biographer, makes a just observation when she argues that Helene's family did not envision her working full-time, even if her liberal education prevented her from becoming a 'conventional, almost submissive, wife, as her mother had been'.[116]

In this respect, Helene's wish to be emancipated brought her in conflict with her mother. She experienced the classic antagonism between her parents' expectations that she become an educated and cultured wife, and her own aspiration of following a—preferably social—profession. Her future husband, by contrast, approved of and even encouraged the emancipation of his future wife and her training as a nurse.

Helene took the initiative to meet Albert again in February 1901. She and some friends, Elly Knapp together with Elsa and Fritz Haas, had founded a cycling club, and she suggested inviting the young man whom she had sat next to at the wedding. Schweitzer sent her a card on 2 March 1901 accepting the invitation. Apparently he remembered very well the girl who had corrected his Alsatian dialect: 'For this card, I wrote three drafts late at night so the sentence structure might meet with your approval.'[117] Thus Schweitzer joined the group's outings, and the bike rides increasingly became 'the occasion that would legitimate our meetings and the more time passed, the less it became its sole purpose'.[118] Helene's first entry in the guest book in the Gunsbach parsonage dates to Whit Monday of 1903, when the cycling club chose Schweitzer's home village as the destination for its tour. What instantly struck Helene about Albert was his visionary rationalism paired with an 'uncommon sensitivity'. She fell in love with him, and he with her. Years later he still wrote her letters from his favourite rock in the hills by Gunsbach, such as the following:

> It seems to me as if you must feel how happy I am. Indeed, I still believe that I can learn everything that I must learn. You know, sometimes the 'universality' of my mind frightens me. I carry it as a burden and tell myself: how happy must be the people who have only one profession, who master one field. But then, when I have the strength again to carry my head firmly on my shoulders, I am proud to have more versatility than the others, and I have confidence in my strength to cope with all the different claims. What joy this is. In the evening, before I go to sleep, I bury my head in my hands and could weep with happiness. [...] You know, you are the only person who can really be happy with me because you live entirely within my own thinking. I feel so strongly, more than I can tell you. That is my happiness. I have been writing to you already for one hour because I pause after every sentence to follow each thought to its end.[119]

Schweitzer, who already in his schooldays had been reluctant to open up to others, shared his thoughts and feelings completely only with two people. The first was his Aunt Mathilde, who had been his closest friend and to whom he dedicated the German edition of his Bach biography 'in grateful memory'. She was the first person he had told of his plans to take in orphans instead of getting married.[120] By November 1902 Schweitzer's relationship with Helene had reached such intimacy that when his aunt died he shared with her the great pain he felt at the 'time of my greatest loss here on earth, where a part of me leaves too'.[121] By this time their relationship had become closer, for Schweitzer had assured Helene of his affections and friendship for her very early in their relationship. On 22 March 1902, on the banks of the Rhine, he told her of his plans for the future, of his wish to serve humanity instead of pursuing an academic career.[122] Helene shared this desire and understood how serious Albert's intentions were, and she offered to become part of his project. Three years later, as Schweitzer was about to enrol as a student of medicine, they made a solemn promise to support each other unquestioningly in pursuit of their ideals:

> But look, at these thoughts that entered into my life, which gradually came closer and closer from some distance and at last finally conquered me. It is my horrible logic that [...] does not allow me any escape and forces me to search for what may fulfil my life! I am at this point. It is difficult to write you this instead of telling it as 'in the beginning' on the bank of the Rhine surrounded by flowers and sun. [...] Earlier I was closer to the goal than you, and now you are active, while I am simply a *privatdozent*—a human who lectures, who does not act. I am so happy for you; now I no longer blame myself for having uprooted you. Now you will find your way. And you will be happy. And if home and family await you, you will be very happy, and if you have to go your way alone, your life nevertheless will be fulfilled. Do you remember that I have a promise from you, from the bank of the Rhine? 'If you need somebody someday, promise that you will call me.' I promised you—and I often think of that. If I ever need you, I will call you, you can be sure. I guard your promise as something precious, like a jewel to pawn.[123]

From the beginning, Albert Schweitzer and Helene Bresslau struggled to come to terms with the realization that their vision of service to humanity would mean that they would have to renounce so much else. Thus, despite her close relationship to Schweitzer after that evening by the Rhine, Helene travelled to England in September 1902 after receiving an offer to teach music, German, and French at a girls' boarding school in Brighton.[124] Yet only a short time later she let Albert know how homesick she was, and she returned to Alsace via London early in 1903.

When Schweitzer, before taking up the study of medicine, declared that Helene was already 'closer to the goal' than he was, he was referring to her appointment on 14 May 1903 making her responsible for orphanages in the old-town district in Strasbourg. Schweitzer also wanted to take in orphaned children, but, as he was the newly appointed principal of St Thomas College, this led to fiery arguments with the dean of the faculty of theology, who was also responsible for the college. Schweitzer requested a larger apartment as well as a fixed salary, for without these he would never be able to realize his plans. The city of Strasbourg also created bureaucratic obstacles for Schweitzer and finally rejected his application to house orphans. As a bachelor he was not considered suitable to raise orphaned children. Thus it was not Albert, but Helene, who was able to put this plan into action in 1903. As an inspector of orphanages, she made home visits that confronted her every day with poverty, malnutrition, and infant mortality. She summarized her vision in terms of a *quid pro quo*: 'We encountered each other with a feeling of responsibility for all the good that we had received throughout our lives and in the awareness that we had to pay for it by means of our assistance to others.'[125]

However, their different assumptions about what was best for them soon brought difficulties. Albert felt that he could not expect Helene to continue a relationship without any prospect of marriage. He was convinced that he could not ask a woman to share a life like the one he had envisioned for himself. He had told his Aunt Mathilde, before he had got to know Helene better, that bachelorhood would be the best path for him to take. He confronted Helene with this frequently:

I have thought about both of us frequently in these days. Always that question: Do I not ruin your life? Your path would be straight if I had not met you, or at least if I had acted with my usual indifference. You certainly would have found a home and a family, all that—and now I think that I have led you astray, and everything I accept from you is stolen from your happiness. That discourages me. I see you leaving for Russia; I know the grief this causes your parents—and if I did not exist, you would remain here; I know this because it is not your destiny to roam and struggle in this world, but to be a true woman in the circle of her family.[126]

But Helene had already explained to Albert on several occasions that she could be content with this kind of idealistic friendship, and these letters must have given her the impression that Albert was distancing himself from her and presuming to determine what was best for her. Helene, for her part, experienced the unusual friendship with Albert, not as a sacrifice, but as reassurance and encouragement for her own vision of helping and serving others.

The relationship between the two of them was indeed socially difficult: she knew that she would not dissuade Albert from his plans, but nor could she marry him—and, from her family's perspective, nor should she. During her tour of southern England, she came to the conclusion that she too would remain unmarried and would work for her living.[127] But when Schweitzer continued to urge her to marry someone else and return to her bourgeois life, she felt increasingly alienated from the one person who had not only helped her envisage a future of serving others but with whom she wished to pursue this vision. Whether it was out of hurt feelings or in order to probe her own thoughts more deeply, she now sought to distance herself from Albert. Her parents forbade her to travel to Russia as she had planned, so she spent the winter of 1903 in Berlin with a cousin of her father's, the painter Johanna Engel. Helene was twelve years younger and called her 'dearest Hans'.[128]

Helene was fascinated by Johanna, an unmarried woman who earned her own money as an artist and lived the free and independent life Helene was struggling to achieve. She did not tell Schweitzer of her plans to go to Berlin until shortly before she left, and he was appalled:

> And the road you want to go—do you know what that is? To be alone in this world—to become an 'old maid', to want to be independent yet not to be able! And you value society—you do not stand above it; you will not detach yourself from it, wall yourself in some occupation—my good, good friend—I fear for you.[129]

Schweitzer saw this stay in Berlin as an attempt at emancipation that was doomed from the start, and he imagined that she would soon be defeated by the social and sexual conventions of their time. This lack of trust and encouragement from her best friend hurt Helene all the more, and the following months were to witness a crisis in their relationship. A last rendezvous at their old meeting place on the Rhine could not take place because of bad weather, and they could hardly meet in public without causing scandalous talk in Strasbourg's society. Instead, Schweitzer wrote four long letters to Helene that weekend. Helene's reply rang of deep sadness rather than of defiance. Schweitzer thought he could not marry Helene, because he and the life he had chosen would not allow it; she did not want to ask him to change his life on her account, although at this time she was more favourably inclined towards the idea of an engagement than he was.

Her response to the four letters came in the form of a short postcard, and on 2 November 1903 she made her way to Berlin on her own.

The two were now separated and filled with sadness, which for Helene developed into depression.[130] Yet she remained committed to the idea of working with orphans and visited an orphanage in Berlin to see what she could do in this field of work. While Albert knew nothing of this, she shared her plans with her special friend Elly Knapp, the only person who might have known about her relationship with Albert and was acting as a bridge between the two unhappy lovers. In this period Helene left Albert's many letters unanswered and sent only this short note for Christmas:

> And I thank you for everything—but please do not ask for an answer from me. You are right; there are a few things I have to tell you, but I *cannot* write [...] I *want* you to be *strong* and *happy*, and that is what you must be, and you have all reason to be so. You should never worry about me, never. [...] The person who has been the most for me while I am here is a sixty-five-year-old lady with a young heart. Her name is Mathilde.—All the best!—Farewell![131]

'Mathilde' is, of course, a reference to Schweitzer's aunt. Those who argue that Helene submitted to a traditional female role by remaining in the shadow of a famous husband and obediently protecting his interests have understood little of this woman's character. Unlike many other women of her time, she attempted to lead her own life as an unmarried woman.

Helene spent Christmas of 1903 in Berlin with Johanna Engel and on 1 January 1904 began a course in nursing at the Stettin City Hospital (now in Szczecin, Poland). While her parents observed their daughter's commitment to social work with growing dismay, Helene quickly recovered both physically and psychologically and, despite the strict routine, felt increasingly comfortable in the hospital in Pomerania. Her only concern was the harsh opinions of the hospital's pastor, a strictly devout and priggish man. It was not without irony that Albert Schweitzer, at the end of an eight-page letter, the first of the New Year, noted: 'Was it interesting, the 'Pastor's Hour'? I cannot well imagine you there, for we are both heretics and may well daunt a respectable servant of the Lord. But we too know him, our Lord, and serve Him and must both suffer and fight in His service.'[132]

What displeased Helene about her work in the hospital was that it seemed to suppress any form of individualism. Her choice of profession as well as her training in Pomerania were an expression of her desire to be independent, and yet working in the hospital required her to submit her personal interests and hopes to the daily routine. Despite this dissatisfaction, Helene completed her training in the hospital successfully.

At this time her father had a breakthrough in his career and in February 1904 became the first unbaptized Jew to become chancellor of a university in the German Reich, a further instance of the liberalism of the newly founded University of Strasbourg. One year earlier, despite being a long-time member, he had been bypassed in the election for editorial chairman of the prestigious *Monumenta Germaniae Historica*, an action that was intended to prevent a Jew from becoming the head of an important research institution on German history.[133] In response, Harry Bresslau stepped down as head of the editorial department of the *Monumenta*, an office he had held for fifteen years. His appointment as university chancellor must have been the cause of all the more satisfaction.

Bresslau and his family felt they would not be discriminated against in Strasbourg, and they felt German—at least more German than the Alsatian Albert Schweitzer, as an exchange about politics between Albert and Helene shortly before the onset of the First World War was to show. In April 1902 Helene completed her nursing course in Stettin and moved to Hamburg to live with an aunt—to the delight of her parents, as they hoped she would once more get used to the life of a marriageable woman in bourgeois society and would prepare for the social duties befitting a university chancellor's daughter. That Helene had completely different plans for her own future and that she wanted more for her life than fulfilling the conventional social duties expected from a daughter or wife was better known to Albert at this point than to her parents.

She wrote often to Albert during her stay in Hamburg on topics related to questions of religion and civilization. She shared the views of her future husband that to be a follower of Christ could only mean consciously making Christ's life an example for her own. The behaviour of a Christian was determined not by expectation of life after death, of heaven or hell, but by the desire to serve others in the spirit of Jesus. In spite of all their other differences, in their beliefs about religion and the world Albert and Helene felt very close to each other. Their plan to serve others, their approach to life, and their ethical beliefs had, after all, been what first bound them together that day on the Rhine in 1902.

Helene returned to Strasbourg for the start of the winter semester and, as was expected of her, took part in her father's social events. Her reunion with Schweitzer immediately after her return was not one of unrestrained joy. Instead, probably owing to pressure from her parents, it was at first rather distanced. As Verena Mühlstein points out: 'It was unimaginable what shame it would bring to the family if Helene became known as Schweitzer's sweetheart.'[134]

While we may smile about these sentiments today, they presented a very real problem for Albert Schweitzer and even more so for Helene Bresslau. It was not so much that his reputation in the faculty of theology was at stake, but that Helene's social standing would be compromised. To the aggravation of her parents, Helene proved she was serious about her independence, and on 1 April 1905 she accepted the post of Second Inspector of Orphanages in Strasbourg. She was encouraged by the mayor of Strasbourg, Dr Rudolf Schwander, who was himself deeply engaged in social concerns. Helene was now responsible for 1,200 children living under the guardianship of the state,[135] and had to visit more than 200 homes every month.[136] Her responsibilities were broad and promised little recognition from society, as her main concern lay with single mothers and their children. The mothers were often servant girls who had become pregnant and then been fired, and the children were often poorly taken care of and ill. Unlike her parents, Schweitzer supported Helene's decision and encouraged her to accept the post.

In December 1904, after his plans to take in orphans had failed, Schweitzer informed Helene that he was considering offering his services to the Paris Missionary Society. Their shared plan began taking on more shape in early 1905. Helene again assured him of her full support, which led Schweitzer to make his final decision to take up the study of medicine in March 1905. Following this decision, their correspondence shows little doubt that, with their new training in medicine, they were planning to go to Africa together. This brought them again much closer to each other, and the crisis seemed resolved. It was with renewed certainty and determination that Schweitzer took up his studies of medicine, and Helene continued her work as an orphanage inspector.

As she would do later for the German edition of the Bach biography, Helene edited Schweitzer's *The Quest of the Historical Jesus* in 1905 and 1906, not only correcting orthographic errors, but also discussing theological questions with him. In 1906 Helene's parents finally came to accept their daughter's relationship with Schweitzer, which they had long known about, but had frowned upon when no engagement took place. In the autumn of 1906 Albert and Helene took their first trip together to Paris.[137] Schweitzer gave her lessons on the organ, and Helene gave him an advanced training course for orphan inspectors. This allowed them to bridge the long and strenuous period while Albert was studying medicine.

Helene was just as active as Schweitzer was. In late 1907 she was involved in overseeing the construction of a home for single mothers on the outskirts of Strasbourg. The additional work resulted in her suffering a breakdown. To recuperate she visited her future parents-in-law in Gunsbach over Christmas. She soon recovered and resolved to join Albert and his brother on a skiing holiday—a highly unusual sport for a woman in those years, yet one that she had mastered years previously. Still, while skiing without poles, she took a bad fall and sustained a serious injury to her back.[138] Schweitzer, with a lifelong distrust of sports ('Football? That's where they chase a ball—are there people who have nothing better to do than chase a ball?'),[139] was more alarmed than Helene was. His concern was justified, though, as she would suffer from back pains and insomnia all her life. Nevertheless, Helene continued working full-time after her accident. She was not to remain the only emancipated woman in the Bresslau family. In 1908 her older brother married her friend Luise Hoff, who taught at the school of commerce in Strasbourg. In the same year, Elly Knapp, another friend, married an editor from Berlin, Theodor Heuss. This small group of self-confident women was to be very important to Helene throughout her life.

Helene's visits to Gunsbach became more frequent, although it is hardly surprising that—not yet engaged—she wondered whether his family, especially his reserved mother, might consider her 'too German, too Jewish, and too cosmopolitan'.[140] But with time

Schweitzer's mother got used to her son's choice, and Helene's relationship with Schweitzer's father had been a warm one from the start. Christmas was celebrated most years in Gunsbach.

Their plan to go to Africa was set. In order to get her certificate in time for their departure, Helene began her one-year training course as a nurse on 1 October 1909 at the Civic Hospital in Frankfurt am Main. She had resigned from her post as orphanage inspector in April 1909. A working day at the hospital might last anything up to sixteen hours, and the salary was hardly more than a pocket allowance, but, as she had done in Stettin, Helene persevered and survived this difficult time. At the end of September 1910, she sat her nursing exam, while Schweitzer was earning the fees for his medical exam at the French Music Festival in Munich.

Then something happened that would have a graver impact on her life than even her skiing accident: she fell ill with tuberculosis. Presumably she had caught the infection in a milder form during her training in Frankfurt around 1910, but the stay in Africa would make it much worse.[141] It takes little to imagine what this meant for the couple's plans in a time before antibiotics when tuberculosis was considered untreatable. In February 1911 Helene entered a sanatorium for treatment that would last four months. On New Year's Day 1912 Schweitzer sent the following lines to Helene, both a retrospect of the past year as well as a preview of the one to come:

> Now 'our year' is here ... how will we be when it has run its course? [...]
> How privileged we are that we can work together, that we have carried
> out what we had planned ... Oh, how different this is from last year,
> when I was full of fear, full of fear ... will you ever know what I suffered
> for you?[142]

At this point Helene had apparently recuperated, yet Schweitzer must have known that a complete recovery was highly unlikely. The word 'tuberculosis' is not mentioned anywhere in their letters. Verena Mühlstein accounts for this by pointing out that in those days tuberculosis, on account of its high risk of infection, was stigmatized as otherwise only sexually transmitted diseases were. At the same time, Schweitzer seems to have anticipated a recovery at least in the long run, as he had informed the director of the Paris Missionary Society, Alfred Boegner, that he need not arrange for a nurse as he had already found one. He can only have been referring to Helene, who, had she still been unwell, he surely would not have put at risk in the African climate.

On 22 December 1911, Albert formally asked Helene's parents for her hand in marriage. They gave their consent in full knowledge of the pair's unconventional plans, to which they assented with heavy hearts. Albert and Helene were married on 18 June 1912 and made their final preparations for departure.

There has been much speculation about the nature of the relationship between Albert Schweitzer and Helene Bresslau. Many of Schweitzer's biographers unjustly relegate Helene to a supporting role. Yet both husband and wife seemed to encourage this impression by never speaking or writing publicly about their long friendship or marriage. In his autobiography, for example, Schweitzer keeps silent about their relationship, with the exception of the following sole reference:

> Last of all I left my residence on the S. Thomas Embankment, in order that with my wife—Helene Bresslau, the daughter of the Strasbourg historian, whom I had married on June 18th, 1912—I might spend the last months, so far as I was not obliged to be travelling, in my father's parsonage at Gunsbach. My wife, who had already before the marriage been a valuable collaborator in the completion of manuscripts and correction of proofs, was a great help again with all the literary work which had to be got through before we started to Africa.[143]

Schweitzer's proofreader—that was all the public knew at first of Helene Breslau. These lines sound unusually businesslike and reserved for someone whose private correspondence to his wife is full of emotion. The tone seems at odds with the fact that the couple wrote each other letters on an almost daily basis, even during the most strenuous times while he was studying medicine. Helene would never see Lambarene as a 'great adventure', but instead as the place in which she could realize her vision and work as a nurse alongside her husband—until tuberculosis finally forced her to return to Europe. It was not so much a life in the shadow of her 'great husband' that distressed Helene. Instead, it was the recurring lapses in her health that prevented her from building their shared vision together—even being forced to surrender this position to other younger women—that troubled her much more. As a result, her relationship with Schweitzer's secretary Emmy Martin, a former opera singer and the widow of a pastor, was often strained. And it was not relieved by Emmy Martin being an invaluable assistant for her husband and often being mistaken for his wife, a circumstance that was facilitated by Helene's frequent inability to travel with her husband. The assessment of Boris M. Nossik that Helene came 'close to the German ideal of a wife, who is selflessly devoted to her spouse' could not be farther from the truth.[144] On the contrary, this married couple was made up of two people who for a long time kept their personal relationship to themselves and later were reluctant to discuss their 'long-distance relationship' in public. At the same time, their correspondence reveals that both were emotionally very sensitive. She must have felt all the more hurt by the accusations that Schweitzer's scarce references to personal matters in his *Memoirs* were an expression of his emotional coldness. The German magazine *Der Spiegel* wrote in 1960:

> The death of his mother (who was run down on a road in Alsace by a German cavalry horse during the First World War), the birth of his daughter, his own marriage—each of these three events he writes only one sentence about in the otherwise almost endlessly sprawling body of his works. The strength of Schweitzer's moral sensitivity is powerful—yet he only turns to the individual person when he sees him suffering.[145]

Claus Jacobi of the German news magazine *Der Spiegel* was sent to Lambarene with the assignment of writing a front-page story on Schweitzer to expose a man who was increasingly revered as a saint.[146] However, though keeping a critical distance as a journalist, Jacobi was eventually deeply affected by this man's charisma and works—as were most visitors to Lambarene. Jacobi admitted that he found it impossible to destroy the 'myth' of Schweitzer. Yet the editorial staff of *Der Spiegel* found it necessary to include criticism, in particular Schweitzer's paternalistic relationship with Africans (an account of which will follow) and Schweitzer's apparent emotional coldness towards Helene, evidence of which was drawn from her being mentioned only once in his autobiography. They overlooked the fact that Schweitzer had always been very reserved in emotional and personal matters. Once he noted:

> A person should not desire to penetrate the being of another. Analysing others—except to help the mentally unfit—is an ignoble pursuit. There is not only a physical but also a mental modesty that we must respect. [...] We can do no more than let others guess at our spiritual being and guess theirs in turn.[147]

3

The Spiritual Adventurer

From Strasbourg to the Jungle and
Back Again (1912–1917)

Departure to Equatorial Africa

The Paris Evangelical Missionary Society sent Schweitzer to a missionary station in Lambarene in what was then French Equatorial Africa (since 1960 Gabon). It was founded as a Presbyterian institution by the American physician and missionary Dr John Nassau in 1876 after a group of Americans had begun missionary work on the Ogowe River in 1874. The French-speaking Congo was claimed by France as a colony in 1892, and the Paris Missionary Society took up its work there, albeit initially without a doctor. Schweitzer, a fully qualified physician willing to work without payment, must have seemed heaven-sent. But his experiences in the Strasbourg faculty of theology were to repeat themselves in Africa, where he would soon meet the limits of what the 'orthodox' pietistic mission would tolerate. Schweitzer was to take an 'examination of faith', something that he refused to submit himself to. The situation was not improved by Schweitzer's assertion that in times of need one should not—on theological grounds—reject even a Muslim should he offer single-handedly to take over a hospital on the Ogowe. The conflict was finally resolved when Schweitzer offered to visit each member of the committee personally in order that each member could decide 'if I really pose such a threat to the souls of the Negroes and the reputation of the Mission'.[1]

It became evident in the course of these conversations that many members feared that Schweitzer, as a liberal academic theologian, might lead the missionaries astray. As a result, Schweitzer was made to promise that he would act solely as a doctor in Lambarene, and would, as a theologian, 'être muet comme une carpe' (be as silent as a fish). Still, his appointment was preceded by a serious conflict that was to remain an issue for many years. Schweitzer declined to become a naturalized French citizen, which would have meant giving up his German citizenship. The protocol of a meeting of the mission records this refusal as being criticized by the Geneva-born Pastor Sautter.[2] At the end of the day, it was Schweitzer's private conversations with high-ranking members of the Paris Missionary Society that finally led to a positive vote.

Schweitzer and Helene were initially sent to the station in equatorial Africa for two years, not as missionaries, but as 'independent medical aides'. In November 1911 Schweitzer managed to convince Minister Lebrun of the French Colonial Office in a private meeting to accept his German licence to practise medicine. There were now no legal obstacles to his working in Africa. In 1912, he began organizing material for Lambarene that had been paid for by donations. He was deeply moved when he realized that German colleagues at the University of Strasbourg were also generously contributing towards the construction of a hospital in a French colony.[3] Schweitzer also raised money before his departure by means of extensive concert tours. It was primarily as a result of these donations that in February 1913 he could seal and ship seventy cases containing materials and medication (bearing the inscription 'ASB') via Bordeaux to Africa. The boxes were constructed so that they could easily be transformed into pieces of furniture.

Schweitzer was worried about the possibility of a war and packed into his hand luggage 2,000 German marks in gold rather than in banknotes. He had given much thought to the possibility of a war breaking out, not only on pragmatic, but also on political, grounds. This shows that Schweitzer was already thinking in political dimensions even before the outbreak of the First World War. He credited himself with the fact that he had 'for many years worked to improve understanding between Germany and France'.[4] In 1913, like many others, Schweitzer still believed war could be averted. Yet his fears about the German military build-up were only too justified. Gunsbach was in the middle of military operations, and Schweitzer's mother was to be killed by a shying cavalry horse in July 1916. A further dimension was added to this tragedy by the fact that when Schweitzer last saw his mother as he was leaving Strasbourg for Bordeaux on Good Friday, 23 March 1913, she had neither accepted nor even understood her son's decision to go to Africa. Instead, she saw this move as an incredible waste of his talents. Suzanne Oswald, Schweitzer's niece, remembers this day vividly: on the day of his departure, Schweitzer came down and asked to have his favourite Gugelhupf cake as a parting meal, but his mother 'pursed […] her lips and left the room. This was bitter for the son. But he knew what he was doing to her.'[5]

Many people in Gunsbach had come to the train station to bid him farewell—with the exception of his mother. There is something of the Old Testament in this scene, where the son is denied the blessing he so longs for from his mother. Schweitzer wanted to maintain a close relationship to his family, his home village, and the entire region, and, as a symbolic expression of this relationship, he obtained a ninety-year lease on the Kanzrain, 'his rock' overlooking Gunsbach, on which he had sat so often as a child and on which he had composed so many letters to Helene as well as parts of *The Quest of the Historical Jesus*.

Before his departure Schweitzer wanted to bring clarity to his academic status. In December 1912, the imperial governor of Alsace-Lorraine, Count von Wedel, had conferred on Schweitzer 'the title "professor" in consideration of his academic achievements'.[6] Heinrich Julius Holtzmann did not live to witness this 'small consolation', having retired in 1904 and died in 1910. Yet what seemed like an advance in his career was in fact the opposite. While Schweitzer could now call himself 'professor', he was informed that his request for a two-year leave of absence had been denied. Going to Africa thus meant giving up his *venia legendi*, his permission to lecture at the university. This decision against his leave of absence can only have taken place after consultation with the faculty of theology, whose members were not all favourably inclined towards him. In June 1912, a first request for a leave of absence had already been denied. Not even the intervention of the university's president, his father-in-law, Harry Bresslau, could alter the decision. Schweitzer's return to academic theology was therefore barred, and his departure to Lambarene meant bidding a final farewell to university life in Strasbourg.

Schweitzer hardly ever used the honorary title of professor that had been bestowed on him. Many letters were addressed to him in

formally correct terms as 'Professor Schweitzer', but he would usually
sign his name with 'AS', 'Albert Schweitzer', or 'Dr Albert Schweitzer'.
There is one telling exception. In a birthday letter of May 1921 to the
theologian Adolf von Harnack, whom he greatly admired, he
announced that he was working on his philosophy of civilization and
soon wanted to return to his humanitarian work, 'be it in equatorial
Africa, where I was, be it somewhere in the Pacific Ocean. But prior to
that I will surely see you. With best wishes, your Prof. Dr. Albert
Schweitzer.'[7] Schweitzer would never go to the Pacific Ocean, nor
would his idea of a Lambarene branch in Cameroon become reality.
Instead in 1924, as before in 1912, he chose Lambarene over a career
in academic theology.

It was not only his mother's silence that made things difficult for the
departing couple. In February 1913, Schweitzer gave the eulogy for
Helene's younger brother Hermann after he had died during an append-
ectomy. This must have made it all the more painful for the Bresslau
family when their daughter departed for Africa a mere month later.

Those who point out that the couple had initially planned to spend
'only' two years in tropical Africa may not adequately appreciate what
this departure really meant.[8] In Libreville, Gabon, 14 out of 100
Europeans died in 1903.[9] Lambarene was in the interior of the
country, and the climate is marked by nearly 100 per cent relative
humidity with tropical nights that are hardly cooler than the stiflingly
humid days. Equatorial Africa was at this point almost unknown to
Europeans. Malaria, bilharziosis, yellow fever, and other diseases
were a constant danger; indeed, they wiped out entire missionary
stations in West Africa and the Ovamboland. Such diseases were far
more common near the equator than in colonies in a more moderate
climate, such as South West Africa, Morocco, or in the South Pacific.

The Schweitzers had therefore been sent to a missionary station
with the harshest climate imaginable. Even two years spent there
could be long and dangerous, and there was a chance that they
would not return. On 26 March 1913, the couple left Pauillac Bordeaux at 4 p.m. and set sail aboard the *Europe* via the Bay of Biscay
towards Gabon. After a rough journey they landed in Dakar, Senegal,
and first stepped onto 'the soil of Africa to which we were to dedicate
our lives, and we felt it as a somewhat solemn occasion'.[10] The next
leg of their journey was a rough one, and Schweitzer became seasick

and learned the importance of securing baggage on sea voyages. Their ship finally reached Libreville on 13 April 1913, where they were greeted by an American missionary named Ford with a bouquet of flowers and fruit, produce of the thriving garden of the Baraka Mission. These abundant gifts of nature reassured the couple, yet formed a distorted and idealized image of their new home. Schweitzer's station in Lambarene had to be built from scratch, and the climate there was far more demanding than on the coast.

On the following day their ship reached Port Gentil at the entrance to the Ogowe River near Cape Lopez, and the travellers had to board the small paddle steamer *Alémbé*. The captain advised them: 'Breathe—for one last time feel the fresh sea breeze! In Lambarene you will long for it often enough.'[11] This would prove to be true, and the Schweitzers would often spend their holidays recuperating on the Gabonese coast. On 16 April 1913, the steamer arrived at the landing in Lambarene, where there were the French office buildings and trading houses. For the last part of their journey, they travelled by canoe the remaining two miles to the missionary station.

News of Schweitzer's arrival had already spread in Lambarene and the surrounding area. He was enthusiastically greeted by several school classes as well as the missionaries Ellenberger and Christol, both from the Paris Missionary Society at the old station in Lambarene, called 'Andende' by the Africans. On top of three hills and surrounded by gardens of fruit trees stood the small white houses of the station. The grounds of the mission measured 600 by 200 yards. Founded directly on the Ogowe River in Gabon, part of French Equatorial Africa, the missionary station of Lambarene lay less than 40 miles from the equator and over 120 miles from the Atlantic coast. The climate was almost unbearable for Europeans. Instead of the promised hut of corrugated iron, Schweitzer had to set up his medical clinic in the station's chicken coop for the first couple of months of his stay.

The African landscape overwhelmed Schweitzer. His first descriptions of it call to mind the young schoolboy who had been so fascinated by 'the sad Negro of Colmar'. Schweitzer wrote glowingly about his first cruise on the Ogowe River:

> In every gap in the forest a water mirror meets the eye; at every bend in
> the river a new tributary shows itself. A heron flies heavily up and then

settles on a dead tree trunk; white birds and blue birds skim over the water, and high in the air a pair of ospreys circle. Then yes, there can be no mistake about it! From the branch of a palm there hang and swing two monkey tails! Now the owners of the tails are visible. We are really in Africa![12]

Schweitzer published these recollections of his first cruise in a book entitled *On the Edge of the Primeval Forest*, which was published in 1921 and sold over half a million copies after 1945, making Schweitzer a well-known name throughout German-speaking countries.[13] The subtitle, *Experiences and Observations of a Doctor in Equatorial Africa*, describes how Schweitzer understood his work there—not as a theologian, or missionary, or philosopher, but as a doctor. The popularity of these accounts explains why Schweitzer's initial reputation was as a 'jungle doctor' in Europe, and not as the author of books on theology or ethics. Schweitzer offered his readers the exotic experience of a 'dark continent', but at the same time gave an insight into its harsh realities:

So it goes on hour by hour. Each new corner, each new bend, is like the last. Always the same forest and the same yellow water. The impression which nature makes on us is immeasurably deepened by the constant and monotonous repetition. You shut your eyes for an hour, and when you open them you see exactly what you saw before.[14]

The working conditions awaiting Schweitzer at the missionary station were extremely difficult and largely consisted in treating the alcoholism and venereal disease that the flourishing trade in timber had brought to this part of Africa. Moreover, traditional village social structures had been destroyed—something that was happening all over Africa:

Now the voyage continues. On the banks are the ruins of abandoned huts. 'When I came out here fifteen years ago,' said a trader who stood near me, 'these places were all flourishing villages'. 'And why are they so no longer?' I asked. He shrugged his shoulders and said in a low voice, 'l'alcohol [...] If we had stopped here in daylight,' said the merchant to me, 'all the Negro passengers (there were about sixty of them) would have gone ashore and bought spirits. Most of the money that the timber trade brings into the country is converted into rum. I have travelled about in the colonies a great deal, and can say that rum is the great enemy of every form of civilisation.'[15]

Schweitzer's reaction to his first day on the Ogowe is typical: 'Thus with the ennobling impressions that nature makes are mingled pain and fear; with the darkness of the first evening on the Ogowe there lowers over one the shadow of the misery of Africa […] and I feel more convinced than ever that this land needs to help it men who will never let themselves be discouraged.'[16]

Lambarene, a Hospital in Africa

From the day of their arrival in Lambarene, Albert and Helene were left in almost all respects to manage by themselves as best they could. The area was under the military control of the French naval base at Libreville, but French administrators only passed through the Ogowe region. Libreville owed its name to slaves from a captured slave ship that had settled there in 1849. With the abolition of slavery after the American Civil War, the transatlantic slave trade slowly declined, and with it Cape Lopez as one of the main trading ports on the West African coast. Yet the inland slave trade on the Ogowe continued into Schweitzer's time without interference from the French colonial government. When it received complaints that French factories or shipments of goods had been plundered, Libreville did little else than send small cannon boats up the Ogowe to fire sporadically at some villages.[17]

In short, there could be no talk of a properly run central government that controlled its borders and maintained order. In the past, Europeans had also become entangled in tribal conflicts. Lambarene was situated on the border between two tribes, the Fang and the more Europeanized Galoa, whose numbers had been decimated by ethnic conflict in the nineteenth century. In order to be successful in Lambarene, Schweitzer had to be aware of this background and avoid getting caught between the two tribes.

Schweitzer had his German prayers translated into both Fang and Galoan for his African patients. He was wise enough to visit the surrounding villages soon after his arrival in order to find workers and establish personal relationships. However, unlike his predecessor Walter Munz and even though this was required of many missionaries, he never made any attempt to learn an African language. This would later give rise to accusations that he had displayed a

typical colonial attitude. He also had strict rules of conduct on the
hospital premises: 'No spitting on hospital grounds!' and 'Return tin
medicine boxes!'

Like Albert, Helene was overwhelmed by the natural beauty of
Africa, and she soon made her peace with their hut's leaky roof and
the enormous ground spiders. Their diaries portray a couple working
closely together and tackling the unaccustomed challenges of everyday
life with realism and humour.[18] Helene's records suggest that, while at
first the work in Lambarene was extremely strenuous, these years were
emotionally among the most fulfilled of their marriage. An ordinary
day for the couple would begin with the morning bells at 6 a.m. and a
chorale by the children. They simply ignored advice from the missionaries that they should take a few weeks to get accustomed to the
climate and concern themselves only with the most urgent cases. By
the second day queues had started forming in front of the Schweitzer
house. However, as the cargo boxes were not scheduled to arrive until
two weeks later through the Catholic Mission, Schweitzer had to treat
patients with the limited medical supplies available in his first-aid kit.
The seventy boxes duly arrived in the night of 26–27 April 1913.
Among the items was the termite-proof piano with organ pedals that
Schweitzer had received from the Paris Bach Society (and that can still
be seen in the Albert Schweitzer Central Archive Gunsbach).

The greatest problem facing Schweitzer after his arrival was that
the African translator they had hired abandoned him. Luckily, one of
his first patients, a French-speaking Catholic, Joseph Azowani, not
only acted as a translator for Schweitzer, but was also to become his
first medical assistant. Meanwhile, Helene assisted Schweitzer during
operations and as a hospital nurse while also supervising the administration of both the hospital and their own household. Though
illiterate, Joseph proved very skilful and quick to learn, especially in
the field of anatomy, even if the former cook would often localize pain
in his patient's 'cutlet' or 'loin' or note when a patient's pulse rate was
high that his or her 'clock' was too fast.[19] Soon Schweitzer was able to
entrust him with carrying out other medical procedures. He was also
learning from Joseph much about traditions, culture, superstitions,
taboos, and local medicine men.

Joseph Azowani was not the only African with whom Schweitzer
formed close bonds during these first months. This belies the criticism

that is occasionally voiced that Schweitzer's relationship with the black population was an entirely instrumental one in that they only served him as workers. Another relationship was formed with Emile Ogouma, a trader in timber. His line of business was of the utmost importance to the construction of the hospital, as the wood industry in the rainforest was strictly regulated. About half of the rainforest was divided into concessions among Europeans, and in the other half Africans were permitted to cut their own wood. Schweitzer and Ogouma took advantage of this regulation. In his book *On the Edge of the Primeval Forest* Schweitzer focuses on the trade in timber and rainforest clearance in 15 of its 176 pages.[20] African-cut timber was cheaper to buy than timber from export-oriented European traders. Schweitzer made the most of this opportunity by keeping on good terms with the African workers and with timber traders such as Ogouma, maintaining these connections as part of his social network. This was how he acquired inexpensive building material for his hospital.

It was due to a tragedy that Schweitzer acquired his second African medical assistant, a man named N'Kendju. Following one of the frequent hippo attacks on the river, a friend of N'Kendju died from his injuries. Before returning to their home village, the uncle of the deceased man needed, as tradition dictated, a scapegoat, and, owing to his presence at the scene of the accident, this person was to have been N'Kendju. Schweitzer, who had attempted to save the man's life, stepped in front of the boy and threatened to report the uncle to the local magistrate. The uncle gave way, and Schweitzer gained another local assistant.[21]

By April 1915 Schweitzer's household was made up of their dog Caramba, fifty-two chickens, three goats, two ducks, a sheep, an antelope, a cat, and a parrot.[22] In the following decades monkeys bearing such names as Antigone, Cosima, Penelope, and Heloise and wild pigs named Thekla and Schufterle were raised in Lambarene. The Wagner-lover Schweitzer named his pelicans Parsifal, Tristan, and Lohengrin and made them famous in a best-selling book. Occasionally they would accompany him on his ward rounds.[23] From the beginning Helene occupied herself with the upkeep of the fruit orchard.

Schweitzer soon gained a local reputation as a doctor and was known in the area as the white 'Oganga', which is Galoan for 'fetish-man'. The first patients to visit Schweitzer in his hen coop turned surgery came with the typical tropical illnesses that Schweitzer had studied in Europe and which he had been lectured on in two-hour sessions each morning by an experienced military doctor aboard the *Europe*.[24] Most common were operations on incarcerated hernias. These were simple to treat but, if left untended, could, like appendicitis, prove fatal. Skin and elephantiasis ulcers, leprosy, sleeping sickness, scabies, dysentery, malaria, heart disease, venereal disease, toothache, and broken bones were also among the many ailments he was called upon to treat.

Schweitzer's first big logistical task was the construction of a medical treatment room to replace the chicken coop. And for this purpose he had been granted 4,000 French francs by the mission. With his three doctoral degrees, he now became a master builder and a somewhat impatient worker foreman. Once again he proved a quick learner, for he soon mastered the principles of construction in a tropical climate. The long huts had to be built on an east–west axis in order to prevent the sun from hitting the entire roof at once, otherwise the temperatures inside would quickly become unbearable.[25] Surrounded by trees offering some shade, the houses were to have neither windows nor walls. Instead, they were enclosed by mosquito nets and raised on posts forged of charred hardwood as a protection from termites. Schweitzer's double-roof construction allowed air to circulate naturally within the room instead of accumulating beneath the ceiling. The floor and roof trusses were also made of wood, while the roof was made of corrugated iron so that the heavy equatorial rains could easily drain off. His buildings were very durable on account of their solid termite-resistant columns and were fairly cool owing to the double roof construction. For his innovative construction techniques for the tropics, Schweitzer was awarded an honorary doctorate in engineering by the University of Braunschweig in 1961.

He managed to get the most out of daylight hours by introducing his own 'Schweitzer time' in Lambarene, which, like daylight saving time in Europe, could be moved forward or backward according to season. One could certainly say that Albert Schweitzer did things his own way, even in Africa.

The presence of the new doctor, however, also created new problems. People who were critically ill were increasingly left in front of the hospital by relatives expecting that Schweitzer would somehow take care of them.[26] Moreover, the lack of space meant that recovering patients would have to watch others dying in the same room, and so Schweitzer soon decided to build a special surgical hut to handle the high number of hernia operations he had to perform. Schweitzer also quickly procured the necessary materials to build an additional emergency and operating room, which measured a mere 13 square metres.[27] For the production of termite-resistant hardwood, he needed money and, above all, many African workers.

The new hospital soon proved highly popular, so that he and Helene—alongside the extensive construction work they oversaw— treated over 2,000 patients in the first nine months.[28] Helene operated the anaesthetic machine, a donation from Europe, while Joseph stood at the operating table as Schweitzer's assistant.

With time, Schweitzer became increasingly acquainted with the history and way of life of his new surroundings: he learned about slavery and cannibalism, about taboos and the unbroken power of the local medicine men, who increasingly became his rivals. In the beginning it was mainly Joseph who explained to Schweitzer his patients' way of life and thinking. He tried to make him understand that, if he accepted as patients those who were already dying or were hopeless cases, his reputation would suffer in comparison with 'the fetish-men, my colleagues',[29] since these

> act like some professors at European hospitals do who do not want their statistics spoiled. And should the unforeseen occur and a patient dies at his hands, then he saves his reputation by immediately finding out who has put the deadly curse on the ill man. Africans believe that knowledge of medicine means first and foremost that the doctor knows if the ill person will die or not and that he does not waste his talents on somebody who is practically dead.[30]

By following advice such as this and because of the numerous hernia operations that allowed so many to survive, Schweitzer's reputation soared in his first months in Lambarene. People would talk with the greatest respect of how Schweitzer administered anaesthetics to a patient: first, the doctor would kill the patient, then remove his ailment, and finally reawaken him to life. Some of the thirty to forty patients he treated in the course of a day also had a clear idea of what his work was worth.[31] One person insisted on paying the ridiculously low sum of 40 francs for an operation—as that was the cost of the thread Schweitzer had used to stitch his wound closed.

The manner in which Schweitzer organized the hospital's accounts and the patients' files suggests that he expected Lambarene to be more than a temporary stop. He clearly expected to be treating patients more than once:

> Each patient is given, on leaving, a round piece of cardboard on a string of fibre, on which is the number under which his name, his complaint, and the medicines given him are recorded in my register, so that if he comes back I have only to turn to the page to learn all about the case, and be spared a time-wasting second diagnosis.[32]

Schweitzer not only established an efficient hospital administration; he also cultivated an almost pedantic frugality, which was, however, necessary in a remote missionary station. He took scrupulous care that all tin boxes and bandaging equipment were returned, considered shaving soap too great a luxury, and used as scrap paper the back of official documents sent to him by the French colonial administration, old calendar sheets, or old lumber bills—for paper was a scarce commodity in Lambarene—and he needed it to record his thoughts on the philosophy of civilization.[33] Money was always an important factor in his decisions, as an item from Europe on its arrival in Lambarene—after paying shipping, customs, and breakage—cost three times the original price. Schweitzer was not pathologically stingy—as some have claimed—since until the late 1950s he had almost continuously to deal with financial difficulties.

Schweitzer also developed a habit of keeping the complete details of the hospital's finances to himself, even when donations had become abundant after he had been awarded the Nobel Peace Prize. His daughter Rhena was not shown the hospital's books and finances until shortly before his death. Schweitzer's unwillingness to talk about the hospital's financial situation may have been rooted in the precarious times he faced between 1913 and 1917. When he left Gabon for Europe as a French internee in 1917, his charitable work for the Paris Missionary Society had left him with over 21,000 francs of debt, which he only managed to pay off with difficulty after the war.

Albert and Helene celebrated their first Christmas in Lambarene together with the Morels, a married missionary couple. Although the climate and hard work increasingly got the better of Helene's health, in the beginning neither her back nor the tuberculosis seemed to cause too much trouble. Sunday afternoons were usually spent taking walks or river cruises into the jungle. Despite her training as a nurse, she even grew accustomed to the poor standards of hygiene as best she could. When Albert saw the cook's son pick sand fleas from his foot with a kitchen knife and chastised him only mildly, Helene remarked indignantly: 'This is how African he already is.'[34] Joseph was able to take their places for routine procedures, and the couple could take a three-week leave to recuperate by the seaside. White patients, too, were now coming to Lambarene to be treated and were looked after by Helene. After fifteen months the Schweitzers felt at home in Lambarene, and the mood was easy and relaxed.

The Outbreak of War and Deportation

Things changed dramatically with French mobilization on 2 August 1914. Helene and Albert held German passports and were considered 'hostile foreigners', which made them, at least officially, enemy aliens. An initial plan to leave Lambarene for Cameroon failed after they were informed by the district captain Cortot that, though they would be permitted to move freely within the premises of the station at Lambarene, they were prohibited from leaving it.[35] They were also forbidden to practise medicine and make contact with Europeans and Africans, and the couple were placed under the supervision of four African soldiers and an officer.[36] This prohibition on practising medicine, however, was soon reversed when all four soldiers sought treatment from him. Schweitzer had a hard time getting over the rapid deterioration of his friendly relationships with several of the French missionaries with whom he had worked well and without the expected disagreements about religious doctrine. A missionary named Ottmann, who was a French patriot, completely reversed his attitude towards Schweitzer and made his daily work a trial, even though Schweitzer by no means approved of German activities in Europe and had declared that the 'worst crisis in history' was taking place.[37]

On account of her own background and her family's political leanings, Helene was in general more positively disposed towards the politics of the German Reich. Yet she kept her opinions to herself, and at first the situation in Lambarene improved. However, with the outbreak of war, Alsace became enemy territory, and goods and medical equipment from Germany were no longer permitted to enter the French colony of Gabon. As a result, Schweitzer was forced to run up debts to purchase what was absolutely necessary for the hospital. By the first Christmas of the war, things at the station had deteriorated dramatically, since, even with the money he was able to borrow, he could not guarantee that enough food from the coast was delivered to Lambarene. In 1915, the situation became critical, when improperly sealed food supplies were infested by ants and termites. To make matters even worse, Joseph Azowani, Schweitzer's first medical assistant, quit his job when Schweitzer was forced to halve his salary.[38] This was a personal disappointment for Schweitzer, because the two had worked well together. He also continued to suffer owing to the tension between him and his French missionary colleagues. This conflict with the Paris Missionary Society would continue into the 1920s. And, finally, the poor supply of food led to both Albert and Helene suffering bouts of tropical anaemia, which were accompanied by the usual symptoms of extreme fatigue.

Schweitzer heard little from home during this time, and the information that did reach him by telegraph via Libreville and Cape Lopez was usually several weeks old. By 1915, the front line that separated French and German troops led directly through the Munster Valley. Only a few miles from the German-held Gunsbach, a battle was fought on the Lingenkopf between 20 July and 15 October that claimed the lives of over 17,000 French and German soldiers in less than three months. On 3 July 1916, Schweitzer's mother became an indirect victim of the war. On their way home from Walbach to Gunsbach, Schweitzer's parents sought shelter from a storm under an umbrella when two Germans passed them on horseback. A third man's horse shied and knocked Adele Schweitzer to the ground. The two doctors who were called to the parsonage from Strasbourg and Sulzbach could do nothing to save her life, and on 4 July at two o'clock she succumbed to her head injuries without having regained consciousness.[39] Schweitzer only learned of this in a letter from his father, which arrived on 15 August 1916. He replied:

There are strange omens: as a ship's siren sounded in the distance,
I knew it would bring me news of this death. Through the room her

picture greets me, the picture we today adorned with palms and orange blossoms. I am still too deeply moved to account to myself for everything, and all I see is the corner of the graveyard in its summer bloom, and I think about how it will be when on returning home together with Helene I shall greet her there.[40]

Schweitzer wrote these lines well aware that his mother had had difficulties coming to terms with his decision to study medicine and leave for Africa. Soon the family had to mourn another victim when in the summer of 1917 Helene's cousin Richard Isay died from battle-field injuries.

As if this were not enough, in the years 1916 and 1917 Helene suffered increasingly from the tropical climate and had to spend ever more time recuperating on the coast. In mid-October of 1916 Albert and Helene set off for N'Tshengue at the mouth of the Ogowe River in order that they might regain their strength there over a period of nine months. This was perhaps the most untroubled period the couple were to spend in Africa. There, in a house belonging to a European friend of Schweitzer's, on the western coast of Africa and in the midst of the turmoil of the First World War, Albert Schweitzer began writing down his thoughts on the philosophy of civilization. This work was born in crisis.

In 1917, working conditions in Lambarene deteriorated further for Albert and Helene, as, after Georges Clemenceau had taken power in France, the colonial government increased surveillance of enemy aliens in the French Congo with the intention of deporting them to France. In 1917 the order came that all 'hostile foreigners' were to be shipped immediately to Bordeaux. With a baggage allowance of only 110 pounds per person, this meant Schweitzer had to leave for an undetermined length of time all his other possessions and the expensive medication in Lambarene stored in corrugated iron huts that were hardly weatherproof. Some household effects were hastily sold, so that at least part of the 21,000 francs of debt might be repaid to the Paris Missionary Society. In order to save the German drafts of his *Philosophy of Civilisation* from confiscation, in two long nights Schweitzer wrote a short summary in French and gave the original manuscripts to the American missionary Ford for safekeeping. The American considered Schweitzer's liberal thoughts so harmful that he would have liked to throw the manuscript once and for all in the Ogowe, yet 'he was willing, in the spirit of Christian charity, to keep it, and send it to me at the end of the war. I could therefore somewhat reassured set out with my wife on the journey to Bordeaux that had been imposed on us.'[41] Only in the summer of 1920 did he have the manuscript in his hands once again.

Schweitzer's relatives were not aware of developments in Lambarene. His last letter, written on 12 December 1916 and sent with the International Prisoners' Service of the Red Cross, probably did not arrive until 18 March 1917. After this letter, Louis Schweitzer heard nothing more of his son until 10 December of that year.

The forced return to Europe almost took a tragic end. When the convoy of about twenty ships with which the Schweitzers were sailing left Dakar in Senegal in the autumn of 1917, a U-15 submarine was lying in wait at the harbour entrance. The submarine commander was Martin Niemöller, who was later interred in a concentration camp by the Nazis for his convictions as a pastor of the Confessing Church. In their correspondence in 1961, they confirmed this near fateful encounter, when Niemöller could have torpedoed the ship carrying Albert Schweitzer.[42] In the end, the convoy was not attacked, and the the *Afrique* brought the Schweitzers as enemy aliens to Bordeaux in mid-November 1917.

4

It Is Good to Preserve Life

*Albert Schweitzer's Philosophy
of Civilization*

'We are all of us just nothing but Epigoni'

Schweitzer used the war years of 1914 to 1917 to lay the foundation for his study of the philosophy of civilization, *The Decay and Restoration of Civilisation*. It adds special significance to his reflections that during a time of war he was studying the importance of civilization and ethics for human coexistence. It is equally significant that he was diagnosing this cultural decay while he was thousands of miles removed from war-ravaged Europe. Schweitzer evidently belongs—in a manner very different, say, from Kant—to that kind of practical philosopher who makes everyday human experiences, rather than categorical systems, the starting point for his thinking. In the light of the butchery taking place not two miles from his home in Gunsbach, Schweitzer formulated his key question: how could this happen? What spiritual aberrations had, together with the political developments, allowed the world to plunge into such a catastrophe?

This was the topic of his first work on the philosophy of civilization, a draft entitled 'Wir Epigonen' ('We Inheritors of the Past'), which, though completed in 1915, was never published. His next work, which had the working title 'Civilisation and the Civilised Nation', aimed to shift the focus away from the 'Epigoni' (that is, from those who inherit past glories)—the key insight unexpectedly revealed to him in Clara Curtius's Berlin salon in 1899.

After his arrival in Africa, Schweitzer began thinking about the core issues of his philosophy of civilization. The breakthrough came, according to Schweitzer, on a cruise on the Ogowe River in September 1915. Since the outbreak of war he had been working on the Epigoni book, which was to explain the ongoing political crisis as rooted in the prevailing world view. However, he was not yet able to explain how a world- and life-affirming ethics for the individual could be established on the basis of these depressing political experiences. This 'iron door' opened in 1915:

> For months on end I lived in a continual state of mental excitement. [...] I was wandering about in a thicket in which no path was to be found. I was leaning with all my might against an iron door which would not yield. [...] I was staying with my wife at the coast of Cape Lopez for the sake of her health—it was in September 1915—when I was summoned to visit Madame Pelo, the wife of a missionary, at N'Gômô, about 160 miles upstream. [...] Slowly we crept upstream, laboriously feeling—it was the dry season—for the channels between the sandbanks. Lost in thought I sat on the deck of the barge struggling to find the elementary and universal conception of the ethical which I had not discovered in any philosophy. Sheet after sheet I covered with disconnected sentences, only to keep myself concentrated on the problem. Late on the third day, at the very moment when, at sunset, we were making our way through a herd of hippopotamuses, there flashed upon my mind, unforeseen and unthought, the phrase Reverence for Life. The iron door had yielded: the path in the thicket had become visible. Now I had found my way to the idea in which world- and life-affirmation and ethics are contained side by side! Now I knew that the world view of ethical world- and life-affirmation together with its ideals of civilisation is founded in thought.[1]

Once he had the principle of Reverence for Life, everything else fell into place, and he was able to develop an entire work on the philosophy of civilization:

> Now there stood out clearly before my mind the whole Philosophy of Civilisation. It divided itself as if automatically into four parts: (1) on the present lack of civilisation and its causes; (2) a discussion of the idea of Reverence for Life in connection with the attempts made in the past by European philosophy to provide foundations for the world view of ethical word- and life-affirmation; (3) exposition of the world view of Reverence for Life; (4) concerning the civilised nation.[2]

Except for the fourth and final section, which was never written, Schweitzer put his ideas on paper over the course of the following decades. Schweitzer's appealing claim that he experienced a revelation on the Ogowe River, however, should be treated with scepticism.

In fact, Schweitzer had already used the term Reverence for Life in the winter semester of 1911–12 in a lecture on 'The results of critical history of theology and the natural sciences for the evaluation of religion'. In this lecture he had declared:

> What life is is not only a riddle to us but a mystery—we only know it through intuition and are worlds away from creating it, for example, with the forces of nature at our command. This is the source of the *Reverence for Life*, which animates even the most convinced of materialists when he avoids treading on a worm on the road or tearing off flowers without reason. And this reverence is the keynote of all culture—in it lies the greatness of Indian culture.[3]

Between September and November 1915, Schweitzer, working mostly in the evenings, began writing the first part of his philosophy of civilization. He was supplied with the necessary literature by Professor Strohl from Zurich and his uncle Auguste through the Red Cross, while Helene took care of hospital business as well as circumstances would allow.[4] The last of Helene's diary entries for their first stay in Lambarene, dated 21 November 1915, simply reads: 'Albert is reading the first part of his Epigoni to me.'[5] Schweitzer worked on this draft until his deportation in the autumn of 1917. In 1920, he completely reworked 'We Inheritors of the Past', without ever publishing the original manuscript.

The reason Schweitzer never published this text was that—as it had been written during the war—it was very pessimistic. He was not alone in this pessimism. Nietzsche, Spengler, and Cassirer all wrote about the decline of the West at this time as well. Schweitzer's philosophy teacher Wilhelm Windelband, one of the most important neo-Kantian philosophers of civilization, also shared in this 'civilizational pessimism'. And in Berlin in 1899 Schweitzer had also attended lectures by the sociologist and philosopher Georg Simmel , who had written about the 'tragedy of civilization'. Schweitzer had then an affinity to the topic, one that was also academic. 'We Inheritors of the Past' differs substantially from Schweitzer's later work written in the 1920s on the philosophy of civilization. This first draft focuses almost exclusively on the 'decline of civilization' and pays little attention to the 'rebuilding of civilization'. The first volume of Schweitzer's philosophy of civilization from 1923 is fittingly entitled *The Decay and Restoration of Civilisation*, and consists of a heavily revised version of 'We Inheritors of the Past'. The second volume bears the title *Civilisation and Ethics*, and thirteen of its twenty-one chapters record the history and development of the principle of Reverence for Life.[6]

The inherent pessimism of 'We Inheritors of the Past' makes it difficult to relate this first work to Schweitzer's later three books on the philosophy of civilization, since these later volumes trace the source of ethics not to society, but to the individual and their ethical responsibility. Schweitzer's concept of Reverence for Life necessarily leads to a life-affirming ethics and world view, while the 1915 edition of 'We Inheritors of the Past' is a pessimistic analysis of its present day. From the first chapter onwards, the tone is gloomy, almost hopeless:

> The belief in the possibility of change is also opposed by the singular and undissolvable relationships that exist between our spiritual and our public life and continually and apparently unstoppably do damage to each other. This is a characteristic of our spiritual decadence. [...] The political catastrophe that has descended on the civilized nations of Europe also displays this double image. In its origins it is the expression and consequence of the decline of civilization that has taken place. Yet at the same time it is a starting point for its further decline. Outward events have wreaked such havoc on our ethos that we have fallen far beneath its original state. [...] What should have led to complete resignation has surpassed it. The decline is so quick and affects all circumstances and events that it is impossible for the individual, however much he should want it, to withdraw into himself and preserve for himself what has been lost to the world. A spiritual decadence that is consummated in the course of two or three generations affects the individual differently than one, such as the Greco-Roman, that was protracted over centuries.[7]

Schweitzer's analysis of the decline of Western civilization resembles that of Oswald Spengler's *The Decline of the West* (1918–22). Schweitzer's critical analysis may be justified by the First World War, yet the question 'how can we restore our civilization?' plays only a subordinate role in 'We Inheritors of the Past'. The reason is not that Schweitzer did not have an answer to this question. Schweitzer was 'an individualist through and through, meaning not only by nature but also on account of his experiences and thinking he was a natural born and sworn opponent of all collectivism'.[8] He explained this relationship in a sermon in St Nicholas on 4 May 1919:

Man must never stop being man. In all of your actions you should *never be impersonal energy*, the *executive organ* in any affair, an *agent of society*; instead you must always grapple with your personal morality, as uncomfortable and as confusing as this may be for you, and attempt in everything you must do, you must attempt to act in a humane way and bear responsibility for the lot that you afford another man.[9]

In another sermon, Schweitzer summarized his basic problem in understanding society and organizations as a collective construct:

Were not many organizations that we had created to counter the poverty of the time almost like idling mills? Every organization, including those that have charitable goals, is in the long term only worth as much as the tireless human energies within them, for *personal initiative*, the varied and adaptable power of the individual, is the element every real achievement is built on.[10]

In both sermons Schweitzer does not speak in the abstract of society as a whole, nor of its collective rise or decline; instead, he speaks of the individual as constituent of all social action. An individual must never be released from personal ethical responsibility for his own actions, even if that person has apparently acted in the interest of his company, society, or country. Neither a concept of political or economic order, nor acting for the supposed common good or out of economic necessity releases the individual human being from moral responsibility for his actions. 'You are nothing, your people are everything' is the opposite of individual ethical responsibility. With the premise that, as each of us is a creature made in the image of God, a person is always responsible for his own personal ethics, and we are committed to reverence for all life, Schweitzer made a philosophical contribution in his later works to the development of what he called a 'civilized nation', rather than offering only an analysis of its decline as he did in 'We Inheritors of the Past'. This was the main reason why he chose to reconceptualize 'We Inheritors of the Past' in his later philosophy of civilization.

Schweitzer's philosophy of civilization was to consist of three separate parts, some of which existed only as drafts. By 1923, he had completed the first and second volumes of *The Philosophy of Civilisation* with the titles *The Decay and Restoration of Civilisation* and *Civilisation and Ethics*. These were written not as academic essays, but instead as an everyday ethics for the twentieth century—and as such they were virtually ignored by academic philosophers, with the notable exceptions of Ernst Cassirer and Karl Löwith, or disparaged as popular philosophy.[11] Nearly 100,000 copies were sold of the two volumes.

Schweitzer worked on a third volume of *The Philosophy of Civilisation* between 1931 and 1945 in an attempt to broaden the scope of European thinking by examining Indian and Chinese thought. It was published in German only after Schweitzer's death with the title *Die Weltanschauung der Ehrfurcht vor dem Leben (The World View of Reverence for Life)*, appearing in 1999–2000 as four consecutive parts in the published works from Schweitzer's estate, *Werke aus dem Nachlaß*. The edition includes diverse pieces of text and an extensive appendix of documents, showing the fragmented character of the work.[12] To date there is no English translation of this third part of his philosophy of civilization.

A planned fourth part to his philosophy of civilization on the 'civilized nation' was never to be completed. Schweitzer now saw the first and second parts of his philosophy of civilization as a project countering the 'fatalist interpretation of history' of his time.[13] In particular, it was directed against Oswald Spengler's *The Decline of the West*, which Schweitzer thought a 'dismal romance': 'On Spengler: he beats time to world affairs like a child beating time to a passing military band. He acts like a woman well paid to wail and lament at the funeral ceremony of our civilization.'[14]

His personal relationship with Spengler was nevertheless amiable. Both authors shared the publishing house C. H. Beck. One day they met an editor, who strode to lunch flanked by the two writers, causing Schweitzer to remark: 'This scene brings to mind a farmer parading his two milk cows.'[15] Although Schweitzer believed that Spengler's *The Decline of the West* was in dire need of a life-affirming corrective, this did not affect his friendship with the historian, as can be seen in a letter of 1932: 'Dear Herr Spengler, a thousand times thank you for sending me your complete political writings. It is very valuable to have a complete overview of your position. I am so absorbed in your enthralling account that I am neglecting my own work over it. Warmest regards, your devoted Albert Schweitzer.'[16]

Nevertheless, Schweitzer takes, with a reference to Spengler's the 'funeral ceremony of our civilization', the opposite approach: 'the ethics of the individual is a string quartet; the ethics of society is military music.' Schweitzer was an antipode to Spengler, who was 'no different from Hegel, but without his optimism'.[17] Schweitzer's ethical concerns were twofold. First, his attempt to create a paradigm shift in traditional philosophy was influenced by his time in Africa. After the slaughter of a whole generation in the course of the First World War, reflection on ethical questions now no longer took place in a 'park', but in a jungle, a 'wilderness' through which Schweitzer attempted to blaze a spiritual and cultural trail towards civilization. Secondly, his compass in this undertaking, as it had been in *The Quest of the Historical Jesus*, was to begin with a thorough history of the problems facing humanity, a historical overview that he had developed more thoroughly in 'We Inheritors of the Past'. This text from 1915 remained a draft because he touched on a large number of diverse topics, all of which seemed to him relevant to the topic. For example, he criticized the concept of freedom and civilization embraced by the Catholic Church;[18] he condemned excessive European nationalism as a cause of the war ('such an unfettered national feeling bordering on mindless as that which had arisen in Europe over the last decades cannot be found in any peoples of the past'[19]); he preferred a monarchy to a parliamentary republic as a form of government ('the real advantages that a republic might have over a monarchy are more than amply made up for by the better stability and continuity of the latter. [...] The character of the true monarchy is its veracity'[20]); and he predicted the depopulation of the civilized nations.[21] In addition, in 1915 Schweitzer was much more rigorous in his fundamental criticism of the decadence and nationalism that marked the political culture of Europe than he was in his later philosophy of civilization.

In the original manuscript of 1915–16 his explanation of the differences between European 'civilised nations' and African 'non-civilised nations' is followed by a chapter entitled 'Civilised Nations and the Colonies'. In this final chapter, which has not been published to date,[22] Schweitzer essentially justifies the primacy of the colonial powers in terms of their higher civilization, a line of argument that also served Schweitzer in his objection to equal civil rights for Africans. Here, Schweitzer firmly rejects political independence for the African colonies and shows himself to be a paternalistic advocate of what he envisaged as a more responsible form of colonialism, one that would raise the level of civilization in the countries it rules. Although he approved of 'moderate' corporal punishment for Africans, as he was convinced that short-term prison sentences would have no effect on them, at the same time he repeatedly emphasized that the exercise of power by the colonial government must serve the interests of Africans and their cultural development. Any form of colonial and European decadence was to be censured.

These considerations are developed throughout this work, leading Schweitzer to the conclusion that it would be best to shelter Africans from the symptoms of decline Europe was experiencing. At the same time, he thought that any progress in civilization could come only from an enlightened form of Western civilization and not from any African counterpart. What may at first appear like a contradiction can be explained if we realize that Schweitzer felt closest intellectually to the eighteenth-century Enlightenment and thought that the ethics of late Stoicism was 'the leaven that ferments the thinking of modernity'.[23] This affinity to the Stoics and the Enlightenment becomes apparent in 'We Inheritors of the Past', where Schweitzer attempts to define the concept of civilization and its roots 'in the Renaissance, the Enlightenment, in rationalism and the great philosophy of the late eighteenth and early nineteenth century'.[24]

Schweitzer saw his philosophical home in a symbiosis of the Enlightenment and classical Stoicism. Remarkably, however, Schweitzer did not acknowledge the substantial role that the experience of living in Africa must have played when writing 'We Inheritors of the Past'. It was common at this time to contrast the decadent and nationalist European with the African 'child of nature'.[25] Claus Güntzel has aptly described this phenomenon with the remark that Schweitzer, who as a zealous European propagated his ideals unmodified in a non-European environment, was a 'colonialist critical of colonialism'.[26] Although he was far more critical of the colonialist enterprise and of European civilization than most other Europeans in Africa, he maintained a lifelong and deeply held conviction of the blessings and superiority of the European Enlightenment and its antique roots. The at times sprawling and not always systematic critique of civilization in 'We Inheritors of the Past' is connected to Schweitzer's work after 1923 by a shared approach to practising philosophy based on elementary life experiences.

What exactly constitutes this 'elementary' aspect of Schweitzer's thinking, which makes it so readable for non-philosophers and so banal for some philosophers, can be seen in his admiration for Goethe as a natural scientist. Schweitzer gave a total of four major lectures on Goethe, the first in 1928 when receiving the Goethe Prize from the city of Frankfurt. Just as he had always claimed that Bach had funded his studies of medicine, Schweitzer added that Goethe had financed his house in Gunsbach. The second and third were in 1932 on the hundredth anniversary of Goethe's death, when he gave memorial addresses in Frankfurt and in Ulm, and the fourth in July 1949 on the bicentennial anniversary of his birth in a talk in Aspen, Colorado, on 'Goethe: His Personality and his Work'.[27] Although each speech differed in important ways, all four reveal his fascination with Goethe: 'When I myself became aware of this and turned back to this nature philosophy [...] then I realised that Goethe was the man who had held out at the abandoned post where we were once more mounting guard and beginning to work again.'[28]

'Work'—for Schweitzer this was Goethe's scientific and philosophical justification of a life-affirming ethics and, above all, its practice. As director of the Weimar Court Theatre, as poet, scientist, and politician, Goethe was so close to Schweitzer because his thinking was more elementary, more practical, and less speculative than that of academic philosophy. Moreover, Schweitzer did not need to develop his ethical concept of reverence himself, as he found it together with a ready theory in the second book of Goethe's *Wilhelm Meister's Journeyman Years*:

> 'Reverence!' Wilhelm was startled. 'Reverence!' they repeated. [...]
> The religion founded on reverence for that which is above us we call the ethnic religion: this is the religion of the multitude of peoples, and the first successful liberation from servile fear. All the so-called pagan religions were of this sort, whatever names they go by. The second religion, based on reverence for that which is equal to us, we call the philosophic religion, since the philosopher, who locates himself in the middle, must draw all the higher elements down to him, while elevating lower elements to his own level, and only in this middle position does he merit the name of sage. Since he can survey his relationship to this kind, and thus to all mankind, and his relationship to all other earthly contexts, essential and fortuitous, he alone lives the truth, in the cosmic

sense. But now we must speak of the third religion, which is based on reverence for that which is below us. We call this the Christian religion, because in it that kind of attitude is most strongly manifested. It is an ultimate to which humanity could and had to attain. But what must it have required, not only to leave the earth behind and to claim a higher birthplace, but also to acknowledge lowliness and poverty, scorn and contempt, humiliation and misery, suffering and death, as divine.[29]

Goethe's concept of reverence influenced educational theories in the nineteenth century. It is also found in Schweitzer's sermons in 1909–10.[30] Long before 1915, Helene Bresslau's enthusiasm for Goethe had led to him read his work. In his talk 'Goethe: His Personality and his Work', Schweitzer identified the philosophies of Plato, Hegel, Schelling, and Schopenhauer as 'dogmatic', while claiming that Goethe was closer to the 'non-dogmatic philosophy' of natural philosophers such as Heraclitus, Thales, or Anaximander.[31]

It was the phrase 'in the beginning was the deed' from Goethe's *Faust* that explains to a great extent why Schweitzer felt that he and Goethe were kindred spirits.[32] Schweitzer, like Goethe, clearly preferred non-dogmatic philosophy, a sort of Stoic natural philosophy. Even so, Schweitzer retained a lifelong respect for Kant's intellectual genius and the Enlightenment as a major achievement of Western civilization. Yet Kant's philosophy did not form an elementary part of Schweitzer's thinking about the world and nature, nor for the ethics he derived from this thinking, unlike mystical religious experience, which did not compete with elementary philosophy, but rather complemented it. Kant lacked something that Goethe had: namely, an awareness for 'something pristine and natural, pagan, which all people bear in themselves from birth', the fateful, the imperfect.[33] Obversely, for Goethe doing what was morally right was the consequence of his most inner feelings, and not only the result of rational calculation or duty.

Schweitzer developed this idea in the third part of his *Philosophy of Civilisation*, and in doing so drew near to a philosopher who, despite their differences in ethics, had an early and lasting influence on Schweitzer: Friedrich Nietzsche. Schweitzer had already read him when he began studying at university in 1893, and this philosopher would become a yardstick for his own thinking.[34] Schweitzer differentiated between 'two types of personality'. A 'natural personality' displays a unity of instincts, impulses, and abilities, while a 'thinking personality' relates to his world through reason. Schweitzer's ideal symbiosis of both types comes close to Nietzsche's idea of the *übermensch*, although this 'superior man' who undertakes a 'transvaluation of all values' at the expense of the weak was diametrically opposed to Schweitzer's ideal of the ethically ennobled individual.

Schweitzer and Nietzsche were connected by the belief that a human being's nature and will to live should not be suppressed, but should instead be developed through thought. Both were convinced that the one intrinsic determinant of the individual is his 'will to live'. It was this sense of vitality and the power of the human will that fascinated Schweitzer as a young man about Nietzsche (to whom he bore a striking resemblance as a student). The essence of Schweitzer's ethics was that the nature of a human being could be realized only as an individual, and not as part of an amorphous mass of people. And it was his belief that this realization of the 'idea of being truly human' had to be moderated by human reason that brought him back to Kant.

Nietzsche was to leave a permanent mark on Schweitzer's later work on the philosophy of civilization, but his influence on Schweitzer's thinking was already evident in a crucial passage of 'We Inheritors of the Past': 'Individualism, if it is not to be more than just an expression, recognizes the danger facing the individual from a collectivity as it threatens to absorb him. The great thing about Nietzsche is that he proclaimed that morality and personality belonged together in a time that had lost all consciousness of this.'[35] In the original manuscript, this passage is directly followed by two sentences: 'By this deed he joins Socrates and Jesus as the third moralist of humanity. His voice is heard with theirs and can never again be disregarded.'[36] Helene commented in the margin: 'Oho!' Schweitzer later deleted these two sentences. His praise of Nietzsche was not a passing whim, as a letter to Helene from 1903 shows:

> I read Nietzsche: *Beyond Good and Evil*—this great and beautiful call to life, to acceptance of life; I hear miraculous strange harmonies that would be mine, too, if my duty would leave me time. [...] It is strange, I can hear the words of Jesus better because I hear that great joy with which He proclaimed them. Some of this laughter is in *Beyond Good and Evil*, this new testament of the pride of human nature, which was supposed to be killed. In Nietzsche was something of the spirit of Christ;

to say this is a sacrilege. It is, however, true; in the end, only the blasphemous is true. But he lacked action; for this reason, his 'pride' paced inside a cage like a captured lion; instead of coming out of his cave to attack his prey, he tore himself to pieces in the end. But he was noble, this man. Had he lived twenty centuries earlier, he could have become St Paul.[37]

It is easy to imagine the reactions that this surprising comparison between Nietzsche and Jesus—or Schweitzer's characterization of Nietzsche as a thwarted St Paul—would have caused among his colleagues in the theology faculty. Schweitzer did not hide his enthusiasm for Nietzsche from his students. In his lecture on 'The Results of a Critical History of Theology and the Natural Sciences for the Evaluation of Religion', given in the winter semester of 1911–12, he declared:

The three great masters of ethics are SOCRATES, KANT, and NIETZSCHE; roughly speaking: SOCRATES made ethics an independent subject and freed himself from tradition, KANT proved its absoluteness against all those views seeking to reduce it to ideas of society or utility, and NIETZSCHE—perhaps the greatest ethicist of all, at least the one who has most to say to those who encounter him openly and are not trapped in his words—he actually proclaimed the entire living human being to be the object of ethics.[38]

Such passages explain why Schweitzer read Nietzsche so intently, even if he came to fundamentally different conclusions in his ethics. The theologian Tom Kleffman notes that Schweitzer's interest in Nietzsche constituted no less than an 'incision in his life, a turning point' that released Schweitzer—and other theologians such as Paul Tillich—'from the unfamiliarity of a traditional, imposed Christian system of belief and its morality'.[39] Schweitzer's principle of reverence for all life stood in fundamental contrast to Nietzsche's writings on the *übermensch* and his ethics of the strongest; yet in his Goethe address in 1932, Schweitzer again returned to this 'elementary' aspect of Nietzsche's philosophy that he had already admired in Goethe. This elementary aspect was for Schweitzer the key to answering the question of how morality and human nature could finally be integrated—a question that Schweitzer believed classical philosophy—but not Goethe—had failed to answer:

Here Goethe takes a very simple path. He does not bother about the derivation and origin of ethics, which the men of his time are attempting to explain, but takes the ethical thoughts which have appeared in mankind as a natural revelation. For, he says, Nature-God reveals itself not only in fundamental physical phenomena, but also in the fundamental phenomena of ethics. [...] So the wind of love blows through the thoughts of Goethe, as it comes out of the prophetical religion of Israel, and out of the religion of Jesus. He who saw even before Nietzsche that the great problem is how man's realization of nobility, which is self-realization, and his achievement of goodness are related to each other—and therein lies his own peculiar philosophical significance![40]

In this sense, Schweitzer's Reverence for Life was not banal, as it was sometimes accused of being, but was instead something elementary. Neither is it part of a speculative philosophical theory; it is an expression of a Stoic natural philosophy, a practical philosophy in the style of Goethe. It was Schweitzer's goal to combine the natural and the moral—and the link was his ethics of love based on the life of Jesus of Nazareth.

Reverence for Life

Schweitzer had already developed the concept of Reverence for Life for his students in the winter semester of 1911–12. It was not an abstract commandment; it was a formula spoken in the awareness that life is displaced by other life.[41] While some had criticized his ethics as being too strongly oriented towards Nietzsche's thinking, Schweitzer claimed he had only radicalized the Golden Rule.[42] For Schweitzer all human beings strive to place themselves in a relationship to the world, and they do this in an existential sense through thinking and knowing—as in Descartes proposes in his maxim: 'I think, therefore I am.' Schweitzer, however, rejected this path, for, if the relationship of the self to the world begins with abstract thinking, then a person finds him- or herself 'irretrievably circling the abstract'.[43] On the contrary,

the most immediate fact of man's consciousness is the assertion: 'I am life which wills to live, in the midst of life which wills to live,' and it is as will to live in the midst of will to live that man conceives himself every

moment that he spends in meditating on himself and the world around
him. [...] Man has now to decide what his relation to his will to live
shall be.[44]

People may negate their will to live, as Schweitzer thought Schopenhauer and Indian philosophy had inconsistently done.[45] Or they
may affirm it, and in so doing act 'naturally' and 'honestly'. 'The
affirmation of life' in Schweitzer's ethics describes not an instinct,
but rather an ethical decision that may be reasonably expected of all
human beings: namely, to treat their own lives and all other life with
reverence, so as to give it its true value. To affirm life, for Schweitzer, is 'to deepen, to make more inward, and to exalt the will to
live'.[46] And yet Schweitzer's ethics demand that a person meets all
life with the same reverence, not despite of but because of his own
will to live:

> At the same time the man who has become a thinking being feels a
> compulsion to give to every will to live the same reverence for life that
> he gives to his own. He experiences that other life in his own. He
> accepts as being good: to preserve life, to promote life, to raise to its
> highest value life which is capable of development; and as being evil: to
> destroy life, to injure life, to repress life which is capable of develop-
> ment. This is the absolute, fundamental principle of the moral, and it is
> a necessity of thought.[47]

Schweitzer conceded that in nature the existence of one creature is
often asserted at the expense of another, a 'puzzling and horrible law',
which even someone who approaches all other life with reverence is
subjected to. Yet a person who thinks and acts ethically will not accept
the brutal logic of 'eat or be eaten':

> But as an ethical being he strives to escape whenever possible from this
> necessity, and as one who has become enlightened and merciful to put a
> stop to this disunion [*Selbstentzweihung*] of the Will-to-Live so far as the
> influence of his own existence reaches. He thirsts to be permitted to
> preserve his humanity, and to be able to bring to other existences
> release from their sufferings.[48]

At this point Schweitzer is surely also describing his own motivation
for going to Africa as a doctor. Friedrich Nietzsche is completely
different: he too affirms the elementary within nature, but, given the

right of the strongest, he saw no need for mercy. For Nietzsche, prevailing ideas of morality are mainly a product of the experiences of inferiority felt by those who are somehow disadvantaged.[49] They seek to compensate the permanent abasement in their lives by postulating their superiority in another area, that of morality. To this end, they have cunningly worked out a justification for their own—from Nietzsche's perspective implausible—moral superiority. In contrast, he argued that it had originally been 'the noble, powerful, high-stationed, and higher-minded' that set themselves and their actions up as good—'in contradistinction to all the low, low-minded, common, and plebeian'. From this 'pathos of distance' they first took the 'right to create values and to coin names for values'.[50] Only in comparison with these 'natural' values can, in Nietzsche's view, the perversity of the subsequent invention of morality be understood: 'The wretched alone are the good; the poor, impotent, lowly alone are the good; the suffering, deprived, ill, ugly alone are pious, alone are blessed by God, blessedness is for them alone.'[51] With this first 'transvaluation of all values' begins for Nietzsche the 'slave revolt in morality', 'that revolt which has a history of two thousand years behind it and which we no longer see because—it has been victorious'.[52]

The whole history of ethics—which for Nietzsche can be largely traced back to the Socratic–Platonic tradition, on the one hand, and the Judeo-Christian tradition, on the other—is under this omen. Once this was understood, the question could no longer be—as it would later become for Schweitzer—about developing a new ethics or reorienting moral attitudes, but about their abolishment. The goal becomes a state of existence 'beyond good and evil'.[53] In this concept of life Nietzsche thought he had found the key to the 'transvaluation of values'. The condemnation of traditional morality, which is born out of a spirit of resentment, is justified because it opposes life and natural selection. The sole aim of the weak is to domesticize life, which is in its superiority spontaneous, natural, and dynamic, and to confine it in a corset of abstract conceptions of justice.

Schweitzer's view of Reverence for Life, on the contrary, knows no 'resentment'. Each life has the same value. As Schweitzer grew older, his early enthusiasm for Nietzsche waned, and he began to emphasize the disparity between them.

Civilization and ethics are intimately related for Schweitzer. In the third part of his *Philosophy of Civilisation*, which he worked on during the Second World War and so once again during a time of crisis, he asked:

> What is true civilization? Generally speaking, civilization is progress, the material as well as spiritual progress of the individual and of nations. The spiritual is essential […] The highest civilization is not the one in which the greatest material progress is realized, but rather the one in which we achieve and realize the noblest form of humanity. Spiritual and ethical ideals make up the essence of civilization. Everything that takes place in the history of humanity has its last and central reason in the thoughts in which the generations concerned live.[54]

This 'noblest form of humanity' was another expression Schweitzer borrowed from Goethe. In another place, Schweitzer described the ethical development of man as 'the highest value'.[55] However, this by no means made him an advocate of the material value ethics, as put forward by Max Scheler or Nicolai Hartmann in the early twentieth century. They created, in Schweitzer's opinion, a system of hierarchies of value with their speculative philosophy and 'lay teachings on revelation'[56] instead of concentrating on practical values, as he was doing in Lambarene.

Philosophy of Civilization and Religion

Schweitzer saw no contradiction between his philosophy of civilization and his mystical theology: they complemented each other well, but a person does not need to be a Christian to live by the principle of Reverence for Life. What Schweitzer calls 'life affirmation' or 'optimism' finds expression in the New Testament: 'For whoever wants to save his life will lose it, but whoever loses this life for me will save it' (Luke 9:24). In Schweitzer's view, classical philosophy 'cannot conceive of the immense impact of Jesus' commandment of love. The ethics of becoming perfect.'[57] Nevertheless, in order to emphasize the universality of this principle, he chose to refrain from references to Jesus when he spoke in lectures on Reverence for Life:

> It has until now been my principle in philosophy never to say more than what is absolutely logical in the experience of thinking. Therefore, I never talk of 'God' in philosophy, but of the 'universal will to live';

this appears to me as two things, as the will of the Creator outside of me, and as the ethical will within me. [...] Therefore I would rather limit myself to describing the experience of thinking and leave pantheism and theism in an unresolvable conflict within me. [...] If I talked in the traditional language of religion, then I would use the word 'God' in its historical certainty and uncertainty [...] I would not avoid forgoing an understanding of the world. Not move beyond the conflict between pantheism–theism.[58]

In a philosophical sense God has a place in Schweitzer's philosophy of civilization, but at the same time his ethics of Reverence for Life has no need for a risen Christ or a God as the Father, the Son, and the Holy Spirit.[59]

Religion and ethics for Schweitzer were based on experience and the subject, and in this sense they were 'elemental'. Those who would sever academic discourse on ethics or philosophy from human experience— something Schweitzer accused almost the entire philosophy of the nineteenth century of doing—misunderstood the nature of ethics and religion. In his thesis on Kant's philosophy of religion, Schweitzer severely criticized the term 'transcendental' because it creates a distance between religious experience and human existence, relegating experience to a numinous, metaphysical epistemology. 'It is the stupidest thing Kant ever invented—transcendental!'[60] This recourse to experience made it impossible for Schweitzer clearly to demarcate the boundaries between theology, a philosophy of civilization, and ethics. For Schweitzer as a theologian, the principle of Reverence for Life was not a religious concept in the Christological sense but a secular, universalizable equivalent of Jesus' ethics of love, which was independent of the historical circumstances of his time and could serve as a universal model of ethical life for humanity today. This was precisely what Schweitzer had attempted to demonstrate in *The Quest of the Historical Jesus*.

Schweitzer considered it a 'logical necessity' that consciousness of the individual's own will to live—'I am life that wills to live'—should be followed by the identification of this same will in others, and that this will must then be experienced as a universal will to live, as 'reverence for all' life. This 'logical necessity' is, however, implausible: many people, perhaps even the majority, value their own life above all else, and their conclusion is therefore precisely not that other life must also have the same value. It is this kind of hierarchizing thinking that Schweitzer attempted to overcome by referring to God's universal 'will to love', which, though revealed in the life of Jesus of Nazareth at a specific time, is timeless. In this sense, Schweitzer understood Jesus as a teacher and a model for others; with his life Jesus showed that ethics is 'active self-sacrifice for the sake of others'.[61]

Christians, Schweitzer believed, had acknowledged this ethical revelation. Yet he believed that beyond all religious and ideological boundaries all human beings endowed with reason could recognize one another as ethically thinking individuals, as brothers and sisters. The knowledge of this natural fraternity of humanity was preserved in the world religions. Schweitzer thus devoted much time, even at an advanced age, to studying the ethics of world religions and their impact on both civilization and human coexistence, for example, in his *A History of Chinese Thought*.[62]

Schweitzer was aware that such an interreligious ethics and philosophy of civilization would have little appeal for academic philosophers. Nor did he receive much encouragement from theologians in this quest for a universally valid ethics. Karl Barth complained that Schweitzer thought it was the human being who decided when ethical principles should be followed, and that Reverence for Life, rather than God, stood at the centre of Schweitzer's thinking.[63] Schweitzer had made a brief acquaintance with Barth in Munster in November 1928 and when Barth fell ill in 1965 sent him two short, friendly notes wishing him a quick recovery. The human being had too much of an active part in Schweitzer's theology for Barth's liking, while God and Jesus were reduced to passive foils for ethical conduct. However, Barth expressed a curious mixture of rejection and admiration when in his last lecture in Basel in the winter semester of 1961–2, he asked:

> Could it not be that such a problematic theologian as Albert Schweitzer—always seen from a theological perspective—might not have chosen the better part, and with him the first of the best, who have tried here and there, without any theological reflection, to heal the wounded, feed the hungry and thirsty, make a home for children without a home?[64]

For his part, Schweitzer objected to the one-sided 'dogmatisation' of Jesus in Karl Barth's so-called dialectical theology, which had a broad following in Germany after the First World War. Although New Testament scholars such as Rudolf Bultmann attempted to go against this trend by 'demythologizing' the gospel, Schweitzer argued that they failed to reach the simple Christian with their message. In the 1950s he wrote to a friend who was a pastor in South Africa:

> Since I know of you, I live in constant worry that the love for truth you share with me will be your doom. Should you ever find yourself without work, you must let me know. Dear Bultmann has caused much harm with the term 'demythologization'. He has made people nervous. Jesus is no myth and never was 'mythologized', only dogmatized, for in adopting the idea of logos from Greek theology, Greek metaphysics has also found its way into the dogmatic conception of the person of Jesus. It is therefore rather a de-dogmatization of the person of Jesus. I have disliked the term demythologization from the beginning and fully understand the aversion felt by the Christian conscience. So promise me that you will never speak this word again; speak only of the Jesus of dogma and the Jesus of the Gospels. The Greeks were familiarized with Christianity through the concept that Jesus was logos became flesh. They could not adopt the concept of the Jewish Messiah. [...] We, however, are used to the idea that the Kingdom of God is where the spirit of Jesus will come to rule the world. Out of all Protestant heretics I am therefore the best-behaved and most ecclesiastical...and can invoke Mark and Matthew better than the church.[65]

In Schweitzer's philosophy of civilization, the determining factor was not the Christian belief in the forgiveness of sin or the resurrection, but the pan-religious element of life affirmation. Without the human affirmation of life, ethics remained a 'romantic ruin that offers no harbour in the storm of life'.[66]

This thought might explain Schweitzer's peculiar judgement that the Danish theologian Søren Kierkegaard was a 'psychopath', whose theology was marked by a 'dysfunction of the will to live'.[67] Schweitzer's evaluation of Schopenhauer's philosophy follows a similar direction; although he admired Schopenhauer for his formulation of elementary problems, he rigorously rejected his world- and life-denying system of ethics:

> Schopenhauer does not think out the pessimistic world view in the large and quiet fashion of the Indian sages. He paces agitatedly amidst it like a nervous and sickly European. Where the former move with majestic

step on the ground of the knowledge which they have attained and which has made them free, and pass from the ethical into the supra-ethical, leaving good and evil behind them as alike over-past, he shows himself a poor Western sceptic. Incapable of living out the world view which he preaches, he hangs on to life as he does to money, prizes the sweetness of rich cakes as he does that of love, and despises rather than sympathizes with mankind. [...] 'To present the whole world abstractly, generally, and distinctly, in the forms of ideas, to paint it as a reflected copy in a set of permanent rational images always ready to hand, this I say, and nothing else, is the task of philosophy.' It is in such paragraphs that Schopenhauer's philosophy really commits suicide.[68]

Schweitzer set his concept of individual life against those of Kierkegaard, Schopenhauer, and others. And by no means did he apply this concept just to human beings.

The Importance of Animals

How human beings treated animals was not incidental to Schweitzer's ethics; on the contrary, it was a test case for the rigorous application of his principle of Reverence for Life. He saw that the cardinal error of all philosophical systems of ethics since Aristotle was their exclusive concern with the relationships of human beings to each other while ignoring the status of animals and plants.[69] When in 1915 Helene recorded that there were fifty-two chickens, three goats, two ducks, a sheep, an antelope, a dog, a cat, and a parrot belonging to their household in Lambarene, this is more than a quaint description of the animals he kept: it is part of the lived principle of Reverence for Life.[70] Everything that Schweitzer observed in his Reverence for Life also applied to animals—although at times there were practical problems, sometimes of a special variety. And so, for example, when ants crossed his desk in Lambarene, Schweitzer did not stop them but instead set out sugary syrup for them as food. He hung his manuscripts on a clothes line to keep them safe from the animals that went in and out of his study. When he preached in Lambarene at Christmas, he spoke—as did his much revered Francis of Assisi—to all creatures. When it came to killing an animal or a plant, Schweitzer made a clear ethical distinction:

1. Albert Schweitzer began his schooling in 1880.

Source: S. Poteau, D. Mougin, and C. Wyss, *Albert Schweitzer: Von Günsbach nach Lamberene* (Günsbach: Edition AISL, 2008).

2. The parsonage in Gunsbach, Albert Schweitzer's childhood home, around 1890.

Source: S. Poteau, D. Mougin, and C. Wyss, *Albert Schweitzer: Von Günsbach nach Lamberene* (Günsbach: Edition AISL, 2008).

3. Albert Schweitzer (*left*) as a 17-year-old grammar-school student with a friend, in 1892.

Source: S. Poteau, D. Mougin, and C. Wyss, *Albert Schweitzer: Von Günsbach nach Lamberene* (Günsbach: Edition AISL, 2008).

4. Albert Schweitzer (second from left) on a bike tour, 1893.

Source: S. Poteau, D. Mougin and C. Wyss, *Albert Schweitzer: Von Günsbach nach Lamberene* (Günsbach: Edition AISL, 2008).

5. Albert Schweitzer at 34 years old.

Source: S. Poteau, D. Mougin, and C. Wyss, *Albert Schweitzer: Von Günsbach nach* Lamberene (Günsbach: Edition AISL, 2008).

6. Helene Bresslau as a nurse at 31 years old.

Source: S. Poteau, D. Mougin, and C. Wyss, *Albert Schweitzer: Von Günsbach nach Lamberene* (Günsbach: Edition AISL, 2008).

7. Albert Schweitzer, his mother, and brother Paul in Gunsbach, around 1913.

Source: S. Oswald, *Mein Onkel Bery: Erinnerungen an Albert Schweitzer*, 2nd edn (Zurich: Rotapfel Verlag, 1972).

8. The mission station in Andende near Lambarene, 1913.

Source: S. Poteau, D. Mougin, and C. Wyss, *Albert Schweitzer: Von Günsbach nach Lamberene* (Günsbach: Edition AISL, 2008).

9. Helene and Albert Schweitzer (on the right) with other Europeans in tropical dress, around 1913.

Source: S. Poteau, D. Mougin, and C. Wyss, *Albert Schweitzer: Von Günsbach nach Lamberene* (Günsbach: Edition AISL, 2008).

10. In 1914 Albert and Helene Schweitzer were confined to Lambarene as enemy aliens.

Source: S. Poteau, D. Mougin, and C. Wyss, *Albert Schweitzer: Von Günsbach nach Lamberene* (Günsbach: Edition AISL, 2008).

11 and 12. In 1917 Helene and Albert Schweitzer were deported from Lambarene and interned as German civilian prisoners of war in Garaison in the French Pyrenees.

Source: S. Poteau, D. Mougin, and C. Wyss, *Albert Schweitzer: Von Günsbach nach Lamberene* (Günsbach: Edition AISL, 2008).

13. Albert holding his 3-year-old daughter, Rhena, in 1922.

Source: S. Poteau, D. Mougin, and C. Wyss, *Albert Schweitzer: Von Günsbach nach Lamberene* (Günsbach: Edition AISL, 2008).

14. Schweitzer (standing on a ladder) also helped in the construction of buildings for his hospital, in winter 1926–7.

Source: S. Poteau, D. Mougin, and C. Wyss, *Albert Schweitzer: Von Günsbach nach Lamberene* (Günsbach: Edition AISL, 2008).

15. The Alsatian sculptor and painter Otto Leiber (1878–1958) made a bust of Albert Schweitzer in Königsfeld, in 1929.

Source: S. Poteau, D. Mougin, and C. Wyss, *Albert Schweitzer: Von Günsbach nach Lamberene* (Günsbach: Edition AISL, 2008).

16. The Schweitzers in Edinburgh, 1932.

Source: S. Poteau, D. Mougin, and C. Wyss, *Albert Schweitzer: Von Günsbach nach Lamberene* (Günsbach: Edition AISL, 2008).

17. Albert and Helene Schweitzer having a beloved picnic on the banks of the Ogowe, 1942.

Source: S. Poteau, D. Mougin, and C. Wyss, *Albert Schweitzer: Von Günsbach nach Lamberene* (Günsbach: Edition AISL, 2008).

18. Schweitzer delivering his Christmas message in Lambarene, around 1950.

Source: S. Poteau, D. Mougin, and C. Wyss, *Albert Schweitzer: Von Günsbach nach Lamberene* (Günsbach: Edition AISL, 2008).

19. At his desk in Lambarene, in 1951.

Source: S. Poteau, D. Mougin, and C. Wyss, *Albert Schweitzer: Von Günsbach nach Lamberene* (Günsbach: Edition AISL, 2008).

20. Albert Schweitzer and his Hungarian colleague Emerich Percy examine a patient suffering from elephantiasis.

Source: S. Poteau, D. Mougin, and C. Wyss, *Albert Schweitzer: Von Günsbach nach Lamberene* (Günsbach: Edition AISL, 2008).

21. Albert and Helene Schweitzer in Oslo to receive the Nobel Peace Prize, 1954.

Source: S. Poteau, D. Mougin, and C. Wyss, *Albert Schweitzer: Von Günsbach nach Lamberene* (Günsbach: Edition AISL, 2008).

22. The plain cross at the grave of Albert Schweitzer in the Lambarene cemetery.

Source: S. Poteau, D. Mougin, and C. Wyss, *Albert Schweitzer: Von Günsbach nach Lamberene* (Günsbach: Edition AISL, 2008).

Whenever I injure life of any kind I must be quite clear as to whether
this is necessary or not. I ought never to pass the limits of the unavoid-
able, even in apparently insignificant cases. The countryman who has
mowed down a thousand blossoms in his meadow as fodder for his cows
should take care that on the way home he does not, in wanton pastime,
switch off the head of a single flower growing on the edge of the road,
for in so doing he injures life without being forced to do so by
necessity.[71]

Such ethical dilemmas arose when Schweitzer, who was not a
vegetarian, wrote about his hunting experiences in Africa for his
European readers,[72] the proceeds of which went to finance Lambarene.
Though he owned a gun and killed snakes or birds of prey that robbed
the nests of the weaver birds in front of his house, he would not shoot
other birds or monkeys. He proceeded with a peculiar gentleness when
he was building.

A feeling for poor creatures may be awakened even in the wildest of
men. I realize this when I set poles. Before a pole is placed in a hole,
I inspect it to make sure that there are no ants, toads, or other animals
inside and lift them out with my hands so that they should not be
crushed by the pole or later perish when the stones and earth are put in
the hole. I explain what I am doing to those who are working with me.
Some smile sheepishly; others are indifferent to the saying they have
heard so often and let it pass by.[73]

On other occasions though, Schweitzer speaks of his 'helpless rage' in
the 'fight that has to be carried on in Africa with creeping insects' that
continuously attacked his supplies of food.[74]

The problem with an ethics extending to all of creation is that it can
make clear-cut distinctions only in theory. Practically, and especially
in Africa, this kind of ethics proved highly elusive—as Schweitzer was
well aware. For animals killed humans, and humans killed animals to
consume their meat for food. Yet, for Schweitzer, killing was the
opposite of the principle of Reverence for Life, and so each time an
animal was slaughtered it was preceded by an ethical decision. The
killing of any animal—even if it were only an ant—required a convincing justification.

Schweitzer's world view was not a collection of static rules, exceptions, hierarchies, and virtues, but instead a deep belief that, when a

person becomes conscious of the consequences of his actions, he should be capable and, above all else, free to act ethically. For Schweitzer, 'a mentality of thoughtlessness' and a growing 'loss of common humanity' in the sense of a lack of concern for one's fellow creatures were more dangerous than a bad person.[75] He rejected the biblical injunction giving human beings dominion over the earth when it was understood to mean unconditional human mastery over nature.

Schweitzer spoke out most decisively on animal welfare in his comments on bullfights and falconry. In 1931, he responded to an article in the Swiss magazine *Atlantis* welcoming the reintroduction of falconry. The magazine published Schweitzer's letter to the editor in March 1932 under the heading 'Falcon Hunting Revisited'.[76] Unlike the authors of the article, Schweitzer could see nothing 'romantic' about this type of hunting and criticized that, under the guise of a love of nature, people were eagerly watching 'a weak creature tortured by a strong one until it falls prey to it'.[77] Someone who truly loves nature, on the contrary, is a person who 'feels himself inwardly united with everything that lives in nature, who shares in the fate of all creatures, helps them when he can in their pain and need, and as far as possible avoids injuring or taking life'.[78] The struggle for survival, while a painful and cruel part of creation, is not a spectacle to be enthusiastically watched.

In 1964, only months before his death, and now in the public spotlight, Schweitzer positioned himself even more decidedly on animal rights in an essay entitled 'France and the Bullfighters'.[79] Schweitzer condemned this so-called sport for its pitiless exploitation of animals. He was surprised that the Christian religion had never taken up the question of animal rights. With the exception of Francis of Assisi, who had little impact on church teachings, it had never seriously addressed the responsibility of human beings to protect each and every creature. Schweitzer observed that in Eastern religions there was a much more positive attitude towards animal welfare. One week after his ninetieth birthday, a passionate appeal for animal protection and welfare by Schweitzer was published by the German weekly paper *Christ und Welt*.[80] We should have not only 'reverence for life' but also 'compassion for all life', for 'compassion knows no bounds'. While Schweitzer did distinguish between 'higher' and 'lower' creatures, ethically all creatures were, following Francis of Assisi, equally 'brothers'. The only path to real humanity is by way of this insight. How a person treats animals reveals the degree that person has internalized the principle of Reverence for Life. In this goal of promoting the absolute protection of life, Schweitzer was willing to be mocked as 'the saviour of worms'. He had already developed an intense relationship with animals in his early years in Gunsbach, but he cultivated it only when he came to Lambarene.

5

The Iron Door Yields

Crisis and Breakthrough
(1917–1932)

Return to Alsace

The Schweitzers were deported to France as enemy aliens aboard the
Afrique in November 1917.[1] After their arrival in Bordeaux, they were
sent to the barracks on the rue de Belville, where they would be
interned with other foreigners. Schweitzer came down with dysentery,
an infection that would afflict him for several years. After three weeks
Albert and Helene were transferred to Garaison, a camp on the site of a
former monastery in the Departement Haute Pyrénées. Here Albert
Schweitzer was hit by possibly the worst personal crisis of his life. It was to
last from his being taken prisoner in 1917 up until 1920. James Bentley
in his biography of Schweitzer convincingly shows that during his internment he was already suffering from depression.[2] Helene, whose health
was fragile after the exertions of living in Africa, once again con-
tracted tuberculosis in the inhospitable climate of the Pyrenees. This
recurrence was to prevent her from ever again spending a prolonged
period with her husband in Africa after 1924. The heavy toll this
period of internment took on Schweitzer's psyche is perhaps best seen
in a photo, possibly the saddest portrait of him, from the year 1918. As
he was unable to play his beloved organ in Garaison, he would
practise by using a bare table.[3]

Schweitzer was co-opted by the camp administrator to be the
unofficial doctor, but in his spare time he worked on his philosophy
of civilization, drafting the chapters on the civilized nation.[4] Helene's
family was able to provide the couple with some money to ease
their stay. At the end of March 1918 they were moved to St Rémy

de Provence, a camp that housed 150 prisoners from Alsace. It struck Schweitzer as strangely familiar.[5] It turned out that Vincent van Gogh had once been a patient in St Rémy when it was a sanatorium and had portrayed it in a famous drawing. Schweitzer was allowed to visit van Gogh's room: 'Like us, he [van Gogh] had suffered from the cold stone floor when the mistral blew! Like us, he had walked round and round between the garden and high walls!'[6] Helene became pregnant during their time in St Rémy. Although the pregnancy was unplanned, their only daughter Rhena was to be a great source of happiness for the two of them. However, the pregnancy posed a serious risk for the mother, who was approaching 40 and already in poor health.[7]

Before the First World War drew to its close, the Schweitzers were released from the camp as a result of their ill health.[8] In July 1918 they set off via Lyons, Zurich, and Constance to return to Alsace. Their daughter was born on 14 January 1919, without any complications for the mother and in the presence of Albert Schweitzer.

Rhena Fanny Suzanne Schweitzer was named after a family friend, Fanny Reinach, and her godmother, Suzanne Oswald, née Ehretsmann, Schweitzer's eldest niece. Suzanne Oswald notes in her memoirs that the dark-haired girl 'received the mysterious name Rhena'.[9] Yet the origin of the name is simple: the Schweitzers would have named a boy 'Rhenus' in memory of that evening on the bank of the Rhine when first they shared their dream of serving others and promised each other their unconditional support and friendship. When a baby girl was born, 'Rhenus' became 'Rhena'—in fact, a common first name of that time, even if Rhena Schweitzer was never very fond of it.

Strasbourg made a bleak and desolate impression on Schweitzer. Owing to the danger of attacks from the air, the city lay in complete darkness on their arrival. Their eagerly anticipated return to Gunsbach was fraught with administrative difficulties, as the village was in the zone of military operations. Trains still ran as far as Colmar, but from there the couple had to travel the remaining 10 miles towards the slopes of the Vosges Mountains on foot. As the last inhabited village before the trenches, Gunsbach had been severely damaged in the war, but Albert and Helene were glad to be back safe and sound at the parsonage, which now housed soldiers alongside the family.

In Gunsbach, Schweitzer's depressive mood improved, but slowly: 'I kept hoping in vain that among my native hills I should get rid of my languor, together with the now slight, now severe attacks of the fever from which I had begun to suffer in the last weeks at S. Rémy.'[10] Schweitzer's health was not only troubled by the long-term effects of his bout with dysentery; he also suffered from a rectal abscess, which was surgically treated on 1 September 1918 by Professor Scholtz in Strasbourg.

Aside from problems with their health, the Schweitzers were plagued by a feeling of having to start again from the very beginning. In order to begin repaying his staggering debts from Lambarene and provide for his pregnant wife, Schweitzer took on a position that had been arranged for him by the mayor of Strasbourg. He became an assistant doctor in the women's ward for dermatology and venereal disease at the Municipal Hospital in Strasbourg, and he was also once again appointed curate at his old church of St Nicholas. He held both positions until April 1921. Moreover, St Thomas College placed the unoccupied parsonage of St Nicholas at the couple's disposal.

When it came to finding a position after five years in Africa, the Schweitzers were hardly received with open arms on their return to Alsace. A teaching post at the university was now unthinkable for someone of German heritage, and the years 1918–19 were far from easy, not only for Albert and Helene, but for most Alsatians. To make matters worse, Schweitzer had to undergo another operation in Professor Scholtz's clinic in Strasbourg, while his wife was struggling with tuberculosis, an infection that became increasingly worse.

However, this did little to diminish Schweitzer's intellectual productivity. On the contrary, he intended to work his way back to health. While recuperating in the clinic in Strasbourg, he completed a twenty-nine-page manuscript 'Notes and Sketches for Ethical Work' and dated it 8 July 1919.[11] In the expectation of being able to continue his work on the Epigoni manuscript, which he had left behind in Lambarene with the American missionary Ford, he immersed himself more completely than ever before in his philosophy of civilization and its relationship to world religions. He attempted to show that 'world affirmation' could be found in each major religion and was the driving force behind all civilizations.[12] As appreciative as Schweitzer was of the 'ethical tendency of Hinduism', he was critical of Islam. Impeding its expansion had been one of the reasons he had offered the Paris Missionary Society for wanting to go to Africa:

> Islam can be called a world religion only in virtue of its wide extension. Spiritually it could not develop to be such because it never produced any thinking about the world and mankind which penetrated to the depths. If ever any such thought stirred within it, it was suppressed in order to maintain the authority of traditional views.[13]

Schweitzer appreciated the mystical elements found in Islam, which, for example, Al-Ghazali had attempted to introduce to orthodox Islam; and he emphasized its ethical orientation, as found, for example, in the religious duty to be charitable.[14] Yet, as a critical theologian of the New Testament, he was disconcerted by the belief in the historicity of the Koran, so that his work *Civilisation and Ethics in the Religions of the World* focused to a much greater extent on Buddhism and Hinduism. The ethical systems of the world religions and the cultural activities of mankind: these were the great themes that occupied Schweitzer while he was an assistant doctor in Strasbourg.

The Lost Penny

After much effort Schweitzer managed to procure a passport in October 1919 and was able to resume giving concerts outside Alsace once again. On returning home he tried to recover the optimism and energy he had enjoyed in the years before the war, but this effort was hampered by his poor health and grim financial circumstances. He felt isolated in Strasbourg and he suffered with the strain of securing a living for his family.

There was a ray of hope a few days before Christmas in 1919, an opportunity that was to change Schweitzer's life dramatically and lift him and Helene out of their seclusion. He received a letter from Lars Olof Jonathan 'Nathan' Söderblom, an archbishop of the Church of Sweden and a liberal theologian with a reputation for being close to the people, inviting him to give a series of lectures at the University of Uppsala over Easter 1920:

> Dear Dr Schweitzer!
> The Olaus Petri Foundation of the University of Uppsala is honoured to invite you to give a series of lectures at our university in one of the

coming years on the subject of the person of Jesus, or the importance of the eschatological anticipation of the Kingdom of God for our time, or the function of religion today, or another topic of your choosing (gladly also touching on church music). [...] The salary for eight lectures is 2,000 Swedish Krona [...] The Olaus Petri Foundation had already had the intention of inviting you before the war.[15]

Söderblom, who had been pastor at the Church of Sweden in Paris in 1894, had studied under some of the same lecturers Schweitzer would later have and had received his doctorate from the Sorbonne in 1901.[16] Schweitzer assumed that the invitation, which he erroneously dated to January 1920 in a letter to Hans Walter Bähr, was motivated by Söderblom still believing him to be under arrest in France and attempting to secure his release.[17] Schweitzer recalled what an offer such as this meant to him at the time:

Thus on the evening of 23 December 1919, on returning home in the lowest of spirits to the parsonage of St Nicholas in Strasbourg that I inhabited as curate of this church, I found a letter bearing several large seals. On reading it I was so moved that tears sprung to my eyes. So I was not completely forgotten, as I had supposed! Ever since the war I had felt, in my seclusion at Strasbourg, rather like a coin that had rolled under a piece of furniture and has remained there lost. I had, after all, been given the opportunity to speak of the thoughts on the ethical world view which I had been carrying around with me over years! Also, the lectures were to be published! Having resigned myself to writing down this work only for myself, I could hardly believe this![18]

Söderblom's invitation was soon followed by others. Only a short time later, the University of Cambridge invited Schweitzer to give a series of lectures on civilization and ethics and, as a result, other universities approached him as well. After receiving an invitation from Mansfield College of the University of Oxford, Schweitzer voiced his suspicions in a letter to Söderblom that his Swedish mentor might have had something to do with all this.[19] These invitations enabled Schweitzer, who had chosen to renounce a university career, to gain an international reputation and profile as a scholar. Especially in England, there was extensive interest in Schweitzer as a theologian and philosopher of civilization.

A letter to Söderblom's wife Anna after his sudden and untimely death on 26 June 1931, composed after Schweitzer had held a memorial service for his mentor in Lambarene, expressed the extent of his gratitude towards Söderblom: 'What part the dear Archbishop played in my life you know. To him I owe that I was able to return to Lambarene—to him that I was allowed to present my philosophy of civilization for the first time—never can I forget what he meant to my life.'[20] Throughout his life Schweitzer felt an intimate connection to this brother in spirit, to his pragmatic commitment to ecumenism, to the League of Nations, and to his passionate calls to end the First World War. For these efforts the charismatic Swede had been awarded the Nobel Peace Prize in 1930—just before his death.

Schweitzer later discovered that he himself had been repeatedly nominated for the award over the years by Söderblom's friends from Sweden, Switzerland, and Germany. They had petitioned the Nobel Committee, although Schweitzer had specifically requested that they let the matter rest. When Schweitzer heard he had not been able to deter his admirers from their plan, he turned in August 1938, almost in despair, to his Swedish benefactress Baroness Greta Lagerfeld and asked her to prevent the prize from possibly going to him. He feared that the prize money and the ensuing fame would rob him of his most faithful friends and supporters in Alsace and Switzerland, who at this time also provided the majority of his European assistants. They might also assume that he would no longer have need of financial support.[21]

Over Easter 1920 Albert and Helene travelled as Söderblom's guests to Sweden for three months, where Schweitzer's lectures and organ concerts were very well received. He was aware of the significance his Olaus Petri lectures at the University of Uppsala would have for his future career and prepared them carefully, focusing also on the style of their delivery. In spite of his high, somewhat reedy voice, Schweitzer was well aware that he was rhetorically gifted. He worked with an interpreter, the theology student Elias Söderstrom, who would not only translate his speech sentence by sentence but also mimic his intonation: 'He catches it like a ball that he throws on at once to the audience.'[22]

The wonderfully resonant tones of Swedish organs were also well suited for Schweitzer's rendition of Bach. After only a few weeks of his

lecture and concert tour through this country, which had escaped the
ravages of war and was still wealthy, the greatest part of Schweitzer's
debts had been paid. When he left Sweden in July 1920, Schweitzer
had firmly made up his mind 'to take up again my work in Lambarene.
Till then I had not ventured to think of it, but had got used to the idea
of becoming a lecturer at the university again. Some hints I had
received before departing for Sweden pointed to Switzerland as the
country I might set my hopes on.'[23]

Schweitzer was referring to the honorary doctorate he had received
from the University of Zurich in 1920 and his friendly relations to
members of the faculty of theology in Berne. What Schweitzer owed
to the faculty of theology in Zurich can be seen in the dedication of *The
Mysticism of Paul the Apostle* from 1930: 'To the Faculty of Theology at
the University of Zurich in grateful memory of the love I was given in
the most difficult of times.'[24] This first honorary doctorate was an
important motivation for him, for 'in learned circles I could have
believed myself entirely forgotten'.[25]

In Sweden Schweitzer's benefactress Baroness Greta Lagerfeld
from Gammalkil suggested that he write a popular book on his
African experiences and invest the profit in rebuilding the hospital.
He followed this advice and finished writing *On the Edge of the Primeval
Forest* one month after his return from Sweden. It was first published in
a Swedish translation, later in the German original in Switzerland,
and afterwards in all major languages. It contained photographs of
Lambarene taken by Richard Classen, a native of Hamburg who had
spent time in Gabon in 1914 as a timber merchant. The book made
the name Lambarene familiar to over 100,000 readers in Germany
alone by 1927. In clear and simple language Schweitzer critically
examined European clichés about Africa, covering a diverse range
of topics from polygamy to witchcraft and from the slave trade and
problems of colonization to the African mentality. Above all, he
proved a keen observer and an excellent narrator. He could write
about the timber trade as effortlessly as about life in a missionary
station in equatorial Africa. The book was a commercial success
beyond all expectations and secured the continuation of Schweitzer's
work in Lambarene.

After their return from Sweden in April 1921, Schweitzer resigned
from his posts as curate and assistant doctor at the hospital and

together with Helene moved back into his father's parsonage in Gunsbach. During his stays in Strasbourg to use the library there for research on his *Philosophy of Civilisation*, he slept in the attic of a parsonage. On Palm Sunday in 1921 Schweitzer accompanied the first ever performance of Bach's St Matthew Passion on the organ in Orféo Catalá, Barcelona. Further lectures on the philosophy of civilization and the early Christians secured a livelihood for his family. In November 1921, Schweitzer visited Sweden again. January and February of 1922 were spent in Britain giving lectures at Mansfield College, an Oxford college with a Protestant tradition, and at Selly Oak College in Birmingham, which had been founded by Quakers. His topic in Cambridge was the importance of eschatology, and in London he talked about the Apostle Paul.[26] Finally, he travelled once again to Sweden via Switzerland, which had become a reliable base for him after his contact with Bishop Söderblom. The entire summer of 1922 was spent working on his *Philosophy of Civilisation*, completing the first volume, *The Decay and the Restoration of Civilisation*, and the second, *Civilisation and Ethics*, in early 1923.[27]

While still correcting the proofs, Schweitzer was already packing cases for his second prolonged stay in Africa, planned for 1924. Directly before his departure, he prepared a short fifty-nine-page version of *Christianity and the Religions of the World*, based on the lecture he had given to an academic audience in Birmingham.[28] The writing of his *Memoirs of Childhood and Youth* came as a spontaneous impulse during a visit to a friend, the pastor and psychiatrist Oskar Pfister, who had encouraged Schweitzer to tell him about his early years and recorded everything so that it might be published in a youth magazine. The result of the two-hour conversation was the book.[29]

James Bentley claims that Schweitzer visited Pfister as a patient. This is, however, hardly likely, as Pfister's daughter recalls the sociable character of the meeting. What is more, one of Pfister's letters from 8 May 1922 mentions only transcribing Schweitzer's memories and treating his writer's cramp.[30] The time of the meeting also speaks against Bentley's claim. Schweitzer did indeed confuse the date of his visit to Pfister, writing of his visit in his autobiography as taking place while he was passing through Zurich 'in the early summer of 1923'. In fact, the meeting had taken place on

26 May 1922.[31] The confusion over the date ten years after the
event seems just as unintentional as the mistake over the date of his
preliminary examinations in medicine in his curriculum vitae. James
Bentley, however, interprets the confusion, not as a lapse of memory, but as a deliberate attempt on Schweitzer's part to conceal his
appointment with a psychoanalyst—just as Helene had kept her
tuberculosis a secret for fear of being socially ostracized.[32] While it
is true that in 1919 Schweitzer was under some pressure on account
of his health and the situation within his family, and this did have an
impact on his psychological well-being, improvement was brought
on, not by sporadic contact with his friend Oskar Pfister, but by the
support offered by Nathan Söderblom.

Schweitzer's lectures and organ recitals between 1920 and 1922
had been financially rewarding enough not only to allow him to repay
his Lambarene debts completely, but also to have a house built in
Königsfeld in the Black Forest, where he wanted Helene and Rhena to
live during his stays in Africa. Since the German economy lay in ruins,
he was able to buy the house at a bargain price. In Königsfeld Rhena
could attend a good yet strict school run by the pietist Moravian
Church. Like Schweitzer, the Moravians resisted interpreting ecclesiastical dogma too strictly, yet their biblical literalism was very different
from Schweitzer's reading of the Bible. Rhena did not always like the
severity of the teachers at the school, but she managed reasonably
well.[33] Unlike her daughter, Helene never did feel at home in the
Black Forest.

After leaving his wife and daughter well cared for, Schweitzer could
set off on his second voyage to Lambarene in 1924 without a guilty
conscience, although the separation burdened the couple—above
all Helene.

Back in Lambarene

On 14 February 1924 Schweitzer left Strasbourg for Lambarene. He
was accompanied by Noël Gillespie, an Oxford student and the son of
Alsatian–American parents, who was to act as his assistant. While
Helene's health did not permit her to travel with them, she planned
on joining her husband the following year. In the meantime, she
and Rhena returned to Königsfeld in Baden. Although Schweitzer

regularly wrote her loving letters, letting her know how much he missed her, this did not altogether improve Helene's psychological state. Her situation was aggravated by insomnia, presumably a result of her chronic back pain and her psychological condition. A visit from her friend Johanna Engel, who joined her in the Black Forest for several weeks, provided her with some relief.

Verena Mühlstein correctly points out the tragedy of Helene's situation. She did not want to tell her family and friends of her misery at her husband's absence and her inability to join him. This situation was to characterize her life. When, after Albert's fiftieth birthday, she found out that younger women were accompanying him to Africa in her stead, her world collapsed. Other women were now carrying out the work that she and Albert had promised to share in 1902:

> The following months are arguably the darkest in Helene Schweitzer's life. Week by week she sinks into deeper depression. Sometimes she fears that in her longing for her beloved Albert she will lose her sanity. The depression is increased by the fact that her father-in-law, with whom she had always been on good terms, is very ill following a stroke, and the health of Harry Bresslau, who has bladder cancer, has deteriorated rapidly.[34]

Helene hardly ever mentions the state of her health in letters to her husband. Her medical records, kept by her physician Dr Max Gerson, show that tests for tuberculosis were positive from 1925 onwards. She either still had tuberculosis or was suffering a relapse. This made a return to Lambarene for the time being out of the question.

Her father-in-law Louis Schweitzer died in May 1925, and her own father Harry Bresslau was soon to follow him in October 1926, aged 78 years. One can but guess what this meant to Helene, to all intents and purposes a single mother, infected with tuberculosis, and increasingly lonely. In spite of all her suffering, she desperately wanted her husband to rebuild the hospital in Lambarene, and she supported this work with her remaining strength, always hoping that she could at some point return to Lambarene. In August 1926, she even completed a three-week course in tropical medicine at the Institute for Medical Mission in Tübingen. But her home would always be in Europe. Meanwhile Schweitzer, some might say stubbornly, did not deviate from his plan to rebuild Lambarene—if necessary without his wife and daughter. In letters he certainly claimed to be suffering from Helene's absence, yet this did not deter him from continuing in Lambarene without respite from 1924 to 1927. As he had learned of his mother's death in 1916 while working in Africa, so he received news of the deaths of his father and his father-in-law.

But Schweitzer considered his work in Lambarene supremely important. This has brought him both much admiration and much criticism. How could he have made his work more important than his family? Helene supported him and tolerated his priorities from the outset, albeit with a heavy heart and at the price of struggling with depression. Helene's early hopes that she was to be an integral part of the work in Lambarene proved mistaken, and it took a long time for her to accept that she and Albert would never lead a normal married life together. Schweitzer could only intuit his wife's condition from her letters, since she presented herself as stronger and more robust than in fact she was. He also simply lacked both time and energy to spare too much thought on domestic problems in Europe, as he was completely immersed in the problems around him. On the sea voyage to Lambarene in 1924, he had with him four sacks full of letters, all of which he intended to answer personally.[35]

After his arrival in Lambarene on 9 April 1924—one day before Easter—all he found left of the hospital were the corrugated iron barracks and the hardwood framework of one of the large bamboo huts. He had to start all over again, beginning with repairing the doctor's bungalow and rebuilding the hospital huts. Schweitzer had planned to continue work on his *Mysticism of Paul*, but there could be no thought of it at this point. During the day he was a doctor and at night a builder, although almost no labourers were available as they were all working in the timber trade.

Despite the rising numbers of patients, things soon began to look up. In 1925 Schweitzer managed to add to his team two doctors, Victor Nessmann, a former fellow medical student, and Marc Lautenberg, both natives of Alsace. Moreover, there were now two nurses in Lambarene, Mathilde Kottmann, a qualified nurse, and Emma Haussknecht, a former teacher, also both from Alsace. With the help of these dedicated volunteers, a new hospital with improved medical facilities was built further upstream and closer to the village of Lambarene. The construction of a new hospital had become necessary because the old one on the site of the Andende mission station could not be enlarged since it was hemmed in on every side. As a result not only was there no room to provide housing for the ever-increasing numbers of patients, but it was also impossible to build the isolation ward desperately needed after the particularly severe dysentery epidemic following a famine in 1924–5. There was also no room to house the increasing number of psychiatric patients; the old site only had two cells available.

Schweitzer later faced accusations that over the years he had neglected to improve medical standards in his hospital. The care afforded to his psychiatric patients, however, shows that in some respects he was ahead of his contemporaries. While in parts of Europe psychiatry was still in its infancy, and comprehensive psychiatric care was unheard of, Schweitzer's new hospital had from the outset provided assistance and support to psychiatric patients. This was especially important in Africa, where sufferers from psychiatric illnesses were often disowned or even put to death by their families.[36]

With the arrival of the two new doctors in 1925, Schweitzer left most of the medical work to Nessmann and Lauterburg and in the following eighteen months dedicated himself almost entirely to recruiting and training African labourers for the construction of the new hospital. The philosopher became a foreman. He reported on his everyday life and work in *More from the Primeval Forest*, a sequel to *On the Edge of the Primeval Forest*.[37] How is Christmas celebrated in the rainforest? How do European doctors cope with the tropical climate? How are snake bites and black water fever treated? Who are the Leopard Men? What are superstitions and taboos about?[38] The aim of these booklets was to increase moral and financial support for his work in Lambarene. 'We trust in them [our friends in Europe] as we dare what we dare and undertake what must be accomplished if pain and suffering in this unhappy country are to be effectively fought.'[39] Publications such as *On the Edge of the Primeval Forest* (the German edition was first published in 1921), *The Forest Hospital in Lambarene* (1938), and stories such as 'African Hunting Stories' and 'Ojembo the Jungle Teacher'[40] financed Schweitzer's work at this point—and they made him famous throughout Europe. He was now better known to his readers as a jungle doctor in a pith helmet rather than as a philosopher or theologian in a lecture hall. However, these publications enabled Schweitzer to extend his planned two-year stay to three and a half years and complete construction of the new hospital.

His secretary Emmy Martin and his brother-in-law Pastor Albert Woytt provided a well-functioning logistical organization in Europe—at first in Strasbourg and then in his home in Gunsbach—that coordinated all donations, requests, and letters. Here, once again, Schweitzer had a small, devoted group of helpers for whom he was a father figure.

On 21 January 1927 the old hospital was moved to the new location upriver. Schweitzer was justly proud of this comparatively modern hospital in the jungle:

> That evening on the last journey we made, I took with me the mental patients. Their guardians never tired of representing to them that in the new Hospital they would live in cells with floors of wood. In the old cells the floors had been just the damp earth. [...] There I was in possession of a Hospital in which, if need be, we were in a position to accommodate 200 patients and those who accompanied them. During recent months the number had been between 140 and 160. Provision was made also for the isolation of dysentery patients. The building for the mental patients was erected from a fund established by the Guildhouse congregation in London in memory of a deceased member, Mr Amrose Pomeroy-Cragg.[41]

Schweitzer was aware of the importance some of his patrons placed on public recognition, and so mentioned this particular contributor by name.

On 21 July 1927, Schweitzer left Lambarene for Europe, taking with him Mathilde Kottman, while leaving Emma Haussknecht behind to manage affairs in the hospital. He spent the next two years travelling throughout Europe on concert and lecture tours. However, Helene again saw her husband only briefly. In August 1928, he was awarded the Goethe Prize by the city of Frankfurt, making him only the second recipient after the poet Stefan George. In his acceptance speech, he emphasized the affinity he felt to Goethe's practical philosophy. Schweitzer was also awarded an honorary doctorate by the Charles University of Prague, where he gave talks on Bach, his work in Lambarene, and the Hellenization of Christianity.[42]

Schweitzer spent the early part of 1929 in Königsfeld together with his family. Here he worked on and finally finished writing *The Mysticism of Paul the Apostle*, begun in 1911 with *Paul and his Interpreters*, so that it could be published in Germany by 1930.[43] On 4 December the Schweitzers, husband and wife together, set off from Bordeaux for Africa. Helene's health did not in truth allow for such a journey, but the bitter experiences of the years 1924 to 1927 led her to risk the consequences so that she could accompany her husband and see the new hospital for herself. The tropical climate required him regularly to exchange his helpers, and he had taken the opportunity while in Europe to engage four Swiss doctors for Lambarene. This would surely not have been possible had it not been for his growing fame.[44]

As was to be expected, Helene was forced to leave Lambarene at Easter in 1930, an event that Schweitzer, failing to mention her illness, downplayed in his memoirs: 'Towards Easter 1930 my wife had unfortunately to return to Europe, since she felt the climate was taking its toll on her.'[45] While an x-ray on her return showed that at least her tuberculosis was no worse, her overall condition was bad enough for her doctor Max Gerson to put her on an eight-month treatment, including a strict low-salt diet.

Albert, though he was only 57 years old, fed the growing interest in himself with the publication of an autobiography, *Out of my Life and Thought*.[46] One important reason for its swift publication was that the Great Depression was making itself felt in Lambarene. A slump in the timber trade in Gabon hit Schweitzer's white patients hard. He wrote home to Helene: 'the largest of firms are unable to pay their bills. Almost all white people are now here to no avail.'[47] Schweitzer needed to write an autobiography in order to have an income.

If in 1919 Schweitzer had still felt like 'a lost penny that had rolled under a piece of furniture',[48] by now he was the famous doctor of tropical Africa. Three main factors had transformed the indebted, ill, and interned man of 1918 into the celebrated recipient of the Goethe Prize in 1928. First, he had regained his health. In his autobiography, Schweitzer quoted his teacher of surgery, who, after he had just passed his state medical examination on 3 December 1910, had remarked: 'It is only because you have such excellent health that you have got through a job like that.'[49] And in a letter of 1937 Schweitzer wrote of himself: 'How I must be thankful to God for my first-rate nerves.'[50] Secondly, the opportunities he had to undertake lucrative concert and lecture tours and write bestsellers such as *On the Edge of the Primeval Forest* were crucial in making Lambarene known to the world and consolidating its finances.

Thirdly, Schweitzer was a brilliant 'networker'. The Albert Schweitzer Central Archive Gunsbach alone stores over 65,000 letters sent to Schweitzer.[51] Letters were his main means of attracting donations. Almost every evening he would sit down at his desk in Lambarene and compose letters by the light of a green petrol lamp. A 'ghost-writer' helped him in this undertaking. Mathilde Kottmann's handwriting bore an uncanny resemblance to Schweitzer's own, allowing her to answer some of the letters addressed to him. This practice was no different from what happens in the offices of ministers or bishops, with the exception that Mathilde Kottmann's letters were handwritten in Schweitzer's name.[52] The writing of another aide in Lambarene, Alida Silver, also became similar to Schweitzer's over the years. Indeed, these women were said to have a 'Schweitzer handwriting style'. Whether he asked them to change their handwriting, or whether they chose to imitate a person they much admired, is unclear. However, the fact that after working together over decades three people should at the end of their lives have almost identical handwriting is in any case telling about the 'spirit of Lambarene'.

Schweitzer knew exactly which contacts he had to cultivate. His correspondents included Alsatian farmers from Gunsbach and American presidents. He received letters from such public figures as the Dalai Lama, Queen Elizabeth II, Wernher von Braun, Albert Einstein, Winston Churchill, Adlai Stevenson, Karl Jaspers, Werner Heisenberg, Karl Barth, Rudolf Bultmann, and even Brigitte Bardot, while exchanging views on topics as diverse as animal rights, the Cuban missile crisis, and dialectic theology. Particularly in his later years, the letters would follow a pattern: he would express gratitude for the friendly lines received, turn to the request that had been made of him, then report on his everyday life in Lambarene, and close the letter with the remark that he should have liked to have written more, but was hindered by writer's cramp. Yet he always took care to give his sponsors enough information about the work in Lambarene so that they continued their financial support.

On the Proper Treatment of Natives

Opinions tend to differ sharply on how Schweitzer saw Africa. Some people think of him as a well-meaning, kindly doctor in the jungle who cared for his African patients with heart and soul. But this 'caring for' already sounds as though he was a typical colonial patriarch, someone who called Africans his 'younger brothers' and led his hospital with a firm hand. His critics say he never truly understood Africa. A third group goes so far as to accuse Schweitzer of being a racist.

One thing is certain: Schweitzer thought that the European colonization of Africa was in principle right, although only on condition that it served to help develop African society rather than exploit it. In his view, Europeans shouldered a heavy responsibility for the development of African society and its economy, 'in which the natives can assert themselves against Western trade'.[53] Although he accused Africans of 'laziness and fickleness', Schweitzer was opposed to all forms of forced labour, and in the name of protecting their culture he recommended prohibiting the import of alcohol from Europe.[54] He saw himself as a purveyor of European civilization', as a helper of Africans, yet also as someone who was culturally superior—an 'older brother' to the African 'child of nature'.[55] Such a paternalistic attitude was typical of its time. However, Schweitzer was in fact fairly liberal in comparison to the approaches favoured by some of his fellow Europeans living in Gabon, most notably in his rejection of violence and coercion as a legitimate method of discipline.

Before his first stay in Africa in 1913, Schweitzer saw Africans above all as victims of colonialism and wanted to protect them from his fellow Europeans. There was little evidence to show he felt a sense of cultural superiority. In 1905, he sent the following thoughts on the topic to Helene Bresslau:

> Thank you for everything you write to me of the Congo. What a brave girl you are! I see you so clearly, as you pose your questions in the middle of the meeting. Do you understand now that it is more a work of humanity than of religion, that in these great rainforests people are needed to guard the Negroes from white predators? What do I care about fever! I will overcome it.[56]

Schweitzer used the German word *Neger* (Negro), which already had a pejorative connotation at the beginning of the twentieth century.

Helene avoided it and instead spoke of 'natives'.[57] Schweitzer's idea of Africa, as was often the case, underwent a dramatic change with his arrival on African soil. He travelled to Africa with a liberal view on the question of race, but changed his mind when he hired Africans to work for him in Lambarene. Like many expatriates, he thought that colonial policy devised in the far-off metropolises of Paris or Berlin had little to do with the reality of the African periphery. This was one reason why Schweitzer came to think differently about race than he had while sitting at the feet of the 'sad Negro of Colmar' in 1890 dreaming about an Africa that had never existed. On the African work ethic, he wrote in *On the Edge of the Primeval Forest*:

> For my part I can no longer talk ingenuously of the laziness of the Negro after seeing fifteen of them spend some thirty-six hours in almost uninterrupted rowing in order to bring up the river to me a white man who was seriously ill. The Negro, then, under certain circumstances, works well, but only so long as circumstances require it. The child of nature—here is the answer to the puzzle—is always a casual worker.[58]
>
> The Negro, then, is not idle, but he is a free man; hence he is always a casual worker, with whose labour no regular industry can be carried on. This is what the missionary finds to be the case on the mission station and in his own house on a small scale, and the planter or merchant on a large one. When my cook has accumulated money enough to let him gratify the wishes of his wife and his mother-in-law, he goes off without any consideration of whether we still want his services or not.[59]

In a different section he noted:

> The Negro is worth something only so long as he is in his village and under the moral control of intercourse with his family and other relatives.[60]

On the topic of compulsory labour he wrote:

> In German Africa, where labour compulsion was enforced in a humane but effective manner, the results were, according to some critics, good; according to others, bad. I myself hold labour compulsion to be not wrong in principle, but impossible to carry through in practice. The average colony cannot get on without having it on a small scale. [...] But the enforcement of general labour compulsion is complicated by the fact that under it men have practically always to leave their village and their family and go to work many miles away.[61]

And, finally, Schweitzer summed up the relationship between black and white:

> The maintenance of the native population must be the first object of any sound colonial policy. Close on the problem of labour comes that of the educated native. [...] Not long ago there came to me a native Government clerk, just at the time that there was also a missionary staying with me. When the clerk went away, the missionary and I said to each other: 'Well, we could hardly compete with him in essay writing!' His chief gives him documents of the most difficult sort to draw up and most complicated statistics to work out, and he does it all faultlessly. But what becomes of these people? They have been uprooted from their villages, just like those who go off to work for strangers. They live at the store, continually exposed to the dangers which haunt every native so closely, the temptations to defraud and to drink.[62]

Once in Africa Schweitzer took the middle ground between his repeated criticism of European colonialism and his—for the time relatively moderate—paternalistic attitude towards Africans. While expatriates commonly meted out severe beatings as a form of punishment, Schweitzer reportedly gave his African employees 'only slaps' or a 'kick in the backside'. Sonja Poteau, also a volunteer in Lambarene, recollected that the Africans he punished were more amused by his disciplinary measures than frightened of them.[63] It was by no means Schweitzer's intention to abuse Africans physically or to establish discipline by brute force. When Schweitzer distinguished between uncivilized, semi-civilized, and civilized peoples, or feared the depopulation of civilized nations, he was displaying an educated European's feeling of superiority towards Africans and revealing himself once more to be a 'child of his time'.[64] Schweitzer's attitude, however, was 'moderate' in that, unlike most expatriates, he never questioned the dignity of Africans. Even liberal academic theologians, such as Werner Picht, published commentaries as late as the 1960s about the work ethic and disposition of Africans that today are justly considered unacceptable. Picht referred to the following anecdote told by Schweitzer:

> The first rains begin in mid-September. It is now essential to store all the wood for building in a dry place. As we have hardly any men

capable of working in the hospital at the moment, together with two helpers I carry the timber myself. In doing so I catch sight of a black man dressed in white, who is visiting a patient. 'Hey there, friend,' I call out, 'won't you help us a bit?' 'I am an intellectual and don't carry wood,' was his answer. 'You're lucky,' I replied, 'I wanted to become an intellectual too, but I never succeeded.'[65]

Werner Picht drew his own conclusions from this episode:

More complicated than the savages are the natives who consider themselves educated. [...] The greatest difficulty lies in the fact that for the natives Schweitzer was with there is no concept for 'fellow human being'. Generally, he can summon compassion and helpfulness only for members of his own tribe. [...] It is therefore no wonder that pity and despair at times form a 'tangled web' in the heart of the jungle doctor.[66]

Picht was trying to explain the frustration Schweitzer experienced in his day-to-day contact with his labourers. However, what he writes in this passage is the verbal equivalent to what Schweitzer did when he occasionally struck his African workers. Neither Picht nor Schweitzer would presumably have thought himself doing anything morally questionable or even racist; instead, both would have emphasized they wanted to teach a lesson.

Schweitzer preached a concept of life that categorically excluded discrimination by skin colour, yet he behaved differently with black people—as he was never seen to slap his white employees. The journalist Norman Cousins is often quoted in support of Schweitzer's alleged colour blindness:

Clara [Urquart] gave another illustration of the fact that his [Schweitzer's] sternness knew no color lines. Once, he became particularly exasperated at an African who was putting boards of lumber in the wrong place. He mumbled that he could almost slap the man. Clara, who was standing nearby, was shocked and said so to the Doctor. 'Well, Clara,' he said, 'I don't think I'm going to slap him. But if I do so, I want you to close your eyes and imagine that I am slapping a white man. In that case, it will probably be all right with you.'[67]

The fact remains, however, that in Lambarene Schweitzer struck only Africans. An odd ethical inconsistency shaped his attitude towards his 'younger brothers'. In that respect, he remained a child of his time.

But the ethical standards Schweitzer was judged by were stricter—and rightly so. Someone 'who looks like a close relative of God' is not supposed to hit black people, especially as the writer in the magazine *Der Spiegel* continues: 'And he behaves like one, too.'[68] But Schweitzer, to the disappointment of his most zealous admirers, failed to live up to the expectations placed on him, and so this side of him is deliberately suppressed in nearly all biographies written about him.

On the other hand, what is repeatedly commented on is Schweitzer's idealistic view of Africa that largely glossed over—if only at the beginning—the cruelty of nature. This is how he recollected his first voyage on the Ogowe River:

> River and rainforest [...] Who can really describe the first impression they make? We seemed to be dreaming! Pictures of antediluvian scenery, which elsewhere had seemed to be only the creation of fancy, are now seen in real life. It is impossible to say where the river ends and the land begins, for a mighty network of roots, clothed with bright-flowering creepers, projects right into the water. Clumps of palms and palm trees, ordinary trees spreading out widely with green boughs and huge leaves, single trees of the pine family shooting up to a towering height in between them, wide fields of papyrus clumps as tall as a man, with big fan-like leaves, and amid all this luxuriant greenery the rotting stems of dead giants shooting up to heaven. [...] We are really in Africa![69]

As for so many other visitors, Schweitzer's first emotion upon arrival in Africa was one of fascination. However, as a doctor his idealism was soon dampened by the suffering a life in this climate caused many of his patients. At the same time, Schweitzer proved to be a perceptive and critical observer of social conditions and was able accurately to describe the causes of problems in Africa. For example, he blamed white expatriates for the rise of alcoholism among the black population and, again in contrast to most missionaries, defended polygamy by arguing 'that we should accept, but try to improve and refine, the rights and customs which we find in existence, and make no alterations which are not absolutely necessary'.[70] But, as regards the relations between the races, he argued:

> What must be the general character of the intercourse between them? Am I to treat the black man as my equal or as my inferior? I must show him that I can respect the dignity of human personality in every one,

and this attitude in me he must be able to see for himself. [...] The Negro is a child, and with children nothing can be done without the use of authority. We must, therefore, so arrange the circumstances of daily life that my natural authority can find expression. With regard to the Negroes, then, I have coined the formula: 'I am your brother, it is true, but your elder brother.' The combination of friendliness with authority is therefore the great secret of successful intercourse. [...] When, before coming to Africa, I heard missionaries and traders say again and again that one must be very careful out here to maintain this authoritative position of the white man, it seemed to me to be a hard and unnatural position to take up, as it does to everyone in Europe who reads or hears the same. Now I have come to see that the deepest sympathy and kindness can be combined with this insistence on certain external forms, and indeed are only possible by means of them.[71]

Schweitzer summed it up in the following words: 'That it is so hard to keep oneself really humane, and so to be a standard-bearer of civil-isation, that is the tragic element in the problem of the relations between white and coloured men in equatorial Africa.'[72]

Some journalists voiced the opinion that he had only an abstract interest in Africans in spite of the good his work was doing them. Gunther criticized:

Schweitzer's interest in Negroes is—aside from healing—practically non-existent. Just as he wrote a book that was much admired in India, *Indian Thought and its Development*, without having ever been to India, so he spent a half of his life in Africa, which is admirable, without ever having learned an indigenous dialect [...] or even having travelled to a country other than Gabon [Schweitzer had also been to Cameroon].[73]

And the *New York Times* wrote in 1965 in its obituary:

His employees were quite familiar with the businesslike and sometimes grumpy and brusque Schweitzer in a solar hat who hurried along the construction of a building by gingering up the native craftsmen with a sharp: 'Allez-vous OPP! Allez-vous, OPP-opp. Hupp, upp. OPP!' When Schweitzer was in residence at Lambarene, virtually nothing was done without consulting him. [...] His autocracy was more noticeable as his years advanced and as his medical assistants grew less awesome of him. Schweitzer regarded most native Africans as children, as primitives. It was said that he had scarcely ever talked with an adult African on adult terms. He had little but contempt for the nationalist movement, for his attitudes were firmly grounded in nineteenth-century benevolence. Although thousands of Africans called him 'le grand docteur', others plastered his village with signs, 'Schweitzer, Go Home!'

'At this stage,' Schweitzer said in 1963, 'Africans have little need for advanced training. They need very elementary schools run along the old missionary plan, with the Africans going to school for a few hours every day and then going back to the fields. Agriculture, not science or industrialization, is their greatest need.' His attitude was sharply expressed in a story he liked to tell of his orange trees. 'I let the Africans pick all the fruit they want,' he said. 'You see, the good Lord has protected the trees. He made the Africans too lazy to pick them bare.'[74]

Claus Jacobi, editor-in-chief of *Der Spiegel*, recollected that, though Schweitzer closely observed his movements at the station, he was surprisingly candid with him. And he treated his African workers in a manner that Jacobi had not expected, slapping them on the face if he felt the pace and quality of their work left something to be desired.[75]

Ultimately, the relations between Africans and Europeans were also a question of morality for Schweitzer, as was his life's work in Lambarene. He would repeatedly emphasize the importance for white men to gain authority among Africans. But respect could not—as many expatriates believed—be won by means of brutality, or by technical superiority, or by ordering the natives about; respect could be gained only by conveying moral authority:

> The child of nature, not having been artificialized and spoilt as we have been, has only elementary standards of judgement, and he measures us by the most elementary of them all, the moral standard. Where he finds goodness, justice, and genuineness of character, real worth and dignity, that is, behind the external dignity given by social circumstances, he bows and acknowledges his master; where he does not find them he remains really defiant in spite of all appearance of submission, and says to himself: 'This white is no more of a man than I am, for he is not a better one than I am.'[76]

As he grew older, Schweitzer's views on racial issues became more problematic. The journalist James Cameron accused him of having open racist tendencies in his book *Point of Departure*, which was published in 1954 following a visit to Lambarene. In the course of his forty years in Lambarene, he argued, Schweitzer had never permitted an African to eat at his dinner table. Moreover, in a conversation with Cameron, Schweitzer went so far as to defend the operations of the South African prime minister and architect of the Apartheid regime, Daniel François Malan (1874–1959).[77] But it is implausible to put Schweitzer in the company of a nationalist and racist such as Malan, who had admired the German Nazi Party, which Schweitzer abhorred. It was instead the case that Schweitzer worried that too close a proximity to Africans would undermine his authority as a white man. But this alone does not make him a defender of Apartheid. In 1951, Schweitzer sought information on South Africa's 'native policy' from a neutral source, Cape Town's Revd Herbert Bahr, to whom he wrote:

> Do please write to tell me how things stand with regard to the problem of indigenous people in Malan's regime. I read and hear so many contradictory things that your advice would be valuable. I have concerned myself with the problem of the indigenous population as it exists here. But that of South Africa is a different one from ours.[78]

Cameron also refers to a derogatory remark Schweitzer made about Gandhi, calling him 'A great educator who let himself be tempted into entering politics.'[79] Yet anyone who has read *Indian Thought and its Development* must know how much he admired Gandhi. A casual criticism expressed to Cameron should not therefore be given undue importance.

Schweitzer's biographer James Brabazon attempted to find out why Schweitzer did not permit Africans to enter the dining room, which he reserved for his white helpers. One reason, Brabazon argues, is that Schweitzer would have been concerned about undermining his own authority as well as that of his white employees. This rule could also possibly be related to the African tradition of sharing meals out of one pot.[80] Brabazon was evidently attempting to defend Schweitzer, who could not imagine taking his meals together with blacks.

However, Schweitzer's basic attitude towards Africans was positive, even if his everyday experiences had slowly transformed him into an 'old hand' who was convinced he knew just how to treat 'the African'. A further reason for Schweitzer's sometimes harsh tone may be that, as the director of an isolated hospital in the middle of the rainforest, he bore responsibility for sometimes more than 600 people.[81] This did not allow for more diplomatic and cautious behaviour, which might be more appropriate in faculty meetings at the university in Strasbourg.

It is hardly surprising that, in addition to admiration, many Africans also expressed harsh criticism of Schweitzer's paternalistic style of leadership during decolonization in the 1950s. These critics also argue that his hospital supported the French colonial system both materially and ideologically. In fact, Schweitzer was highly critical of decolonization:

> He who is acquainted with the colonies and well intentioned towards the colonial peoples cannot accept as the first and most important aim that they should achieve independence as quickly as possible—as though this were all that is necessary. The chief goal can only be that they should assimilate under the most favorable conditions whatever in civilisation is useful and essential to them, thereby becoming people of real worth and humanity. When they have made this measure of progress, they may then decide whether it is imperative that they should govern themselves. It is, however, in no way useful to their development that they should now be brought to consider their independence as the first essential. To the degree in which their attention is fixed upon this secondary matter they will be diverted from preoccupation with what should really concern them.[82]

Schweitzer made no efforts to educate young African doctors or, when the time came, to hand over the administration of Lambarene to Africans. Yet, in contrast to most expatriates, he did not exploit Africans, but instead treated their illnesses. And he did this in full awareness of the guilt that colonial Europe had amassed over the centuries. In 1927, he remarked:

> In the end, everything good that we bestow on the peoples of the colonies is not benefaction but atonement for the great suffering that we white people, from the day that our ships found their way to their shores, have brought on them. The problems facing the colonies today cannot be solved through politics. The change that must come is that white and coloured meet in an ethical spirit. Only then will understanding be possible. Working towards the creation of this spirit means practising future-promising world politics.[83]

6

With Central African Greetings

The Time of the Third Reich (1933–1945)

The Calm before the Storm

Less than four years after Schweitzer had been awarded the Goethe prize by the city of Frankfurt, he was invited back to give a talk on the centennial of Goethe's death in the city's opera house on 22 March 1932. Rhena and Helene were in the audience, and for Schweitzer it had a special meaning that, on the thirtieth anniversary of his first meeting Helene, he was able to talk about Goethe. However, the ceremony took place under police protection for fear of attacks by National Socialist Stormtroopers.

Schweitzer did not only pay homage to the poet, but prophesied a bleak future for the country:

> The city of Frankfurt remembers its greatest son on the hundredth anniversary of his death, once more in the brilliant sunshine of spring— but also in the greatest emergency this city has and Goethe's people have ever known. Many inhabitants of this town, of the Reich, are out of work, suffer from hunger and despair. Who dares measure the burden of worry about sheer existence that we, gathered for this celebration here, have born into this house! The spiritual life is threatened by the material life. So much that was being done recently for civilisation and for culture must now be discontinued. [...] So pressing are the necessities and the anxieties of this time [...] Do we still desire to remain faithful to the ideal of human personality even in the midst of hostile circumstances, or are we now on the contrary loyal to a new ideal for humanity which ordains that man shall achieve a differently ordered fulfillment of his nature in the restless merging of his being in organized society? [...] And now, a hundred years after his [Goethe's] death, it has come to pass, through a calamitous development determined by events and through the influence of that development upon the economic, the social and the spiritual everywhere,

that the material and the spiritual independence of the individual, so far as is not already destroyed, is most seriously threatened.[1]

Schweitzer believed that the humanist ideals of the Enlightenment had been lost in Germany. At the same time he observed that 'not everything in history is ordained to be overthrown in the process of constant change', but rather 'that ideals that carry within themselves enduring worth will adjust themselves to changing circumstances and grow stronger and deeper in the midst of them'.[2] The principle of Reverence for Life could survive because it contains a profound, almost palpable, truth about humanity, a truth not even the Nazis could destroy. However, the extent to which Hitler and his followers would be successful in accomplishing just that was at this point beyond the imaginations of both Schweitzer and his audience. The storm-troopers' threatening presence on this day offered a bitter taste of what was to come.

Early in 1932 Schweitzer moved into his newly built house in Gunsbach, which had finally been completed with the money from the Goethe Prize he had received in 1928. This new residence became his headquarters in Europe and was highly welcome to Schweitzer and his helpers, especially his assistant Emmy Martin. Helene would, however, have ambivalent feelings towards her new home throughout her life. This was the place where the work in Africa was planned and organized, and because of her illness she no longer felt fully a part of this undertaking.

A few months after his speech on Goethe, Schweitzer travelled to Britain, where he was showered with honours: in the summer of 1932 the University of Oxford bestowed on him an honorary doctorate in theology; in Edinburgh there followed an honorary doc-torate in music and theology, and at the University of St Andrews one in law. He made such an impression on the students in St Andrews that two years later they nominated him as chancellor. Schweitzer felt unable to take on this position and turned it down, not only because of his work in Lambarene, but also because he spoke very little English.

In between receiving such honours, Schweitzer used his time in Europe to visit old friends and acquaintances, appraise organs, and give organ recitals.[3] In November 1932 he met Helene in Berlin, where she was undergoing further treatment for tuberculosis under the supervision of Dr Max Gerson. After a relapse in 1930 while she was in Africa, she was admitted to the hospital and put on a strict salt-free vegetable diet and hormone therapy. While she was recovering, she was subject to 'strong irritability, nervousness, and a tendency to grumbling and quarrelsomeness'.[4] That the last weeks of her eight-month stay in the clinic were spent correcting proofs of her husband's autobiography *Out of my Life and Thought* did not improve her spirits.[5] In 1932, a pulmonary cavity was found to have once again grown and the overall state of her health deteriorated rapidly; she was forced to undergo yet further treatment. The couple had originally planned to spend the next couple of months together while Schweitzer worked on his *Philosophy of Civilisation* manuscript. As tuberculosis was a stigmatized illness, she kept the state of her health a secret from her friends in Berlin, which was an exceptional burden for her.[6]

At the same time the political situation in Germany worsened as Hitler seized power at the end of January 1933, which Schweitzer witnessed in Berlin at first hand. A short time later he was once more on his way to Lambarene, and he shared his pessimistic thoughts with Helene:

> Oh, I suffer terribly from these times, I am completely without hope. What will all of this lead to…The situation in France. In Germany Hitler is seizing the reins. They were such dreadful days for me in Berlin. […] In these days the last chances for improving relations were relinquished…The days I spent with you were the most monumental dates in post-war history…God help us out of this…And this terrible pressure that rests on me numbs me in my work. Every day I have to tear myself out of this sadness in order to get to work. Sometimes I am unable […] Now I have barely the strength to hope. I always tell myself, why write this down…Before a new spirit can arise, the madness of these nations will have destroyed everything that still stands… But I always force myself to hope once more.[7]

Helene's poor health had once again forced her to stay in Europe. When her doctor Max Gerson was dismissed on account of his Jewish ancestry, Helene left the hospital. She realized that the popular support for the Nazi Party and the anti-Jewish sentiment in Germany made it necessary for her to depart immediately. Together with her daughter Rhena, she decided to emigrate to Lausanne in neutral

Switzerland. Schweitzer agreed that Rhena 'must spiritually belong to a country whose education system still holds onto the ideals of Humanism'.[8] The majority of Helene's relatives, most of whom were assimilated Jews, were now leaving Europe one after the other.

Schweitzer was repeatedly pressurized to protest Nazi politics publicly. Max Born, whom Schweitzer had met in Königsfeld in the winter of 1928–9, urged him in July 1933 'to return to Europe and call on the civilized world to try and act against this barbarism'.[9] Schweitzer declined, as he considered 'the situation in Germany hopeless and felt unable to leave his African patients'.[10] A letter from 1930 to Jewish acquaintances shows his long-held contempt for right-wing parties and his assessment that party leaders in the Weimar Republic were naive in their actions: 'German party leaders are the greatest idiots in existence. And the stupid anti-Semitic attitude of the right-wing parties is deeply regrettable. For surely these will one day gain power, as German democracy in its foolishness is unfit for life.'[11]

Though Schweitzer declined to condemn Nazi politics openly, he put much effort into persuading family and friends to leave Germany as quickly as possible. The Nazis had already frozen Helene's bank account in Königsfeld, and it seemed only a matter of time until they would seize the house. Helene's brother Ernst emigrated to Brazil in 1934. Schweitzer supported his family with the substantial profits from his books. Meanwhile, in Lambarene the financial situation became dire, and Schweitzer had to contribute to the running of the hospital with the proceeds from his concerts and lectures in Europe.

After his return in 1933 he found reason for confidence in the situation in Lambarene. The newly built hospital served its purpose well, and in the years 1933–4 each of the doctors performed over 500 surgeries, in contrast to a yearly average of around 100 in the 1920s.[12] A donation from a doctor in Alsace along with money given by Schweitzer's relatives made possible the purchase of the first refrigerator.[13]

Only nine months later, in 1934, Schweitzer returned to Europe to spend time with his family and in Oxford, and a short time later at the University of London, to deliver the Hibbert Lectures on 'The Religious Factor in Modern Civilization'. In Edinburgh there followed the Gifford Lectures on 'The Problem of Theology of Nature and Ethics of Nature'. These public appearances in Great Britain were a great success. A brief summary of both lectures, written by Schweitzer himself, was published a short while later in the US magazine *Christian Century*.[14]

Schweitzer felt the effect of the Nazi terror even in England. Requests from German acquaintances and church representatives reached him there, asking that he refrain from visiting them, as they did not wish to be associated with his critical views of the Nazi government. In response, Schweitzer vowed never again to set foot on German soil as long as Hitler remained in power.[15] In this context an anecdote concerning Schweitzer's exchange of letters with Joseph Goebbels, which are still missing, is often related. It was told by, among others, Theodor Heuss, who gave Werner Picht as his source, at the Nobel Peace Prize awards ceremony in 1951. Schweitzer, who was present, did not deny it. When Hitler's propaganda minister wrote to Schweitzer in an attempt to win him as a figurehead for Nazi Germany, he concluded his letter with the Nazi closing *mit deutschem Gruß* (literally 'with German greetings'). Schweitzer is said to have politely refused to cooperate in any form with the Nazis and signed his letter 'with Central African greetings'.[16]

While he was giving lectures in Edinburgh in 1935, Schweitzer met Wilfred Grenfell, who had founded a hospital for fishermen in Labrador, Newfoundland. The two men immediately hit it off, prompting Schweitzer to add to his entry in the guestbook: 'The hippopotamus is delighted to meet the polar bear.'[17] After his lectures, Schweitzer took a private tour of Britain, and then travelled on to Switzerland, where on 14 January 1935 he celebrated, with much attention from the public, his sixtieth birthday. Leaving the turbulence behind, Helene and Albert spent a week in Montreux on the shores of Lake Geneva. These few days were the only ones they spent alone with each other. Here they had the time for long walks as they had used to do on their free Sundays in the jungle.[18]

From Montreux, Schweitzer set off for Lambarene, where the daily routine soon caught up with him. The long waiting lists for operations meant the hospital's capacities had to be increased yet again. A petroleum lamp was procured to allow emergency operations to be performed at night—and was immediately used on four consecutive nights. From 1938 a radio station was built that enabled Schweitzer and his employees in the isolation of Lambarene to keep in touch with world news.[19] In the same year, on the occasion of the twenty-fifth anniversary of Lambarene, some of Schweitzer's former European patients expressed their gratitude by offering to donate an x-ray machine worth 90,000 francs. Schweitzer, however, was able to convince the benefactors that he should be allowed to dispose of the money as he saw fit. He foresaw war in Europe and thought it more prudent to procure as much medication as possible. In January 1939, he travelled to Alsace for a few days to purchase medication and food and returned to Port Gentil immediately on the same ship. This devastated Helene and Rhena, as the original plan had been to have a reunion in Europe in the spring.

The years between 1937 and 1939 ushered in a significant change in the lives of Helene and Rhena. In 1937, mother and daughter had travelled to New York, and, besides meeting relatives, Helene spent her time with Albert's friends, maintaining contacts among Lambarene's supporters, and establishing new ones. She also gave public talks to introduce Americans to her husband's work. During the war Schweitzer expressed his gratitude to these new donors: 'How thankful I am to all my faithful friends that I may now, as in the past, take in and feed all patients in need! We are also once again able to operate more than we were in recent times.'[20]

One of the visitors received by Helene and Rhena was Albert Einstein. He was very friendly, but awkward when it came to making conversation and tried to cover this uneasiness by 'constantly compelling them to take another slice of apple cake'.[21] Rhena, by now 19 years old, had been forbidden by her father from studying medicine—'That is no job for women like you'[22]—and during her stay in the USA she took singing lessons, completed a training course for secretaries, and attended lectures on psychology. Helene had intended to travel from the USA to Africa in 1938, but her former doctor Max Gerson, who had emigrated to the United States, emphatically discouraged her from this plan. Helene ignored his advice, boarded a ship to France, and from there rejoined her husband on 17 May 1938, while Rhena was still enjoying her time in the States. As in the old days, Helene and Albert took short cruises on the Ogowe River in the evenings. But Helene returned to Europe in the autumn of 1938 to be with her daughter, who had returned from New York. Despite their Jewish ancestry, at this point the two could still travel with relatively little risk to Germany on their French passports.

In November 1938, Helene once again travelled to the United States. In May 1939, mother and daughter set off together for Lambarene by way of Bordeaux. Rhena, who was seeing Lambarene for the first time, was deeply impressed. A mere six weeks later the two had to return to Europe because of the threat of war. Moreover, Rhena longed to be reunited with her fiancé, Jean Eckert, an organ-builder she had met two years previously in Gunsbach and who currently lived in Paris. After the outbreak of war he was sent as a civil employee of the French Air Ministry to Blois on the Loire.

Lambarene during the War

The Second World War began in September 1939 and only months later, in March 1940, though far from Europe, Lambarene felt its impact. The passenger liner *Brazza*, which Schweitzer had taken several times for the journey between Europe and Africa, was torpedoed and sank with almost all passengers on board. Although nobody connected with the hospital was on board at the time, all the supplies and the expensive medication that Schweitzer had recently purchased for Lambarene were lost.[23]

Lambarene was short of staff, as some of Schweitzer's employees had returned to Europe at the outbreak of war. The four nurses took over the medical care together with Albert Schweitzer and another doctor, Ladislas Goldschmid, a Hungarian of Jewish descent who had come to Lambarene in 1933. He managed to return to the hospital from a holiday in Europe just before the war began.[24] Anna Wildikann, a Latvian from Riga, had been in Lambarene in the mid-1930s and resumed her work as a doctor there in January 1940.[25] Then, after a long and eventful journey, unexpected support arrived from Europe. Helene had managed to reach Paris from Lausanne shortly before the Germans occupied France. She was met there by Rhena and her newborn baby, and on 10 June the three fled from Paris to Blois, where Jean Eckert managed to find a place for them to stay. But the German troops granted them only a short reprieve. Five days later the family set off—Paris had already been occupied—in the direction of the Massif Central. They found shelter in a village for one night and on the next day made their way towards Bordeaux. As a Jew, Helene lived in the constant fear of being stopped by a police patrol and, in spite of her very good French, exposed as a foreigner.[26] Once in Bordeaux, Helene learned of the armistice between Germany and France. They had to take flight once more, as the Nazis now controlled the complete Atlantic coast. Lambarene was now farther away than ever.

Helene was relatively unmoved when she heard the news that the Nazis had seized her house in Königsfeld: 'I wonder again and again at how one learns to detach oneself from things once held dear.'[27] When Bordeaux was occupied by the German army, Helene made her way to Vichy alone and with great difficulty. However, it proved all but impossible to obtain exit documents. Unoccupied France under the rule of the pro-Nazi Vichy regime was now also passing ever more anti-Jewish legislation. To make matters worse, Lambarene became the setting for a battle between the Free French Forces under General de Gaulle and the Vichy French forces in the Battle of Libreville. With de Gaulle's victory, Lambarene was cut off from continental Europe. Britain and the USA were now the only hope for help, as Lambarene was now subject to the rule of the French government in exile in London and could be reached only with a British visa, something that was impossible to obtain in France. Helene was finally aided by the Schweitzer family's connections: the Swiss ambassador, who was close to the Vichy regime, and Helene's nephew, Pierre-Paul Schweitzer, who had useful contacts with the French government authorities, managed to secure a visa for her. Helene was allowed to enter Switzerland in March 1941. A letter from 9 July 1941 to her sister-in-law Luise Bresslau-Hoff reveals her state of mind. She was living in the constant fear of never seeing her husband again and, disregarding all advice, was determined to get to Lambarene at all costs:

> As we have now not been able to correspond for more than a year, he not being able to leave the hospital while the war lasts, nobody can tell how long it will continue and, in short, this state can simply no longer be borne, especially in view of his age and the length of time he has now been out there—in the sixth year![28]

From Lausanne she travelled to Geneva to secure the help of the International Red Cross in obtaining the necessary documents from

London. After finally receiving permission to leave France and enter one of its colonies, in the summer of 1941, to avoid having to obtain a transit visa for Spain, Helene took a ship from Bordeaux to Lisbon. Her journey was again interrupted for four weeks as she had to wait for a visa to enter Portuguese Angola. Then on 12 July 1941 the time had finally come. Helene sailed to Angola on a Portuguese steamer, and after a surprisingly uncomplicated car journey she arrived in Lambarene on 2 August.[29]

To her great relief she found her husband healthy, yet she saw that the hospital lacked personnel as well as medication and was carrying out only the most essential operations. The outbreak of war and the ensuing difficulties for the hospital had forced Schweitzer to discharge the majority of his patients. The operation logbook recorded only around fifty for 1943:[30]

> It is now necessary to economize on operating materials as we do not know when we will be able to obtain more. We are permitted to undertake only the most essential operations. Generally, we cannot take in any patients who are not severely ill. Our means furthermore do not allow us to feed large numbers of ill people. What sad days we spend afflicted like this! Again and again we must reject the desperate pleas of those who have waited nevertheless, again and again explaining to them the incomprehensible: that they must leave the hospital.[31]

The number of hospital assistants also had to be reduced. Helene's arrival was therefore a great relief to the remaining nurses, as she was able to support them and help in preparations for the operations.

Albert Schweitzer experienced the fighting between de Gaulle's and the Vichy troops at first hand. Although both sides had agreed not to shell the hospital, Schweitzer nevertheless took precautionary measures and single-handedly barricaded the buildings with sheets of corrugated iron to protect against stray bullets.[32]

With the hospital cut off from the outside world, Schweitzer's earlier contacts now paid off. He received two separate offers of financial aid and medication, one from Edward Hume, secretary of the Christian Medical Council for Overseas Work, and the other from the American Everett Skillings; both of them had previously visited Schweitzer in Gunsbach. Schweitzer compiled a list of medication and medical equipment that Hume was to purchase with money raised by

Skillings.[33] This aid, which took a year to arrive in Lambarene, along with other donations from Britain, Sweden, and the USA in the years 1942 and 1943, enabled the hospital to increase the number of patients it could handle. These important supplies were mainly as a result of Helene's commitment and work in creating and maintaining important contacts during her stay in the USA.

Meanwhile, there were far-reaching changes in the political situation. Félix Eboué, the French Governor of Chad, had fought with de Gaulle against Vichy troops and then led support in French Equatorial Africa for de Gaulle's government in exile. Chad was joined by three further French colonies: French Congo, Cameroon (formerly a German colony), and Ubangi-Shari (Central African Republic). De Gaulle met Eboué early in 1944 in order to thank the Africans for their support and hold out the prospect of French citizenship for citizens of the French colonies, and an agreement was signed two years later. Schweitzer, however, viewed this politically motivated concession critically, as he felt it unwise to offer illiterate people the right to vote.[34]

On 14 January 1945, Schweitzer celebrated his seventieth birthday in Lambarene. True to the tradition of St Thomas College, where the birthday boy was allowed to choose what was for dinner, Schweitzer celebrated with a dish of fried potatoes.[35] While French and German troops were still engaged in grim battles near Schweitzer's home in Alsace during the last months of the war, British newspapers were reporting on his work in reverent terms.[36] The end of the war was at hand, but this was no occasion of real happiness for the Schweitzers, as many of their friends had not survived the terror of Nazi rule. Several of Helene's Jewish relations and friends, among them Margit Jacobi, had been killed. Helene's cousin Johanna Engel had taken her own life in 1942 when she was faced with deportation to the Theresienstadt concentration camp. Schweitzer's first assistant doctor, Victor Nessmann, had been murdered by the Gestapo in France in 1944. In despair, Helene wrote: 'Now, as the war draws to its close [...] where is the immense joy with which one had wanted to welcome this end? Everything is covered with too much sadness.'[37]

In March 1945 the couple learned that Alsace had been liberated. News that the end of the Second World War was imminent reached Schweitzer on 7 May 1945. At first he was busy answering letters and treating patients, and the real significance of the new political situation struck him only in the evening. He took up a book by the Chinese thinker Laozi and read:

Weapons are disastrous implements, no tools for a noble being. Only when he can do no otherwise, does he make use of them […] Quiet and peace are for him the highest. He conquers, but he knows no joy in this. He who would rejoice in victory, would be rejoicing in murder […] At the victory celebration, the general should take his place as is the custom at funeral ceremonies. The slaughter of human beings in great numbers should be lamented with tears of compassion. Therefore should he who had conquered in battle bear himself as if he were at a festival of mourning.[38]

Schweitzer was relieved that the war was finally over, yet in the light of the widespread poverty in Europe he had doubts about the future of his hospital. He appealed to his donors to continue to support him:

There is one thing we can assure you of, and that is that this work is necessary, in the future more necessary than ever before. We who know how much physical affliction there is here and what the hospital means to those afflicted, we dare to ask our friends: 'Help that it will remain with them in the future.'[39]

While Schweitzer eagerly anticipated the arrival of new doctors, who in the following year were to carry out roughly 600 operations,[40] Helene longed to be reunited with Rhena and her grandchildren and chose to return to their house in Königsfeld in the Black Forest in the autumn of 1946.[41] They had survived the war. Albert and Helene could look back on five shared years in Africa. It was to be the longest time they spent together.

7

Exorcising the Ghost of
the Nuclear War

Schweitzer in the Cold War
(1945–1957)

The end of the war by no means solved the many problems facing Lambarene. On the contrary, they were exacerbated. In spite of donations from Great Britain and the United States, Schweitzer's hospital was running at a loss. One reason was the absence of qualified employees and the food shortages directly after the war. New drugs for leprosy meant that more and more people went to the 'jungle doctor' hoping for a cure, and the hospital had to bear the burden of feeding these additional patients. As Schweitzer became better known in America, the amount of donations grew rapidly, and without these funds it would have been extremely difficult to have coped with the greater number of patients between 1945 and 1948. Before his visit to the USA in 1949, Schweitzer was barely known to the general public there, and so donations were mainly from individual Christians, churches, and associations. Journalists had not yet discovered Lambarene. This was to change by the late 1940s.

'The Greatest Man in the World'

After the war, interest in Albert Schweitzer surged in the United States. The Albert Schweitzer Fellowship of America was founded in 1940, with the doctor and former missionary Emory Ross as its driving force. This institution alone succeeded in securing the financial sponsorship of several American church organizations for the hospital in Lambarene. Pharmaceutical companies and hospitals also made commitments to Lambarene, while an occasional organist of the New York Philharmonic Orchestra, Edouard Nies-Berger, also a citizen of Alsace, organized charity concerts in aid of the Schweitzers' African project. In 1946, Emory Ross finally had the opportunity of meeting Schweitzer in person when he visited Lambarene together with his wife. Although this spurred his enthusiasm for Lambarene, the fact remained that in 1947 Schweitzer faced one of his gravest financial crises. At one point the situation appeared so hopeless that he even considered closing the hospital.[1] Luckily, things soon began looking up. In the same postal delivery, the Banque Commericale Afrique informed Schweitzer that his account for Lambarene was overdrawn by $1,045, and he also received a letter from the National Bank of Industry and Commerce, telling him that the Unitarian Service Committee in Boston had just transferred the sum of $4,375 to his account.[2] The most pressing debts could now be repaid, and some necessary items purchased for the hospital.

Schweitzer also had Helene to thank that he did not have to close the hospital, as she was the one who had been establishing these contacts in America since 1937. 'In those days I only got the ball rolling', Helene wrote, 'that led to the foundation of the fellowship, which in turn helped the hospital through the war'.[3]

Two American journalists, Charles Roy and Melvin Arnold, both working for the magazine *Christian Register*, were particularly interested in Schweitzer. As Unitarians and Freethinkers, their theological beliefs were similar to his own. Behind the *Christian Register* stood the Unitarian Service Committee, which had begun its financial support of the hospital during the war years. The two journalists now proposed to introduce Schweitzer's ideas to the United States. Following their return to Boston, the magazine published a special edition on Schweitzer in September 1947, which further boosted his popularity throughout the country.

But Schweitzer's name had already appeared in the US press. In 1946, *Reader's Digest* ran a story entitled 'God's Eager Fool—the Story of a Great Protestant Told by a Catholic Priest'. At the same time, in Europe, a survey declared Schweitzer to be a universal genius, alongside such personages as Leonardo da Vinci and Goethe.[4] Praise of Schweitzer reached a peak in a special edition of *Life* magazine of 6 October 1947, which elevated Schweitzer to the status of 'the

greatest man in the world' and a 'jungle philosopher'.[5] The fascination of the press and its readers made the 'Schweitzer myth' unstop-
pable. This unexpected surge in popularity also benefited the hospital
financially, as the number of donations increased rapidly. In the span
of only a few years a small hospital in the African bush was elevated to
an outpost of humanitarianism admired around the world. America's
enthusiasm for Schweitzer soon reached beyond the popular media to
the Ivy League universities. Yale University was prevented from
awarding him an honorary doctorate in theology only by its own
rules against bestowing the honour *in absentia*. Harvard University
invited him to give the renowned Lowell Lectures, and the nuclear
physicist J. Robert Oppenheimer offered Schweitzer a one-year sab-
batical in Princeton. Harvard, Yale, Princeton—Schweitzer refused
all these offers. The curious reason for his refusals was given in a letter
to Albert Einstein, who was currently teaching at Princeton:

> But now that I, compelled by circumstances, have to miss the opportun-
> ity of getting together with you in Princeton, I have no choice but to write
> to you [...] Dr. Oppenheimer must have told you why I cannot come.
> I am no longer a free person: in everything I do, I have to consider my
> hospital and make sure I do whatever is necessary for its survival. Today,
> every enterprise is so thoroughly encumbered by all sorts of rules and
> currency matters and the like that it requires tight reins every step of the
> way. That is why I cannot travel far from Lambarene or for any length of
> time that would prevent my being here when needed. At the moment
> I have no doctors who are fully familiar with procedures here. The two
> doctors assisting me are about to end their two-year period and will be
> replaced by two new ones, whom I have to break in. And as for all the
> administrative work, I have no one who could take care of the necessary
> decisions and responsibilities.[6]

When it came to his work and its advancement, Schweitzer's
decisions were thoroughly pragmatic. He had received an invitation
from the University of Chicago, where he was to have been awarded
an honorary doctorate. Afterwards he was to visit the Institute of
Humanistic Studies in Aspen, Colorado, where he had been asked
to give a talk (in German and in French) at the bicentennial celebra-
tions of Goethe's birthday. Initially he intended to reject the offer, but
when he realized what the fee of $6,100 offered by the Chancellor of
the University of Chicago, Robert Hutchins, who was also chairman

of the US Goethe Bicentennial Foundation, amounted to in French francs, he promptly accepted. Schweitzer used his time in America to visit the pharmaceutical company producing the medication his hospital used, to meet friends, and to thank his donors for their support.

In October 1948, Schweitzer returned from Africa to Zurich. He was present at the baptism of his grandson in June 1949, before setting off together with his wife from Liverpool on the *Nieuwe Amsterdam* to the city that had lent its name to the transatlantic steamer. On 28 June Albert Schweitzer first stepped onto American soil in New York and was met by a large number of reporters.[7] *Time* magazine reported that he 'faced the crouching semicircle around him like an indulgent grandfather playing a strange new game with the children'.[8]

During his travels in the American West, there was an amusing incident when two elderly ladies, mistaking Schweitzer for Einstein, requested an autograph. In reply, Schweitzer wrote down the words: 'Albert Einstein, conveyed by his friend Albert Schweitzer'.[9] Emory Ross accompanied Albert and Helene from New York to Colorado. He recalled admiring Schweitzer's keen intelligence, his knowledge, and the way he could relate to the people he met without having ever been to the USA before.[10] On his arrival he immediately enquired whether there was an organ he could play for an hour or so in order to relax from the strenuous journey.[11]

Schweitzer gave his commemorative speech on 'Goethe, the Man and the Work' on 8 July in the picturesque town of Aspen, Colorado. He spoke in French, with Ross acting as his interpreter. Two days later, when Schweitzer repeated his speech in German, it was none other than the novelist and playwright Thornton Wilder who translated his talk into English.[12] The content was roughly the same as the talk he had given on Goethe in 1932, as he once again took up the relationship between morality and nature, a theme that played such an important role in Schweitzer's philosophy of civilization. The extent of Schweitzer's admiration for Goethe rings out in the closing lines of his tribute: 'This is Goethe—the poet, the thinker and the man. There are persons who think of him with gratitude for the ethical and religious wisdom he has given them, so simple and yet so profound.'[13]

Albert and Helene returned to Chicago directly following the speech, where he was awarded an honorary doctorate by the faculty of law at the University of Chicago. The ceremony was followed by a dinner in the Grand Ballroom of the Stevens Hotel and attended by hundreds of guests. Among those present was the Governor of Illinois, Adlai Stevenson, who would later become the US envoy to the United Nations during the Cuban Missile Crisis, and who would twice run for the US presidency. He would also become a frequent correspondent of Schweitzer's and would visit him in Lambarene. The text printed on the invitations for this event itself deserves some attention, for it represents Schweitzer as the Americans saw him: as a 'man of God'.[14] Mass-media coverage soon ensured that America was fascinated by 'Christ's thirteenth apostle'.[15]

Schweitzer proved he was highly skilled at dealing with the press. His visit coincided with the beginning of the McCarthy era, and inevitably he was asked what his views on Communism were. His quick-witted response was: 'There are no such questions in the jungle!'[16] When besieged by overly eager journalists, he adroitly summarized the essence of his Reverence for Life in one sentence: 'I, Albert Schweitzer, am life. It would be "Reverence for Life" if you were mercifully to let me depart.'[17] As 'one of the most extraordinary men of modern times', Schweitzer made the cover of *Time* magazine at the close of his trip on 11 July 1949.[18] The lead article mainly repeated his life story as related in his autobiography *Out of my Life and Thought*. It is interesting, however, to note that Americans tended to emphasize different aspects of Schweitzer's life from the ones the Europeans did. *Time* magazine largely ignored his academic achievements and instead focused extensively on his life's work serving humanity in Africa.

Schweitzer became a media star in the USA overnight. And, in the interest of securing the funding of his work in Lambarene, he did not object. Although he was irritated by the effusive tone of the praise, he knew from the financially difficult years from 1945 to 1947 that the support it would bring could be decisive to the continued survival of his work in Lambarene. The US media were above all interested in the human factor, and saw his personality and apparent selflessness as his defining character trait. It depicted him as a 'silver-maned, bushy mustached old lion of a man [...] whose thirty-six years of selfless pioneering as a missionary to the natives of French Equatorial Africa are a bright highlight in the relations between the white race and the black'.[19]

From 1949 onwards it would have been easy for Schweitzer to make use of the willingness of international companies to donate money to his cause and turn Lambarene into a fully equipped modern hospital. But having to give his name and turn Lambarene into a moral symbol for the Western world seemed too high a price to pay. Lambarene was not just a hospital for Schweitzer; it was the expression of his personal philosophy of life, and as such could be neither bought nor sold—it could only be lived as authentically as possible. However, this became problematic when Schweitzer was portrayed as little more than the caricature of a do-gooder, when in *Breakfast at Tiffany's* Audrey Hepburn imagines Albert Schweitzer would be the ideal husband, or when in his novel *Fahrenheit 451* Ray Bradbury offers the lukewarm description of him as 'a very kind philosopher indeed'.[20]

The Nobel Peace Prize and its Consequences

At the end of July 1949 Albert and Helene returned to Europe. Three months later, in October 1949, they set off for Lambarene for the eighth time. There Schweitzer was visited by Erica Andersen, a documentary film-maker from Austria, who after initial scepticism was given permission to make a film about Schweitzer and his work in Lambarene. The film was highly praised in the *American Weekly* in January 1957, and it went on to win the Academy Award for Best Documentary in 1958. However, Schweitzer watched the film for the first time in 1959.

Schweitzer spent six months in Alsace from May 1951 onwards, taking short trips to the Netherlands, Scandinavia, and Great Britain. On 28 July 1951—the anniversary of Bach's death—Schweitzer performed a recital in St Thomas in Strasbourg; Erica Anderson was among those present. In repeated visits over the years, she had formed such tight bonds with Schweitzer and Lambarene that she was buried in the cemetery in Lambarene, one row behind Schweitzer's grave.[21] On 16 September, Schweitzer was awarded the renowned Peace Prize of the German Book Trade in St Paul's Church in Frankfurt am Main. He donated the 10,000 marks that accompanied the award to German refugees and needy authors—not to Lambarene. His tour of America had consolidated Lambarene's finances.

In the following months Schweitzer travelled around Sweden, where he received the Grand Medal of the Red Cross of Sweden and was made a member of the Swedish Royal Academy of Music. One popular story about Schweitzer was that at the award dinner, which was attended by the King of Sweden, he was served one course consisting of a whole fish. Unsure of how best to eat it, he waited until no one was looking and quietly slipped the fish into his pocket. The next day a newspaper covering the event reported that Schweitzer had learned impressive skills in the jungle and had devoured his entire fish without leaving even the fish bones.[22]

After returning to Lambarene in December 1951, Schweitzer found the hospital in good condition, yet he was worried by the housing of leprosy patients. He saw no alternative but to build a new leprosy village, a task that was to put a great physical strain on the 76-year-old over the next two years.

On an international level, voices grew louder demanding him to use his impeccable moral authority to engage in politics. Above all, he was urged to call for an international agreement on the control of nuclear weapons. At first he was reluctant and claimed that he lacked sufficient information to enter into such a politically charged debate. But after winning the Nobel Peace Prize he was forced to reconsider the issue.

Schweitzer was well aware that he had been a leading candidate for the Nobel Peace Prize for several years now. In a letter dated 11 February 1952, he had been informed by Max Tau, who had received the Peace Prize of the German Book Trade in 1950, that the 'most eminent Norwegians […] have recommended you for the Nobel Peace Prize'.[23] His principle of Reverence for Life resonated well among Norwegians. In a radio broadcast, the Norwegian poet Gabriel Scott called on his fellow countrymen and women to follow his example: 'Look up to Albert Schweitzer, follow him. Be happy that he is showing you the way!'[24] The committee, however, was of another opinion and decided not to award the prize at all in 1952,[25] a decision that was heavily criticized in the Norwegian press.[26] Apparently the committee gave in to the pressure of public opinion and in October 1953 decided belatedly to award him the prize. According to Schweitzer, no one in Lambarene was prepared for this news: '"Are you coming along to congratulate him?" asked Mathilde [Kottmann].

To this Ali [Silver], who knew nothing yet, replied, "Congratulate him? What for? Which cat has had kittens?"'[27]

Schweitzer informed the Nobel Committee that he would be unable to travel to Oslo as he thought his presence in Lambarene was indispensable as long as the leprosy village was being built. The prize was thus awarded *in absentia* and, as Schweitzer had French citizenship, was accepted on his behalf by the French ambassador to Norway. A whole year went by before Schweitzer and Helene travelled separately to Oslo to accept the Nobel Peace Prize on 4 November 1954. Many of their loyal companions over the years were also present, including Clara Urquhart, Erica Andersen, Charles Joy, and Melvin Arnold. It was expected that, being a French citizen, Schweitzer would give his acceptance speech in French. Against his custom, he decided to read the speech from a manuscript, only to be informed shortly before the event that, instead of the expected eighty minutes, he would only have thirty, and he was forced hastily to cut over half the text he had prepared. The result, read out in a tired and monotonous voice, was not the impassioned appeal for peace his listeners had expected, but instead a classic academic talk problematizing the history of the concept of peace.[28] Nevertheless, this uninspired appeal to humankind's responsibility for world peace was met with a spontaneously organized torchlight procession after 30,000 predominantly young Norwegians gathered in front of the town hall. A collection for Lambarene yielded 315,000 crowns in only three days—more than double the prize money for the award.[29] Just as he had managed to do in America, Schweitzer had successfully gained the enthusiastic support of the Norwegian public for himself and his work. One member of the press went so far as to write: 'God's name was not even mentioned. And yet everyone felt that there was something of God's almightiness and greatness keeping us safe and blessing us when we were in the company of Albert Schweitzer.'[30] The Norwegian theologian Johan Hygen praised Schweitzer in equally enthusiastic terms: 'If this is Humanism, then we should like to be Humanists. If this is Christianity, then we should like to be Christians.'[31]

For Helene the time preceding the award ceremony had been far from easy. Since the news of the Nobel Prize, she had not had a moment's peace in her Gunsbach home, which was also Lambarene's headquarters in Europe. And Schweitzer took on more work when he returned to Germany in May 1954. Now nearly 80 years old, Schweitzer performed his last organ concert in commemoration of Bach's death in St Thomas in Strasbourg. The church was so overcrowded that Schweitzer repeated the performance the following day so that everyone who wanted to attend could also have a seat.[32] For Helene, meanwhile, he barely had any time to spare. She felt forgotten and lonely. Mühlstein has portrayed her situation vividly:

> Photographs from this time show Helene Schweitzer, weak and fragile, next to her husband, who is radiating energy and vitality. One can see the strain involved as she attempts to keep up with him. [...] That Emmy Martin is occasionally even assumed to be Schweitzer's wife, and that she enjoys this mistake, hurts Helene Schweitzer deeply and renders the already troubled relationship between the two women even more frosty. If Helene Schweitzer is present when such a mistake occurs, she immediately and vigorously corrects it. Albert Schweitzer, however, sidesteps such conflict and avoids clearly taking his wife's side. By the way, his reaction is the same when disagreements arise between female employees who have been with him for many years. While he otherwise makes short work of disagreeable employees and is quick to send them packing, he is more restrained in such cases.[33]

In an attempt to avoid conflicts with Helene, Schweitzer received the many visitors wishing to congratulate him on being awarded the Nobel Prize in Emmy Martin's apartment in the Gunsbach headquarters. This made matters worse. The long, simmering disagreement finally boiled over on the eve of the trip to Oslo. Helene flatly refused to accompany her husband if Emmy Martin was to be a member of the party, while Schweitzer believed, given the number of dignitaries he would be meeting in Oslo, he would need his assistant's help. He finally set off for Oslo without Helene, but in the company of Emmy Martin. His daughter, Rhena, informed him that Helene was after all going to Oslo, but she was in a dark mood and willing to go to extremes, even publicly to threaten Schweitzer with divorce. His response was 'Let her!'[34] Helene did not make good her threat, but they did not exchange a single word with each other during the ceremony.

These domestic troubles did not reach the public, so that Oslo remained a high point in Schweitzer's life. Perhaps even more important to Schweitzer than the honour itself was the prize money of $33,000 and a soaring increase in international donations. He was

finally able to complete the *village lumière*, the new leprosy village.
A letter from 5 November 1953 explained how important this was
to Schweitzer:

> My work and my eyes that I must avoid straining condemn me to silence,
> more than I can take responsibility for. I cannot manage to write even
> the most important business letters. I must spend much of my time on the
> construction of the leprosy village. If I don't spend a majority of the day
> on the building site, then work does not advance. Building a whole
> village for 300 people is simply no small undertaking.[35]

Schweitzer, who wanted to devote himself entirely to his new project,
found the Nobel Prize to be also a burden:

> Now the Nobel Peace Prize has come on top of everything else.
> Journalists sent by press agencies are landing in special planes. Tele-
> grams from press agencies in Paris, London, and New York arrive with
> questions that I am supposed to answer by cable. It's touching but
> strenuous. I've been devoting whole days to all this.[36]

It was especially important to Germans that Schweitzer was awarded
the Nobel Peace Prize. Only years after the end of the moral catastrophe that had been the Third Reich, they once again had a 'good
German' to present to the world. The year 1954, when Schweitzer
was awarded the prize, was also the year that saw the 'miracle of Bern',
when the German football team unexpectedly won the World Cup.
Many Germans saw this as an indicator of a new German self-
confidence, and with it a return to the international community. Yet
Germans tended to forget that, since the Treaty of Versailles, Schweitzer
had been a citizen of Alsace and a Frenchman. Sales of his autobiography, *Out of my Life and Thought*, soared to over half a million copies after
1954.[37] His friend Theodor Heuss, Germany's first president, praised
him as a 'role model' for all Germans; the city of Frankfurt made him
an honorary citizen; and the city councillors of Dortmund collectively
donated their personal remuneration to the aid of Lambarene.

A 1964 study found that Albert Schweitzer was most often named
by German school pupils as a role model.[38] And this was at a time
when it was still common for school pupils in the young Federal
Republic of Germany to idolize such figures as the Wehrmacht field
marshal Erich von Manstein, First World War flying aces Manfred
von Richthofen and Ernst Udet, or the president of the Weimar

Republic Paul von Hindenburg in the same breath as the first president of the Federal Republic Theodor Heuss or the first chancellor Konrad Adenauer. Schweitzer was considered a 'role model in terms of personality and morality'. Pupils commented on their choice with such explanations as: 'As an ideal of charity I would like to emulate Albert Schweitzer, but, as his outlook on religion does not correspond with the teachings of my religion, in this matter I would have to be my own self; but otherwise I would almost like to worship Albert Schweitzer.'[39] A different pupil wrote: 'Albert Schweitzer is a great example to me. He helps poor and ill people, and he opposes evil doings in the world. I thought his remarks about the nuclear bomb were simply great! If only everybody thought that way!'[40]

The authors of this study identified what Schweitzer represented to many Germans, especially to the younger generation: He was a man that 'counts as the universal embodiment of an exemplary and ethical life in the post-war period'. The results of this study, according to its authors, represented an educational success on the part of schools that had made great efforts in this period to acquaint their students with the life and work of Albert Schweitzer.[41] And in fact he was almost omnipresent in the media in the year he won the Nobel Prize. In 1954, over a period of several months, the magazine *Revue* published a full-page serialized novel on his life with extensive photo coverage entitled *Albert Schweitzer: The Life of a Good Person* by Robert Jungk under the pseudonym Jean Pierhal.[42] Moreover, in an accompanying column 'The Good Deed of the Week', readers of the magazine were encouraged to find people in their neighbourhood who did good things without seeking praise. Schweitzer was probably aware of the magazine's campaign, as his close friend Erica Andersen supplied the photographic material. However, for Schweitzer, as 'physician of an ailing century',[43] this sudden popularity could hardly have been agreeable, since it went against the core of his philosophy of civilization, which teaches the irrelevance of fame. Serial articles in celebrity magazines promoting his fame were potentially threatening to his authenticity: A 'close relative of the dear Lord God' was not a media star.

News of Schweitzer's Nobel Prize spread around the world and prompted the British journalist James Cameron to visit Lambarene and examine the myth of Albert Schweitzer for himself. Cameron later summarized his impressions in his autobiography, *Point of Departure*.

Schweitzer had to be aware that, given the cynical logic of journalism, a 'Hosanna!' might be quickly followed by a 'Crucify him!' And that is exactly what happened. Cameron was one of the first to draw a highly critical image of Schweitzer, even going so far as to describe him as a racist. He liked Schweitzer's down-to-earth manner and began his article harmlessly enough by saying that one could discuss with Schweitzer any topic from world affairs to the best way to eat a mango. What followed, however, was much more critical in tone. In response to the question when he would collect his Nobel Prize, Schweitzer responded: 'I can't go yet. If I went now the lazy animals would never finish their houses. And they need them so badly!'[44] From this and similar observations Cameron concluded that it was less that Schweitzer existed for his hospital than that the hospital existed for his self-realization. A hospital in the African bush that had been minimally equipped on purpose, for Cameron this was understandable from an ethical perspective, but medically it was problematic. But Schweitzer believed that medicine in Africa must be adapted to the circumstances, habits, and needs of life in Africa. He must also have underestimated what Europeans and Americans would think of his work when he drove on his African workers with words like the following: 'Hurry up! Work like a white man, or can't you do that?'[45] Cameron also disparaged Schweitzer's medical work in Lambarene and accused him of not putting into practice the ethics he preached in his philosophy:

> While the original achievements of Schweitzer were considerable and his sacrifices notable, yet his accomplishments were negligible; his mission an illusion; his hospital in the equatorial rainforest medically valueless, or even dangerous, existing solely as a frame for his immeasurable ego; his own philosophical contribution to the advancement of Africa rather worse than negative.[...] the Schweitzer hospital was no place of light and healing but a squalid slum, from which the Doctor excluded all the advantages he was for ever being offered simply because he did not personally understand them; that his immense personal vanity insulated him from anything less than sanctimonious worship; that his celebrated 'Reverence for Life' contrasted bitterly with the cruel loneliness imposed on his own wife and daughter.[46]

Some critics interpreted Schweitzer's claim that 'simple people need simple healing methods' to mean that he was refusing to give his African patients an appropriate level of medical care and was following minimum standards of hygiene and technology because—as a doctor, colonialist, and philosopher—he was still living in the nineteenth century. Many people were bothered by the fact that Schweitzer had organized his hospital on the model of an African village instead of following the structure of a European hospital. This was the impression Norman Cousins made on his visit to Lambarene:

> The idea of a hospital creates instant images in the mind of immaculate corridors, white sheets, total sanitation. These images were badly jolted when one saw the Hospital at Lambarene for the first time. [...] The sanitary facilities were at an absolute minimum. There were only two outhouses, one for each sex. The sewer underneath was open and sometimes the wind blew from the wrong direction. There were no bedsheets. The Africans brought their own blankets. [...] The difficulty, of course, was with the term 'hospital' as applied to the Schweitzer colony. It created false images and expectations by outsiders. The proper term should be 'jungle clinic'.[47]

The majority of Schweitzer's white staff was made up of highly motivated volunteers. There were, of course, infamous exceptions, such as the 'poor rich girl' Olga Deterding, the daughter of an oil magnate, who proved ill-suited to the occupation of nursing, or Marion Preminger, who sought to impress Schweitzer with the most expensive of presents on his birthday and annoyed those around her when she talked of 'her hospital'.[48] But, although they were reported by the press with much delight, these cases were exceptions. The *New York Times* was able to appreciate the positive aspects of Schweitzer's concept in his obituary in 1965:

> The compound was staffed by three unpaid physicians, seven nurses and thirteen volunteer helpers. Visitors who equated cleanliness, tidiness and medicine were horrified by the station, for every patient was encouraged to bring one or two members of his family to cook for him in the ditches beside the wards. Babies, even in the leper enclave, dropped toys into the dust of the unpaved streets and then popped them into their mouths. [...] Lambarene resembled not so much a hospital as a native village where physicians cared for the ill. Actually, Schweitzer preferred (and planned) it in this fashion on the ground that the natives would shun an elaborate, shiny and impersonal institution. The compound even lacked electricity, except for the operating and dental rooms, and members of the staff read by kerosene lamp. Of

course, it had no telephone, radio or airstrip. Schweitzer's view that
'simple people need simple healing methods', however it might have
outraged medical sophisticates, won for Lambarene a tremendous
measure of native confidence.[49]

Schweitzer had excellent leadership skills. For example, he made a
point of celebrating the birthdays of his nursing staff with cake and
candles. He made sure that his long-term aides could spend time in
Europe for recuperation on a regular basis. And, owing to his system
of 'community sisters', nurses who travelled to visit patients in surrounding area, the hospital soon won a high reputation. In fact,
the quality of the hospital was repeatedly praised on account of its
simplicity. Africans, it was often said, needed not European-style
hospitals, but villages where families were integrated into caring for
the ill. Schweitzer's hospital had come to specialize in the prevalent
tropical diseases: dysentery, malaria, yellow fever, sleeping sickness,
elephantiasis, common hernias, and wounds caused by animals.
Mortality rates in Schweitzer's hospital were considerably lower than
in the local French government hospital. Schweitzer's staff were highly
motivated and highly qualified, so that many white patients chose to
be treated in his hospital rather than in the government hospital in
Lambarene.[50] This may explain why the former French government
doctor in Lambarene, André Audoynaud, in a book published in 2005,
criticized—without however providing any convincing support for his
accusations—how Schweitzer ran his hospital.[51]

While some medical equipment may have been old or in bad shape,
and although Schweitzer may have reacted too late to some medical
advances, the fact remains that, for many Africans, Lambarene was a
place where they experienced compassion. Suzanne Oswald coun-
tered criticism of Lambarene:

> To be sure, there are no white tiles, no glittering chrome—the goats
> run freely around the hospital, and there is no room here for super-
> hygienic demands. [...] Here something African has been made out of
> what is found in Africa. The medical equipment of the hospital,
> however—and this was admitted by a critical Swiss journalist who
> surely had not come to Lambarene to praise it—the equipment of
> the hospital would be a model for any provincial hospital in Europe. All
> diagnostic tools, x-ray and screen devices, all necessary technical facil-
> ities for treatment are available.[52]

A short while after James Cameron's visit, Schweitzer welcomed the well-known American author John Gunther, who intended to write a book about Africa. Schweitzer never imagined that one chapter was to deal with his hospital. Gunther wrote of Schweitzer that he was 'august and good [...] but cranky on occasion, dictatorial, prejudiced, pedantic in a peculiar Teutonic manner, irascible, and somewhat vain'.[53] Gunther found little of the benign, almost naive, mildness or the qualities of the do-gooder that were attributed to him by other, less critical admirers. As Gunther portrays both the positive and the negative sides of Schweitzer's personality, his judgement seems more plausible than James Cameron's. Like other visitors, Gunther seems to have expected Lambarene to be a paradise of benevolence and generosity of spirit. He was deeply disappointed when he received the advice to leave nothing unlocked because theft was a common problem in Lambarene. Yet he also learned to love the idiosyncrasies of the hospital, such as the smoke from the fireplaces wafting through the buildings to keep out mosquitoes. He shared Suzanne Oswald's positive assessment of the medicine practised in Lambarene. At the same time, he was annoyed that Schweitzer wanted to approve quotations before publication and demanded that he delete certain passages in his book. Cameron and Gunther were the first to write about Schweitzer after he had been awarded the Nobel Prize, and it was the beginning of a series of critical journalism dealing with the 'myth of Schweitzer'.

The view Gunther had of Schweitzer's character is corroborated by other journalistic sources, including Claus Jacobi[54] and, before him, Melvin Arnold and Charles R. Joy in 1948.[55] Norman Cousins, however, emphasized that Schweitzer's treatment of Africans was only one side of the coin:

> To get the full picture, one must realise that Schweitzer also treated most whites as his 'small brothers' and one had to find out how the Africans themselves interpreted his manner. [...] When he appeared to be arbitrary or gruff in what he told them to do they would smile broadly and carry out his instructions. Sometimes when he called out sharply, he would have a glint in his eye which they would catch and it would amuse them. [...] They knew he was somewhat short-tempered when things did not go just right; but they knew something, too, about the pressures under which he worked. And what was most important to

them was that they knew the stern manner did not reflect any displeasure by Dr Schweitzer. [...] Once he scolded the wife of one of the patients. Fifteen minutes later he beckoned to her when no one was looking, said he was sorry and gave her thirty francs. 'We do not become angry,' the leper said. 'How could we? Could a man become angry at his own father for telling him what to do?'[56]

Schweitzer was a kind of *pater familias* and felt responsible for all his patients and their families, for his nurses, aid workers, and doctors. He was not willing to waste his time with trivial matters. Cousins observed that

Dr Schweitzer did not intend to use all his time in Africa treating white people for sunstroke; his purpose was to provide medical treatment for Africans. And it became a little wearisome having to go through detailed explanations to each new visitor. Hence his 'take-my-word-for-it' approach. [...] At Lambarene I realised that the criticism of Dr Schweitzer's relationship with the Africans missed an important point. The somewhat arbitrary or paternalistic manner was not reserved for blacks only. Once, while Dr Schweitzer was superintending a jungle-clearing operation, he ordered the blacks to rest. Then he turned to three white members of the staff and to me and said, 'Now it's your turn.' [...] After about ten minutes we looked as though we had been working ten hours. [...] Then the Doctor said we could stop; he just wanted us to have some respect for the requirements of physical labor in Lambarene.[57]

Although for the majority of journalists Schweitzer remained the selfless conscience of humanity, he was increasingly attacked by academics as a medical dilettante or as a calculating, narcissistic tyrant. They argued that he sought international acclaim for his hospital as a humanitarian paradise—not to serve his African patients but for his own sake.[58]

There is a grain of truth in this exaggerated criticism. Schweitzer did indeed run his hospital like a patriarch. Cameron's criticism of Schweitzer as too interested in promoting himself is not plucked from thin air. When Schweitzer slipped into a conversation that he travelled third class on the railway, he wanted his listeners to think he was frugal and unpretentious. And, if one looks at all of the drawings, pictures, and sculptures created by the artist Fritz Behn between 1952 and 1954, or as early as 1929 by sculptor Otto Leiber in

Königsfeld,[59] one cannot avoid the impression that the modesty implied by his dress and manner was at times staged. The criticism voiced by the first journalists to visit Lambarene, admittedly, goes far deeper in its fundamental questioning of Schweitzer's ethos and work in Africa. Schweitzer, however, did not let any criticism deter him from the path he had chosen. His steadfastness—interpreted by his followers as integrity, by his adversaries as stubbornness—had made him what he was.

Schweitzer, Einstein, and the Bomb

The Nobel Prize made Schweitzer world famous. And the world now expected him to comment on the many issues surrounding the question of peace, something Schweitzer had so far been able to avoid in his secluded life in Lambarene. He had no desire to be caught between rival political factions. Although well informed on political events, Schweitzer had at first strictly refused to take a stand on the role of atomic weapons. His attitude gradually changed in the early 1950s. The experiences of the war, the mass murder of Jews, and the tens of thousands of victims of the first use of nuclear weapons were all reasons for Schweitzer to think more seriously about this issue. He read Martin Niemöller, J. Robert Oppenheimer, Karl Jaspers, Robert Jungk, and others. He made his first statement in an essay entitled 'The Concept of the Kingdom of God in the Transformation of Eschatology',[60] written in 1950, but not published until 1953. It echoed the cultural pessimism of his early work, 'We Inheritors of the Past':

> We are at the beginning of the end of the human race. The question before it is whether it will use for beneficial purposes or for purposes of destruction the power which modern science has placed in its hands. So long as its capacity for destruction was limited, it was possible to hope that reason would set a limit to disaster. Such an illusion is impossible to-day, when its power is illimitable. Our only hope is that the Spirit of God will strive with the spirit of the world and will prevail.[61]

The testing of hydrogen bombs by the USA in 1954 convinced Schweitzer to become more active in the atomic debate from both a scientific and a political perspective.[62] For some time he had been engaged in a casual exchange of ideas with Albert Einstein on the subject. The two men had become acquainted in the autumn of 1929, when Schweitzer had visited Adolf von Harnack in Berlin, and had met once again before Einstein emigrated to the United States.[63] Einstein thought that Schweitzer was 'the only person in the Western world who had a moral influence beyond national borders, comparable to Gandhi'.[64]

As Einstein believed that his own warnings were not being heeded, he urged Schweitzer to become involved with the issue. In a letter to Theodor Heuss, Schweitzer gave Einstein's request as the reason for his decision:

> As perhaps you know, I was close friends with Albert Einstein, although we did not see each other often. It was a spiritual friendship. It deeply impressed me that in his last years he suffered so much from the fact that his pleas to abolish nuclear weapons went unheard, despite the high esteem the world held him in. That encouraged me to engage myself further with this question, for which I possessed sufficient scientific and medical knowledge.[65]

After receiving the Nobel Peace Prize, he also felt obligated to stand up for world peace:

> The Nobel Peace Prize, which had been awarded to me, acted on me in the same manner. To speak in the words of St Paul, I 'thought it not robbery' to have received it, but wanted later to do something for peace, that I might belatedly come to deserve a little the means that had enabled me to purchase the corrugated iron roofs for my village of lepers. Thus I came seriously to study the question of the atomic threat, as it existed since 1954 in the rise of radioactivity in the atmosphere following test explosions of the large hydrogen bombs. I have been in touch with scientists concerned with this. I, who initially leaned towards skepticism, increasingly came to realize the danger which humanity is in without being aware of it. And, as I have some standing in the world, friends from Europe and America pressed me to speak on this issue. It was the Americans who finally convinced me. I knew, too, that the US President was beginning to be highly impressed by what he learned from scientific sources about this danger.[66]

On 20 February 1955 Schweitzer wrote the following lines to his 'dear friend' Einstein, who was teaching at Princeton at this time:

> We are spiritually in touch even without corresponding, for we both feel the horror of our dreadful time and are mutually afraid for the

future of mankind. When we met in Berlin, we could never have dreamed that such a bond would ever exist between us [...] it is strange how often our two names are mentioned together publicly. [...] I receive letters asking you and me and others to speak up.[67]

The tests not only posed a political problem for Schweitzer; he was also emotionally affected. The publicist Robert Jungke (writing under the pen-name Jean Pierhal) wrote: 'Almost everybody who met Albert Schweitzer privately between the years 1954 and 1957 was questioned by him about the "nuclear threat" intensively.'[68] After Alexander Haddow, a specialist in cancer research, had proposed in March 1954 that the United Nations should invite scientists to a conference to discuss the consequences of further testing of hydrogen bombs, the London-based *Daily Herald* sought Schweitzer's opinion on this proposal. His response came in form of a letter, which was printed in April 1954, expressing his serious concern over the development and use of nuclear weapons.[69] Moreover, it was the duty of scientists who 'comprehend thoroughly all the issues and dangers involved' to 'tell the terrible truth'.[70] In the summer of 1954 Schweitzer had the opportunity to exchange views at the fourth convention of Nobel Prize recipients in Lindau on Lake Constance, where he met the chemist Otto Hahn and the physicist Werner Heisenberg. This meeting increased his interest in the problem of nuclear disarmament.[71]

Only months later, Schweitzer repeated his appeal for peace and his warning against nuclear armament in his speech at the Nobel Prize Award ceremony on 4 November 1954 in Oslo. For many people he was now a 'conscience' in these matters.[72] In fact, Schweitzer was well aware that his fame was valuable for the anti-nuclear movement, and he planned his political activities strategically. Speaking from places such as Oslo or Lambarene had the advantage that his remarks would not be seen as those of a cold-war warrior, on the side of either the United States or the Soviet Union. He intended to speak on behalf of the scientists who had expressed their fears and concerns to him in letters and make known to the world what, for political reasons, they were unable to talk about openly at conferences or in their own countries. The title page of the *Daily Herald* in April 1954 read: 'The H-Bomb: There is anguish in my heart, says Dr Albert Schweitzer.'[73]

When the article encouraged other experts to join him openly, Schweitzer's strategy appeared to be bearing fruit. After his speech in Oslo, he was met with a wave of sympathy. A few months after the Nobel Peace Prize ceremony, on 21 July 1955, Schweitzer received a letter from the Secretary General of the United Nations, Dag Hammarskjöld. Hammarskjöld asked him to urge the world publicly to work towards a global peace without nuclear weapons. Hammarskjöld admitted that he had 'the—perhaps extremely bold—hope that you will be willing to add your powerful voice to the appeals that are being made for the mutual respect of nations.'[74]

In 1920, as a young man, Dag Hammarskjöld had met Albert Schweitzer while he was giving the Olaus Petri lectures in Uppsala at the invitation of Archbishop Nathan Söderblom, an intimate friend of the future secretary general.[75] Hammarskjöld's father had been governor of Uppsala province and maintained friendly relations with the family of the archbishop. Hammarskjöld and one of Söderblom's sons had been schoolmates, and his mother was already acquainted with the archbishop.[76] During their stay in Sweden, Schweitzer and his wife were guests in Söderblom's house, which enabled Hammarskjöld to get to know Schweitzer privately, too.[77] This meeting was a decisive moment for Hammarskjöld, as can be seen in an essay he wrote in 1951, in which he stressed the role of Schweitzer's ethics in dealing with political problems and in exercising public responsibility. Schweitzer's principle of Reverence for Life was founded on a solidarity that transcended political boundaries.

The close relationship between Schweitzer and Hammarskjöld can be seen in their frequent correspondence, which both wrote in German. Schweitzer made the first step in a letter he sent from Lambarene on 19 December 1953, writing to the newly appointed UN secretary general that he had read in a British newspaper that Hammarskjöld was interested in his ethics. He also asked him to find a position in the United Nations for Dr Goldschmid, a Hungarian doctor who had worked for Schweitzer before and during the war. Schweitzer casually mentioned that he occasionally visited Sweden and was planning a trip to the United States, where the two might have occasion to meet. This second visit to the United States, however, was never to take place. On 13 January 1954 Hammarskjöld replied, thanking him for the congratulatory wishes, and assuring him he would see the directors of WHO, UNICEF, and UNESCO about a position for Dr Goldschmid. Schweitzer had an extensive network and was always trying to recompense those who had done work for Lambarene, often with little pay, by writing recommendations and arranging future employment.[78]

In 1955 Hammarskjöld wrote to Schweitzer once more. An employee of the secretary general, Benjamin Cohen, wanted to stop in Lambarene during a visit to Africa so that he might gather some ideas for the work of the UN Secretariat. Hammarskjöld also expressed the wish that Schweitzer might give a speech at the festivities for the tenth anniversary of the United Nations. According to Hammarskjöld scholar Manuel Fröhlich, the secretary general was forced to abandon this plan because the strain of the journey would have been too much on Schweitzer, who never travelled by plane.[79]

It is not inconceivable, however, that Hammarskjöld had been pressurized by the USA, the most influential member state of the UN, to withdraw his invitation to Schweitzer on account of his criticism of nuclear testing. The unsatisfactory turn of the Korean War and the acquisition by the Soviet Union of nuclear weapons drastically fuelled the political debate in the USA. Anti-Soviet hysteria—forever connected with Senator McCarthy's name—began to take hold of American politics and society.[80] The general perception of a Soviet threat was intensified by the news, which was initially withheld from the public, that the Soviet Union had managed to detonate a hydrogen bomb, something the Americans were only to achieve seven months later. The physicist J. Robert Oppenheimer was accused by the FBI under J. Edgar Hoover of showing Communist sympathies and was accordingly classified as a 'threat to security'.[81] Robert Jungk, who in his 1956 book *Brighter than a Thousand Suns* called for the abolition of nuclear weapons, also came under suspicion. And Schweitzer, too, as an opponent of nuclear weapons, was caught up in this anti-communist witch-hunt, although he had the advantage of working in far-off Africa.

In January 1957, Norman Cousins, the American publicist and editor of the literary magazine *Saturday Review of Literature*, together with the photographer Clara Urquhart, visited Schweitzer in Lambarene.[82] They passed on President Eisenhower's birthday wishes as well as best regards from Indian Prime Minister Pandit Nehru, whom Schweitzer had met in Lausanne in 1936.[83] But above all they pressed him to intensify his public warnings against the nuclear threat. Once more, however, Schweitzer doubted his own competence on the issue and argued that his opinion would surely not be of much public significance. He was finally persuaded to compose a letter to President Eisenhower highlighting the necessity of an effective arms control.[84] Schweitzer acknowledged that he had 'over years gathered material on nuclear energy, both military and non-military'.[85] He also sent to the US president a note of thanks for the birthday letter, as well as a powder made in Lambarene to treat the President's persistent cold. Eisenhower thanked him, but also commented that unfortunately his cold was still not any better.[86] Schweitzer was now a key voice in the nuclear debate, though he was still not entirely convinced that his own efforts were useful. He explained why he nevertheless intensified his struggle:

> All my life [...] I have carefully stayed away from making pronouncements on public matters. Groups would come to me for statements or I would be asked to sign joint letters or the press would ask for my views on certain political questions. And always I would feel forced to say no. It was not because I had no interest in world affairs or politics. My interest and my concerns in these things are great. It was just that I felt that my connection with the outside world should grow out of my work or thought in the fields of theology or philosophy or music. I have tried to relate myself to the problems of all humankind rather than to become involved in disputes between this or that group. I wanted to be one man speaking to another man.[87]

For too long, humanity had been oblivious to the potential dangers posed by nuclear tests:

> As day after day passes, and as the sun continues to rise and set, the sheer regularity of nature seems to rule out such terrible thoughts. But what we seem to forget is that, yes, the sun will continue to rise and set and the moon will continue to move across the skies, but mankind can create a situation in which the sun and moon can look down upon an earth that has been stripped of all life.[88]

Schweitzer had a very clear idea of what form an effective protest against nuclear weapons should take. It should be neither too journalistic and superficial, nor too academic and weighty. As Cousins wrote:

> 'I am worried about present-day journalism,' he said. 'The emphasis on negative happenings is much too strong. Not infrequently, news about

events marking great progress is overlooked or minimized. It tends to make for a negative and discouraging atmosphere. There is a danger that people may lose faith in the forward direction of humanity if they feel that very little happens to support that faith. And real progress is related to the belief by people that it is possible. [...] Some way must be found to bring about an increased awareness of the danger. Anything that is done should above all be simple and direct. It should not be ponderous or academic.'[89]

In Germany anti-nuclear sentiment gathered momentum from the 1950s onwards. Chancellor Konrad Adenauer had downplayed the danger of nuclear weapons in a press release of 5 April 1957. In response to a parliamentary request by Social Democrats, eighteen leading nuclear scientists, among them Otto Hahn and Werner Heisenberg,[90] drew attention to the magnitude of the threat. In the Göttingen Declaration of 12 April 1957, they pointed out that 'each single tactical nuclear bomb or grenade [...] has a similar effect to the first nuclear bomb that destroyed Hiroshima'.[91] Linus Pauling, 1954 Nobel Prize winner in Chemistry and in 1962 in Peace, Albert Schweitzer, and other leading scientists and Nobel Prize laureates attached their names to this declaration.[92] At the same time, Schweitzer maintained a good personal relationship with Adenauer. He wrote to the chancellor in July 1957: 'While working on my speech for Oslo on the danger of continuing the testing of nuclear bombs, I often had to think about the discomfort and problems that it would cause especially you. I really did suffer under these thoughts. But I could do nothing else. [...] I avoided anything overly emotional in my speech.'[93] But Schweitzer's appeal proved successful, increasing public pressure on those advocating the use of nuclear armament.[94]

On 23 April 1957, eleven days after the Göttingen Declaration, Radio Oslo and many other radio stations broadcast Schweitzer's Declaration of Conscience, a speech that was to become world famous.[95] Schweitzer had been urged to take this move by UN Secretary General Dag Hammarskjöld. He had also sent a copy of his speech to the Nobel Prize Committee, asking them to transmit it from Oslo. The committee could not refuse this request to the Nobel laureate.[96] Albert Schweitzer, the 'world renowned theologian and Humanist',[97] now in the role of the 'benign old family doctor [...sat down] at the sickbed of humanity to advise her'.[98] As a physician, his diagnosis was brutally honest:

> The material collected, although far from complete, allows us to draw the conclusion that radiation resulting from the explosions which have already taken place represents a danger to the human race—a danger not to be underrated [...] Particularly dangerous are the elements combining long life with a relatively strong efficient radiation. Among them Strontium 90 takes the first place. [...] What we absorb of radioactivity is not spread evenly in all cellular tissue. It is deposited in certain parts of our body, particularly in the bone tissue and also in the spleen and in the liver. [...] What are the diseases caused by internal radiation? [...] They are mainly serious blood diseases. [...] To the profound damage of these cells corresponds a profound damage to our descendants. [...] We are forced to regard every increase in the existing danger through further creation of radioactive elements by atom bomb explosions as a catastrophe for the human race, a catastrophe that must be prevented. There can be no question of doing anything else, if only for the reason that we cannot take the responsibility for the consequences it might have for our descendants. They are threatened by the greatest and most terrible danger.[99]

The reaction was immediate: Kaare Fostervoll of Radio Oslo announced that the declaration and its translation into various languages had been a complete success,[100] and Otto Hahn declared 'that Herr Schweitzer, speaking with exceptional authority, had made clear to the nations [...] that they must sit down with each other [...] in order that these dreadful tests be abandoned'.[101] Western governments, however, were suspicious of Schweitzer's appeal. The Soviet Union posed a constant threat, and deterrence seemed the only option that would hold it at bay. Schweitzer followed closely the reactions to his speech in the press, and he complained to Norman Cousins that the US media had not afforded his speech the attention it merited. In a letter to Theodor Heuss, Schweitzer wrote about reactions to his Declaration of Conscience:

> Now the London Negotiations about stopping tests have taken place in July 1957. An agreement between them was expected. [...] I have received detailed accounts of the negotiations. They say that Americans had torpedoed the thing by demanding impossible terms regarding inspection, and had generally rejected every proposal. I am confirmed

in my view, as America—or let us say Dulles—is now spreading propaganda in America and Europe that radiation in the atmosphere let off by test explosions, even should it amount to ten times the normal, is completely risk-free. This thesis was championed in their propaganda by people who had a name in nuclear issues. [...] These authorities were physicists who had no concern for the medical aspects of it all! The press in Europe and America was glad to be able to report that it would take a long time until the radioactivity produced by radioactive substances in the air was even worth mentioning. With this exceptionally well-organized propaganda, Dulles has sedated public opinion. Now this propaganda needed to be disproved. The press was thoroughly dismissive. Public opinion was not to be alarmed.[102]

Schweitzer was of course not alone in this struggle. Linus Pauling, since 1946 a member of the Emergency Committee of Atomic Scientists headed by Albert Einstein, asked him to sign a petition addressed to the United Nations demanding an immediate end to nuclear testing. This petition was signed by 9,235 scientists, among them Schweitzer, and handed over to the United Nations by Linus Pauling on 13 January 1958.[103] On 3 March, Schweitzer wrote to the philosopher Martin Buber, whom he had met in 1929 at the thirteenth meeting of the Schopenhauer Society:

I am investing much time into staying updated on the nuclear issue and to help exorcizing the ghost of nuclear war. Politicians do not understand what it is about. Lately they have started becoming even more foolish. A mighty propaganda is released to numb the public! I follow it week by week. [...] Where are we going?[104]

At first, the petition failed to have the hoped-for effect. The nuclear powers did not react and were no closer to coming to an understanding. Schweitzer prepared three further declarations that were broadcast by Radio Oslo on the last three days of April 1958, and read by the President of the Norwegian Nobel Prize Committee, Gunnar Jahn. These three speeches, The Renunciation of Nuclear Tests, The Danger of an Atomic War, and Negotiations at the Highest Level were received enthusiastically by the international public. In the same year they were published under the title *Peace or Atomic War?*[105] and translated into several languages. In a letter of 28 September 1958 Schweitzer thanked his friend Max Tau for having made possible the publication of these three appeals.[106]

Despite initial public support, it was not long before Schweitzer also faced strong criticism. The Swiss newspaper *Neue Zürcher Zeitung* commented on the publication of the speeches in its edition of 10 September 1958 under the headline 'Strange Albert Schweitzer':

> The revered name of Albert Schweitzer should not prevent the con-clusion that this document is worthless from a political, philosophical, military, and theological perspective. The gamble he expects the West to expose itself to is itself already outrageous. His judgement on America and the Soviet Union makes it completely impossible to take Albert Schweitzer's advice seriously.[107]

Schweitzer was also criticized by former allies. A disagreement arose between himself and Dag Hammarskjöld on the political situ-ation in the Congo. On 7 March 1961 Schweitzer sent him a clear assessment of the situation:

> Since things have been going so badly in the Congo, I think of you day by day, sometimes even at night, and I think of everything you must bear and fight for. The ungratefulness and slander you face are incon-ceivable. But they will not prevail. As an old African hand I believe there will be fewer deaths if Africans are left to fight their own feuds than if one intervenes. The presence of Indian troops is a dangerous thing. Who can vouchsafe that the Indian soldiers will really behave as UN soldiers and will be recognized and accepted as such? […] Hope-fully things will turn out better if Africans themselves reach an agree-ment about the collapse of Belgian Congo into five or six nation states. The Belgian Congo was an artificial construction that could endure only as a colony but not as a free African state.[108]

Schweitzer's estimation of the situation apparently annoyed Ham-marskjöld, as is evident from a letter dated March 1961:

> I can very well imagine the dark feelings with which you as an experi-enced African must be following the developments in the Congo. Yet it is my duty to execute the decisions of the United Nations, and in this respect I obviously have to take into consideration the whole situation worldwide. It is therefore inevitable that sometimes there will be the impression that events, seen only individually, make no sense. But I have high confidence that the Congo affair will gradually improve. I hope, as you do, that it will soon be possible for me to visit you in Lambarene; this has been, as you may know, my own wish for a long time.[109]

But this meeting was not to take place. At first, Hammarskjöld could not settle on a date owing to his many commitments. On 13 September 1961, it seemed a meeting was at hand: Hammarskjöld announced he would visit Schweitzer in Lambarene as part of a trip to Léopoldville (now Kinshasa). Almost prophetically he predicted his own fate: 'But in my current life the unexpected occurs only too often.'[110] On 18 September, his plane went down in Ndola, Zambia. The *London Observer* noted that Hammarskjöld's 'Schweitzerian thinking' made him homeless in the midst of all parties.[111] In his ideas he had hoped to find stimulus for international politics. Yet Schweitzer only reluctantly drew the political consequences of his own thinking. He remained a proponent of individual ethics and a critic of state institutions and governments. Unethical government actions were the source of all political evil:

> The objection is raised that, according to all experience, the state cannot exist by relying merely on truth, justice, and ethical consider-ations, but in the last resort has to take refuge in opportunism. [...] It is refuted by the dreary results. We have, therefore, the right to declare the opposite course to be true wisdom, and to say that true power for the state as for the individual is to be found in spirituality and ethical conduct. The state lives by the confidence of those who belong to it; it lives by the confidence felt in it by other states. Opportunist policy may have temporary successes to record, but in the long run it assuredly ends in failure.
>
> Thus ethical world- and life-affirmation demands of the modern state that it shall aspire to making itself an ethical and spiritual person-ality. It presses this obstinately upon the state. [...] The wisdom of tomorrow has a different tone from that of yesterday.[112]

Schweitzer extended his criticism of binding political treaties and rule-making to include Kant:

> Kant published, with the title *Towards Perpetual Peace*, a work con-taining rules which were to be observed with a view to lasting peace whenever treaties of peace were concluded. It was a mistake. Rules for treaties of peace, however ably drawn up, can accomplish nothing. Only such thinking as establishes the sway of the mental attitude of reverence for life can bring to mankind perpetual peace.[113]

The principle of Reverence for Life was, in the end, also a political utopia:

> Only to the degree that they [the nations] submit to the ethos of reverence for life will they be able to trust one another completely. A utopia? If we do not manage to realize this utopia, then all of us will be at the mercy of nuclear weapons and the ruin they promise. Only through the power of the true ethos of humanity can the world be rid of the power of nuclear weapons, and peace begin to reign.[114]

After the Soviet Union had announced in 1958 that it would cease all nuclear testing, the two Western nuclear powers, the United States and the United Kingdom, followed suit. This moratorium lasted for thirty-four months until the Soviets took up testing again in August 1961, and the USA consequently no longer felt bound by the treaty. A wave of protest followed this decision. It was Albert Schweitzer who, in a letter to John F. Kennedy dated 20 April 1962, declared that 'disarmament and effective international control' were the most important goals.[115] In October 1962, the Cuban Missile Crisis spread fear of nuclear war around the whole world. The discovery by American U-2 spy planes that the Soviet Union was stationing nuclear missiles in Cuba led to a series of events that brought the world to the brink of a nuclear war. De-escalation was achieved only on 28 October after both sides had managed to wrest military and political concessions from each other. In the midst of this crisis, Schweitzer wrote to Norman Cousins that 'time works for those who want to abolish nuclear weapons'.[116] On hearing that the USA was considering the use of nuclear weapons to end the Cuba conflict, Schweitzer wrote—without ever posting the letter—to President Kennedy on 24 October 1962:

> You are counted on as a guarantor that nuclear weapons would not be used. We believed this only now to hear the US publicly announce that, should conflict arise as a result of the Cuban Missile Crisis or the Berlin Crisis, it would use nuclear weapons. We are appalled and do not understand this change of policy. In effect, this decision means an end to negotiations. They become pointless. Nuclear weapons become facts. [...] What our time needs is not a politics of power but a politics that looks towards negotiations to bring peace. [...] Now I venture to make my great request to you no longer to claim that the US will use nuclear weapons in a conflict in Cuba or Berlin. Let this declaration be

forgotten, so that serious negotiations on halting nuclear testing and the abolition of nuclear weapons can proceed with a prospect of success. The future of humanity depends on this. If we retain nuclear weapons, they will destroy us.[117]

Instead, around four weeks later on 23 November 1962, Schweitzer composed the following letter, which this time was to reach its recipient:

In the terrible situation in which we find ourselves through the existence of atomic weapons, our last slight hope of avoiding a nuclear war remains in the fact that both the West and the East are determined to make use of atomic weapons only if the other should do so first. Yet you disregarded this implicit agreement when you declared that in both the Berlin and the Cuban crises you would take the initiative and employ atomic weapons should hostilities arise. Do you really want to burden yourself with this terrible responsibility that your country should be the first to use atomic weapons and thus put an end to our last hope of averting nuclear war? [...] Nuclear war is inhumane. [...] In both world wars we sunk deep into inhumanity, and now we resolve to sink even deeper in the course of a coming nuclear war. Something so ghastly must not be permitted to come true. We must cease living in spiritual blindness.[118]

Schweitzer conceded that the United States would be justified in using nuclear weapons only if the Soviet Union had first used them. The West should do what is necessary to avoid falling behind another nuclear power.

At the height of the Cuban Missile Crisis, Schweitzer also composed a letter to Robert McNamara, the US Secretary of Defense, and wanted it published in an American newspaper. When the conflict was settled, however, Cousins refused to aid Schweitzer in this undertaking. Still, Schweitzer persisted: 'We cannot stop publicly criticizing McNamara to the utmost, since he has announced that he would use nuclear weapons.'[119] The Test Ban Treaty, which a commission of the United Nations had been preparing since March 1962, was signed on 25 July 1963, prohibiting all nuclear testing in the atmosphere and underwater, but not underground. Schweitzer saw the 'light of dawn' in this treaty, but voiced the following concern:

The sun can begin to rise only when all nuclear test explosions, including those underground, cease [...] It is and remains regrettable that the great powers could not decide at the Moscow Conference to halt underground testing, as they were not able to come to an agreement on sufficient monitoring nor able to trust each other that each party should keep to the agreement of ceasing underground testing even if comprehensive monitoring was impossible.[120]

Unlike Einstein, who Schweitzer thought had died embittered about political developments in America, Schweitzer was able to witness this success. He wrote in a letter to President Kennedy in August 1963:

I am writing to congratulate you and to thank you for having the vision and courage to initiate a policy of world peace. At last a ray of light is visible in the darkness in which mankind is seeking its path; this glimmer gives us hope that the darkness will yield to the light. The East–West pact that bans nuclear testing in the atmosphere and underwater is one of the greatest events in world history.[121]

A Bell from the German Democratic Republic

When the editor of the magazine *Der Spiegel*, Claus Jacobi, travelled to Lambarene, he made an astounding discovery. In the centre of the village there stood a bell tower with the inscription: 'For peace in the whole world'—donated by the Morgenröthe Press Plant in East Germany. In honour of Schweitzer's eighty-fifth birthday in September 1959, the factory had cast an iron bell and sent it to Lambarene.[122]

Retracing the bell's long journey from Morgenröthe-Rautenkrantz in the German Democratic Republic (GDR) to Lambarene in Gabon, one finds many people not immediately associated with Albert Schweitzer. One is Walter Ulbricht, the head of state of East Germany; another is his emissary Gerald Götting, who would become chairman of the Christian Democratic Union party in East Germany and deputy chairman of the State Council. Schweitzer's connection with East Germany began, harmlessly enough, with birthday wishes sent by Gerald Götting on his eightieth birthday. The note ran: 'We know that in this struggle we are in need of such mental strength and energy as you display in Central Africa among the Negroes—among the victims of inhumane colonial politics—for the welfare of these people and also for the rehabilitation of the name of Christianity.'[123] Götting followed up this letter with another on Schweitzer's eighty-fifth birthday. He also forwarded a message from the German Peace Council announcing the visit of an East German delegation to Lambarene, headed by Götting himself. From the outset Götting had planned this journey with Walter Ulbricht.[124]

One of the most prominent members of this delegation was Robert Havemann. The future civil-rights activist was at the time still a member of the Socialist Unity Party of Germany that governed the East German state from its formation until the 1989 revolution. He was also a delegate to the People's Chamber of East Germany. There is a certain irony in the fact that in Lambarene the delegation was put up in a guest house named *Sans Souci*.

This first journey to Lambarene from East Germany was made into the documentary *Visit to Lambarene* by the East German film company DEFA. Robert Havemann and Gerald Götting collaborated on the screenplay. The documentary portrayed Albert Schweitzer as a 'great humanist' and 'friend of peace'.[125] As Schweitzer's past experiences with photojournalists in Lambarene had been far from positive, he was initially wary of the cameraman, but ultimately let him proceed with his work.

It was the avowed goal of this short film—as it was of the illustrated book published by Götting in 1961[126]—for East Germany, the 'second' German country, to share in some of Schweitzer's fame. And the issue of nuclear power seemed the ideal opportunity to position Schweitzer in opposition to Adenauer's policy of West German rearmament.[127] His eighty-fifth birthday was the official occasion for the visit, and Schweitzer was either not aware of or not concerned by its political dimensions. However, the delegation, bringing fifteen boxes of medication as a gift, was delayed by visa problems at several African borders and arrived a week late.[128] Over the following years Götting would organize several donations of medical equipment from East Germany; at one point he was even treated in a dentist surgery in Lambarene that he had previously been instrumental in equipping. Götting's goal was to improve the political position of East Germany in general and the East CDU party in particular. In a personal interview he conceded that obviously part of the motivation of his visits had been that Schweitzer should feel more friendly towards East Germany.[129]

The production of the short film on Lambarene provides evidence to support this claim. It had been minutely planned in East Berlin, and the approval protocol for this film, which was necessary before it could be shown in East Germany, summarized the government's interest in Albert Schweitzer:

> The small but impressive documentary shows, on the one hand, the hardships of the population living under the yoke of colonialism and their struggle for national sovereignty and civilized progress, and, on the other, the successes brought about by the great humanist Albert Schweitzer. It also covers his letter addressed to the Peace Council of East Germany, in which he expresses his unconditional commitment to the fight for the preservation of peace and his position against the use of nuclear weapons.[130]

The East German government's objective of this carefully planned trip to Gabon was to bring Schweitzer's engagement against nuclear armament in line with its own political agenda. It is astounding how openly Schweitzer behaved towards those who came to Lambarene, even if they had a clear political agenda of their own. After all, he must have been aware that Götting would use the task of delivering Schweitzer's letter to the Peace Council for political purposes. An assessment written by a member of the Ministry for State Security, working under the code name 'Fidelio', shows that Götting was not only representing the interests of East Germany and the SED, but was also systematically promoting his reputation as a well-connected politician:

> Götting uses every chance that presents itself to make strong public appearances as a political figure. This had already been the case before his appointment as deputy leader of the State Council and has since this point in time become increasingly noticeable. One must say that he does it very skilfully and that he does everything in all fields, including the publication of books, with the intention of making a strong public appearance. His connection with Albert Schweitzer has given him many opportunities [...] To come close to as many different groups as possible, he has already arranged a number of lectures on Albert Schweitzer and is very keen on using the topic to make public appearances in different groups, e.g. at Christian meetings. Initially, he attempted to override the party chairman and in public powerfully [...] [At this point the following pages of the report have been removed

and cannot be reconstructed, according to information by the archive of the Centre of the Federal Commissioner for the Records of the State Security Service of the former German Democratic Republic.][131]

Götting's trip to Lambarene involved considerable administrative effort and was fastidiously protocolled by Department V/3 of East Germany's Ministry for State Security.[132] On 18 December 1959, Götting travelled to West Berlin to procure the necessary visas at the Inter-Allied Office, enabling him to travel to Lambarene via third-party countries.[133]

The trip was a complete success in publicly documenting Schweitzer's essentially positive attitude towards East Germany. A biography written by Boris M. Nossik and published in East Germany quotes Schweitzer on the visit of 1961 as follows:

> I am happy to have met you at my age, because from you I hear about the growing resonance of my appeals for Reverence for Life in the socialist world and still more because you give me hope that a time may come when these most humane of all efforts, which will culminate in peace on earth, might become reality in a renewed society.[134]

Of course Nossik did not mention Robert Havemann's visit to Lambarene in his biography of Schweitzer, although Havemann's good relationship with Schweitzer had been the cause of some difficulty before the trip. Early letters from January 1960 suggest that the relationship between these two men must have been very close. Schweitzer's papers contained a remarkable poem by Havemann on Schweitzer and the principle of Reverence for Life entitled 'Albert Schweitzer'.[135] The poem is an authentic impression of Havemann's fascination with Lambarene. The two kept up their correspondence following the visit. Both the go-between Götting and the Ministry for State Security were well informed about the content of these letters, as copies in the archives of the Ministry prove. In a letter written four days before the construction of the Berlin Wall in 1961, Schweitzer asked why he was not included as a member of the next delegation from East Germany, but then, as usual, he talked shop about solar energy and asked about his research.[136] Three years later, in April 1964, after Havemann had aroused the suspicions of East German government with his ideas for a democratic socialism, Schweitzer received a letter marked 'urgent' that he was able to answer via Gerald Götting and the president of the Academy of Sciences of

East Germany only on 25 April 1964. Havemann, who obviously saw
Schweitzer as a close confidante, wrote:

> Dear, most honourable Herr Prof. Schweitzer,
> Last winter semester I gave a lecture series entitled 'Scientific Aspects
> of Philosophical Problems' at the Humboldt University in Berlin and
> although it was most well received by students, it has now been
> heavily criticized by the Party. An interview attributed to me,
> which was printed by a West German publicist without my know-
> ledge or consent following a meeting with me, gave cause for my
> immediate dismissal from my post at the university. Meanwhile, the
> German Academy of Sciences has ensured that I will be allowed to
> continue my research on photochemistry. Yet at the moment the
> conversion of my current corresponding membership to the Acad-
> emy to a full member is being discussed, as is to be done with all
> corresponding members in accordance with the new statute. [...]
> Now those at the top want to prevent my membership on account of
> the political dispute (I have been barred from the SED Party). I am
> not turning to you on account of my person. Nor does the reputation
> of the people who have decided on such a course of action concern
> me. But I think that it lies in the interest of the Academy that it does
> not let itself be used as the executer of such an arbitrary act. After
> close counsel with a highly acclaimed member of the Academy, of
> which you are the sole honorary member, I have decided to compose
> this letter to you.[137]

In desperation, Havemann turned to Schweitzer in his function
as honorary member of the Academy of Sciences of East Germany
with a plea that he should write to the Academy on his behalf by 21
April 1964 to forestall his being expelled. However, Havemann's
letter reached Lambarene only on 22 April, and Schweitzer was
unable to answer in time. But even a timely response would not
have changed things: Schweitzer's letter was intercepted by the
Ministry for State Security. A copy exists in the Ministry's file on
Havemann.[138] The original was handed over to Havemann by
Götting. A note by the minister's deputy sheds light on the sensitive
political dimension of the communication between Havemann and
Schweitzer:

> In the groups of people close to Havemann, speculations are ripe that
> Albert Schweizer [*sic*] will speak up for Havemann and possibly

officially return the honours bestowed on him by the government of the GDR in protest against the dispute with Havemann. In discussions about Havemann's motivation for his behaviour at the Phil. Institute of the Humboldt University, the version was discussed that Havemann probably wants to play the martyr, even wants to provoke direct sanctions against himself, in the expectation that Albert Schweizer [*sic*] will spark off an international protest.[139]

It is remarkable to note how Schweitzer's contact in East Germany, Gerald Götting, reacted to Schweitzer's belated letter. He wrote to Schweitzer, with a degree of cynicism, about Havemann's fate, on 5 May 1964:

I have immediately forwarded the birthday letter to Prime Minister Khrushchev and hope that he has already received it. Your letter to Havemann I have handed over to him. Diverse comments he has made in front of his students and West German journalists have involved him in the 'cold war' against our Republic. He has had to pay the price. He will now be able to commit himself all the more to his proper work in research. Your letter is surely an encouragement for his scientific work.[140]

Schweitzer used Götting to bring Lambarene to the attention of Ulbricht and, through him, the Soviet Union. Götting in turn used his contact with Schweitzer to gain the support of a world-famous moral figurehead for himself and his East CDU party, someone who opened doors in the State Council of East Germany as well as in the churches. Furthermore, he claimed that, in its position on nuclear weapons, East Germany held the moral ground over the Federal Republic of Germany. Meanwhile, neither Götting nor Schweitzer openly criticized the other's ideological position. This resulted in a bizarre situation. Schweitzer did not publicly protest when Ulbricht built the Berlin Wall, but instead sent, unofficially, Götting a list of names, asking that he help these people leave East Germany. Götting gave Schweitzer his promise. The mere fact that it was necessary to give a representative of a government a list of people who were not allowed to leave that country ought to have made Schweitzer think, at the very least, about its moral legitimacy. Yet Schweitzer's letters do not contain any criticism of the border policy of East Germany, although a regime that denies its citizens the right to leave its territory is flouting the principle of Reverence for Life. Although he had directly experienced how this regime dealt with its critical citizens when it isolated Havemann, Schweitzer apparently still considered it beneficial to have direct access to East Germany's top leadership.

On the occasion of the 250th anniversary of the Charité University Hospital, shortly before the erection of the Berlin Wall, Schweitzer received an honorary doctorate from the Faculty of Medicine of the Humboldt University in East Berlin. The dean of the Faculty of Medicine, Louis-Heinz Kettler, travelled to Lambarene to bestow the honour on Schweitzer on 6 August 1961. With the award came a donation from the Red Cross of East Germany in the form of ten crates of medication worth 20,000 East German marks as well as a medal from the Peace Council. Götting noted in his Lambarene diary:

> But this time even the doctor [Schweitzer] has put on a dark suit and a black bow tie. Standing, the doctor listens to the short but sincere speech delivered by Kettler. [...] Schweitzer is deeply moved. His thanks are delivered with memories of his time in Berlin. He remembers with joy the time that was for him so happy at the turn of the century. He talks of his encounters in the house of Curtius, who had discovered Olympia. He says he had seldom been so happy and free. His military service and the difficult years as a student lay behind him and the future awaited him. He recollected, among others, Harnack and the many conversations— Harnack probably sent him the last letter before his death. [...] S. is transformed into the young Schweitzer, who is determined not to live as an 'epigone'. [...] S. attaches great importance to his 'corresponding membership of the German Academy of Sciences' in Berlin. [...] After the prolonged walk, dinner: macaroni, cheese, tomato sauce. Then, like on almost every other evening, S. sits down at the piano. We sang 'nun ruhen alle Wälder' [...] and it seemed to us as if we were sitting in our homeland and were far from the mysterious, fermenting African continent that is heading towards new things.[141]

His comments reveal a mixture of romanticized colonialism and highbrow educational pretension. Meanwhile, Walter Ulbricht wrote the following lines to Schweitzer one month before the official ceremony:

> Allow me to use the occasion of Herr Gerald Götting's visit to convey my heartfelt wishes and above all my sincere congratulations on your

receiving the distinction of an honorary doctorate from the Humboldt University of Berlin. [...] On 9 February 1961 I had a talk with a delegation of Christian citizens of the German Democratic Republic led by the esteemed Professor D. Emil Fuchs about all the questions that touch the common ground shared by forces for Humanism [...] And here I see no cause for disagreement between atheists and Christians.[142]

Schweitzer was apparently flattered by this letter, as his response of 9 August 1961—only four days before the Berlin Wall went up— shows:

> Most honoured Chairman,
> I thank you most sincerely for your kind letter from 20 July 1961. I see from it that you agree with what I have said about peace and also that you look sympathetically on my idea of Reverence for Life. I have read with great interest what you write about the plan for peace and its realization. May it be given to all who give their best effort to the cause of peace that they experience something of its coming and may the insight that if peace is not achieved mankind's existence is at stake be understood throughout the world. With best wishes, your respectfully devoted AS.[143]

It did not occur to Schweitzer that the East German head of state would not treat a letter with a Nobel Peace Prize recipient as private correspondence. Yet Schweitzer's misjudgement can surely not be put down to a lack of political sensitivity regarding Berlin and West Germany. In 1959, Schweitzer had received a most friendly letter from the mayor of Berlin, Willy Brandt, who had described the tension in the city and his will to remain steadfast in this 'current crisis'.[144]

In addition to keeping up with the news, Schweitzer had correspondents such as Heuss, Adenauer, and other politicians who kept him well informed about current affairs in Germany. Yet of all times he chose August 1961 to write a personal letter to the leader of East Germany. Shortly after building the Berlin Wall, Ulbricht forwarded this letter to the press. Although Schweitzer had shown himself to be decidedly pro-Western and agreed that nuclear disarmament could not be allowed to 'put the West at a disadvantage compared to Soviet Russia',[145] many in West Germany mistrusted him and criticized his attitude towards East Germany. Some claimed that by writing this letter he had given up his political neutrality and positioned himself as a supporter of East

Germany and its social model.[146] On his return to Berlin, Gerald Götting wrote a letter to Schweitzer on 21 August 1961, although Schweitzer appeared by now to be wary of GDR rhetoric: 'We arrived here just at a time when our government, at the height of the tension that had been developing in Berlin, had to close our part of Berlin against the disruptive actions initiated by West Berlin.'[147]

To retain Schweitzer's good graces, Götting did attempt—although he was not always successful—to secure the release of those people on Schweitzer's lists. On 25 March 1962, Schweitzer noted the names of twenty-six people who were denied permission to leave despite Götting's efforts.[148] However, this did not deter Schweitzer from immediately having Mathilde Kottmann pass on a further eight names.

In 1962, Götting began publishing Schweitzer's writings in East Germany, paying royalties amounting to 9,000 marks in the form of medication. He said of Schweitzer's works: 'Not only your many friends, but Marxists, too, are very interested in them here.'[149] As a result, Schweitzer became well known in East Germany, while Götting was able to improve his own political position in his dealings with the ruling SED party.

Schweitzer must have been aware that Christians in East Germany faced repression in various ways, as this was reported on in West German newspapers and his correspondents also wrote about it. Götting attempted to gloss over the situation. For example, when Schweitzer asked what truth there was in the rumour that the government of East Germany was planning to tear down the University Church of Leipzig, Götting replied:

> In reference to your letter concerning the University Church of Leipzig and the accompanying telegram, I can inform you that, while it is true that there was a discussion about tearing down the church, as some architects were in favour of enlarging the university, which was destroyed in the war, and wanted to make use of the space taken up by the church in their plans, our official talks have, however, shed light on the matter and the University Church will not be demolished.[150]

In the same letter Götting tried to correct Schweitzer's image of the Federal Republic of Germany. He conceded: 'Sadly, your question on the permission of citizens of East Germany to enter Gabon is justified.'

Yet he argued that West Germany and NATO were doing everything in their power to prevent freedom of transit and international recognition, and West Germany was trying to 'gain possession of nuclear weapons by way of the multilateral nuclear power of the NATO'.[151] Less than four years later, in 1968, Ulbricht approved a plan to demolish the University Church of St Paul in Leipzig. But by then Schweitzer was already dead.

Until 1965, visitors, helpers, and even doctors from East Germany came to Lambarene, despite the notorious troubles with visas. For his ninetieth birthday Schweitzer was honoured by Walter Ulbricht with the following lines, who valued the doctor as a

> great humanist [...] who always stands up for peace and understanding. [...] Your maxim of life has caused you to leave a bourgeois world marked by repression, exploitation, and war to help our black brothers in Africa and found an oasis of humanity. [...] in our socialist state, the German Democratic Republic, we attempt to realize this Reverence for Life with all its possible consequences for society.[152]

Ulbricht went on to voice concern about nuclear armament and general developments within West Germany. Schweitzer knew that East German border guards had orders to fire at so-called deserters, and he must have found it cynical when Ulbricht described East Germany as a country that practised his principle of Reverence for Life. In the course of the Hibbert Lectures in 1934, Schweitzer had still labelled socialism as 'immoral':

> Marxist Socialism does not put forward any ideals for improving the life of the workers and thus does not seek to have any impact, but instead continues to wait for world revolution; this is what makes it so sinister and immoral. It calls on no ideals in places where they are most needed. That is the reason why historically it has not worked as a benevolent but only as a corrosive force.[153]

In his later life Schweitzer's attitude towards representatives of the system he denounces here was at best pragmatic and in any case inconsistent. Between 1960 and 1965, he accepted regular donations from East Germany, such as Ulbricht's gift of medication worth 10,000 marks in March 1962.[154] The first and only delegation from the Soviet Union stayed in Lambarene over Christmas 1961. In addition to the traditional Russian Matryoshka dolls, they presented

Schweitzer with a model of a Sputnik spacecraft, for which he thanked them saying: 'And so a Sputnik has now landed in Lambarene,' and offered in return a sack of bananas.[155]

For Schweitzer's ninetieth birthday, East Germany issued a set of stamps bearing his name and portrait. Showing little foresight, Schweitzer wrote to thank the minister of postal services of East Germany. The commemorative stamps venerated him as a 'Great humanist and physician' on the 10 pfennig stamp, an 'Opponent of war and nuclear death' on the 20 pfennig stamp, and a 'Musician and Bach interpreter' on the 25 pfennig stamp. Unsurprisingly, there was no mention of him being a theologian. An unusual amount of effort was put into the set of stamps. They not only had a distinctive first day cover, but also a special 'commemoration leaflet in honour of Albert Schweitzer', the inside of which bore a copy of Schweitzer's letter to the minister of postal services, dated 12 November 1964, and including the entry stamp of the minister's office. Every stamp collector in East Germany could now read:

> Most honoured Herr Minister,
> So you want to launch letters bearing my portrait! I still cannot believe that you are bestowing this honour on me. If I become vain with age, you bear the responsibility. But what you have done moves me deeply. Your country has been so kind towards my hospital and has shown me so much love. The three pictures displayed on the stamps are very natural and lively. Please convey to the government of your country my deepest thanks for the honour you do me. Excuse my bad handwriting. At my age I have a bad writer's cramp. The quill will not obey the hand. How I should like to come to the GDR to thank you in person. But at my age I must forgo all travel. The work I do here does not allow me to take journeys. I still have to enlarge my hospital. I myself must oversee the construction. With the best of thoughts, yours humbly, Albert Schweitzer[156]

It requires little imagination to appreciate how this text was received in West Germany. Yet Schweitzer must have also been aware of this. James Brabazon's claim that Schweitzer had gone so far as to become an honorary patron of the East German state youth group, the Free German Youth, could not, however, be verified in an interview conducted with Gerald Götting in 2008, nor in the correspondence in the archives at Gunsbach or Berlin.[157]

After the Berlin Wall had been built in 1961 and after the episode with Robert Havemann, Schweitzer must have known that accepting money from a state that orders 'deserters from the republic' to be shot was not only strategically ill-advised, but hardly consistent with his principle of Reverence for Life. Schweitzer's successor in Lambarene, Walter Munz, recalled how Götting would constantly pester Schweitzer with political questions on the inner German relationship and foreign affairs during dinner, trying to get him to take sides. But Schweitzer was unwilling to oblige him.[158] Ironically, on a political level East Germany was treating Schweitzer and his life's work exactly in the way Schweitzer as a theologian had so minutely shown in his *The Quest of the Historical Jesus* can happen: that is, how an ideology can be projected onto a historical person. East Germany was turning the theologian into a humanist advocating East Germany's understanding of peace. Schweitzer's letters and responses, as in the case of Robert Havemann, show that, while he understood he was being co-opted, he did not defend himself.

It appears all the more remarkable that, in a letter to the mayor of Berlin, Willy Brandt, sent on 10 February 1965, Schweitzer assures him that he has always commiserated with the fate of Berlin. The future German chancellor answered Schweitzer: 'From conversations with friends who have met you in the last years, honoured Dr. Schweitzer, I know that you have shared in the fate of Berlin in these past difficult years and that your good wishes were with us: now you have clearly expressed your relationship to this city.'[159]

Perhaps Schweitzer felt he had to document his solidarity with West Berlin, especially on account of his contacts with the leaders of East Germany, and he did this when he replied to Brandt's congratulations on his ninetieth birthday. In any case, the correspondence shows how intensively the question of the two German states gripped him and how effectively he attempted to remain in contact with all parties concerned.

Homo politicus

What makes a person a 'political animal'? The political scientist Franz Walter summarizes his or her characteristics as follows:

> The successful politician of this type combines political instinct, popu-
> lism, a sensitivity to atmosphere and problems, the ability to concentrate

on what is essential, an exceptional media presence, and pragmatism. He must be an immensely multifaceted personality, must be a suitable surface for the projection of a diversity of needs, attitudes, and cultures, must be able to change positions, must be able to adapt immediately to new situations without appearing opportunistic. He should be an embracing integrator but also be able to scout tomorrow's trends.[160]

Following these criteria Schweitzer would qualify as a remarkable *homo politicus*, but one who was wise enough not to get involved in day-to-day politics. As a citizen of Alsace—torn between two power-hungry countries—he must have been born with this political instinct. And, by running a hospital for Africans in a French colony, he automatically found himself in the midst of a proxy political war conducted by the United States and the Soviet Union in Africa. Moreover, Schweitzer was faced with the storm of decolonization that swept the old colonial powers out of states such as Gabon or the Congo. It was possible to remain neutral in such a situation—or at least to make a show of neutrality—as Schweitzer had done. To remain entirely apolitical, however, was not an option. How did Schweitzer come to terms with his role as the 'world's conscience' during the cold war, writing almost identical letters to politicians as different as John F. Kennedy and Khrushchev? The German President Theodor Heuss answered the question whether Schweitzer was a politician with a decided 'no' during his speech at the ceremony for the Peace Prize of the German Book Trade in 1951:

Yet today, at this point in time, the term peace simply means: wishing that war does not happen again, not once more, that the suffering accompanying humanity will not be technically multiplied a thousand-fold, a millionfold. Is the word peace spoken in this room today therefore a political issue? Is Schweitzer a politician? No, he is not. It is true that he tells us that, as a boy, he read an immense amount of history, and history is history of states, condensed politics. Yet, if I understand him correctly—however curious about life he was—he has shielded himself from these issues in order not to be deterred from his own goal in life.[161]

Schweitzer's interest in politics was awoken during his school years living with relatives in Mulhouse. His habit of regularly reading newspapers initially aroused the mistrust of his great-uncle, while his great-aunt suspected that he read the *Straßburger Post*, the *Mulhouse Tagblatt*, or the *Neue Mühlhauser Zeitung* only for the 'serial novels and the murder cases', and would have liked to prohibit him from reading the newspaper.[162] Schweitzer objected—he was just 11 years old at the time—that, on the contrary, he was mainly interested in politics and current affairs. This led to an impromptu oral examination by his great-uncle, a strict schoolmaster:

> And then he began to examine me as to who the ruling princes in the Balkans were, and what the names were of their prime ministers. Next I had to tell him who made up the three last French cabinets. Finally, I had to summarize the contents of Eugen Richter's last speech in the Reichstag. I passed this examination—accompanied by fried potatoes and salad—with flying colours. It was then decided that I might read the papers not only while the table was being set, but after I had finished my lessons. Of course I also used this permission to devour the serial novels in the literary supplement, but politics was what I was really interested in, and from that time my uncle began to treat me like an adult and to talk about politics with me at meals. I inherited this interest in public affairs from my mother, who was a passionate reader of newspapers.[163]

Schweitzer would keep up with political affairs all his life long. He listened to the radio and made a considerable effort to have daily newspapers delivered to Lambarene from the coast. With the notable exceptions of atomic weapons and East Germany, Schweitzer took scrupulous care that he would not be used to advance any political agenda.

He was all the more irritated at being used by political parties in West Germany for their own purposes after making an 'open appeal' on Easter 1962 against atomic weapons (together with Linus Pauling, Martin Niemöller, and Bertrand Russell, among others) or when he supported an immediate ceasefire and the use of an international court of arbitration in the Vietnam War on 3 June 1965.[164] His likeness had already been used, without his knowledge, on a campaign poster of the German Peace Union, a small West German party financed by East Germany. Schweitzer reassured Götting in 1963 that, when worker brigades in state-owned companies asked to use his name, 'I always say yes'.[165] But he wanted his carefully crafted political statements to be understood as non-partisan calls to ethical action. Nevertheless, he was repeatedly accused of taking sides. The Jesuit Father Leppich, who was known in West Germany as 'God's machine gun', called Schweitzer a 'Protestant Free Mason of socialism'.[166] Reactions like these were almost inevitable. As a Nobel laureate, Schweitzer had to address issues that were a 'minefield': racial discrimination, nuclear weapons, the inner-German relationship, the Cuban Missile Crisis, the Vietnam War, global justice, and decolonization. On all these issues Schweitzer carried on an extensive correspondence with leading politicians.

Schweitzer had a knack of identifying politicians whose political careers still lay ahead of them. After the flood catastrophe that struck Hamburg in 1962, he corresponded with a senator of the city who was to become defence minister and then chancellor: Helmut Schmidt. Like Schweitzer, Schmidt thought strategically and was well connected. He used his personal contacts with leading NATO figures to aid Hamburg and requested, without constitutional authorization, over 100 helicopters from the Bundeswehr and the British Royal Air Force. His handling of this disaster gave him a reputation for acting according to his personal beliefs and ethical responsibilities, even in times of crisis. The correspondence between Schweitzer and Schmidt shows how much they held each other in high regard. Schmidt wrote:

Dear Professor Schweitzer,

On returning from a short holiday, I found your kind letter from 3 March. It made me *very* happy, especially as politicians are not very often applauded. As my wife and I (both lifelong friends of Bach's music) have always highly admired you both as musician and as doctor and on account of your entire life's work, your letter was doubly pleasurable. The situation in the disaster region has largely become normal again, although it has not yet been possible to rebuild the dikes south of the Elbe. Sadly, the number of dead has now climbed above 300. This is by far the most depressing fact. I want to wish you— also for your work—all the best from my heart. Your devoted Helmut Schmidt[167]

Schweitzer was able to analyse complex political situations with impressive precision. As a Francophile Alsatian bearing a German passport, Schweitzer had divided political loyalties and he had to find a way to avoid 'falling between two stools'. This can be seen in how he assessed the geopolitical situation in his correspondence with Helene Bresslau from 1911.[168] To begin with, Helene wrote of their plans to travel to equatorial Africa:

Don't you see, the 'devourers of countries' are the French this time; they are not satisfied with what the Algeciras agreements granted them and think they can get what they want because they feel England's jealousy behind them. But Morocco means such a colossal increase in power for France that Germany may indeed feel uneasy at such a shift in the balance, and because it has genuine interests of German subjects to protect—which were threatened already on the previous situation— it probably is justified in demanding reparations. [...] But for us, what would it mean if the Congo were to become German? If I call to mind your reasons for choosing to go there, there are three of them: (1) to rescue the intelligent and educable natives there from the burgeoning influence of Islam; (2) to help the French Protestant mission, *which needs people*; (3) to prove that human labor can and should rise above all the national differences that separate us. *As long as the Fr. mission remains in the country*, all these reasons are independent of the nationality of the region itself. Now if the Congo really were to become German, it seems to me that it is a worthy task for anyone who desires peace and the labors of peace (and then to work with the mission itself) to make it stay in the country. [...] Farewell—and if you consider me a complete baby politically, keep on loving me a little bit anyway![169]

Schweitzer replied, outlining his thoughts on the conflict between Germany and France:

On your letter: I am far from thinking you a baby politically. On the contrary. But this one time you do not see what lies behind it all. The treaties of Algeciras were not a solution, but only a source of further disputes [...] the reason being that Germany wanted to put the thing off so that (1) France would get a lot of trouble; (2) the Mannesmann brothers would buy lots of mines and lots of land; (3) it could arm its own fleet to be able to fight England if need arises. Here under heading number 3 is the fly in the ointment! What Germany wants above all is an Atlantic harbor so that it can make an enormous military harbor out of it. [...] The fact that the only object of Germany's world policies is to get the upper hand over England and threaten it with invasion by a German army is as clear as daylight...And that is the nasty part. Germany has to acknowledge the current state of ownership...but it still wants to triumph over England; then it can take as many colonies as it wants. Hence the coalition against Germany. (Thank God!) […] In the long run, Germany cannot survive this insane rearmament and is bound to collapse. That is why it must risk everything before that happens, a life-or-death risk…only because of insane plans for greatness…That is the one truth.[170]

He continued his letter, highly critical of German and French nationalism:

And with regard to our Congo, if it becomes German, the German God, who made iron grow, will have to come in at the same time. The French missionaries will have to move out of the area at once and leave it to a German society. Then the children will have to learn 'Hail to the victor's crown,' etc., in German right away. By the way, France would do just the same if it took over a German colony. It is the insane nationalism that always comes first. Then there is no place for me. I do not wish to torment myself to pieces in such senseless periods of transition! But we will find something somewhere else. Perhaps the missionary society will settle somewhere else…or, as is more probable, Germany will strike a milder chord and will not get the Congo. […] You know that I do not hate Germany; I honor it. But this delusion of grandeur, to which decency, honesty, morality, etc. are no more than empty concepts, is unworthy of this people. Is this a political letter, my little baby?[171]

Schweitzer attempted to turn Lambarene into a kind of neutral Switzerland in the jungle. He maintained relationships with both Germany and France, and he did not feel he had to choose one over the other. He was also able to avoid taking sides in the arms race. And, especially when he was in Gabon, he considered himself a guest in the country and refrained from voicing opinions on local politics, and he expected as much from his employees. This political neutrality allowed him to continue his work following the inauguration of the first president of Gabon after independence, Léon M'ba, whom he knew personally.[172] He wrote home to a friend in Strasbourg:

It is my strategy never to respond to an attack, whatever kind it may be. This has always been my maxim, and I have adhered to it faithfully. Nobody can fight against silence in the long run. It is an insuperable opponent. And I do not need to be defended. I am destined to go my way without fighting.[173]

As a world citizen Schweitzer knew that national boundaries have little to do with one's ethical responsibilities. He managed to stage himself *as if* he were a politician without acting *as* a politician. The older he became, the more he resembled the image many had of him: that of the wise old 'jungle doctor'. The extent to which he fascinated his contemporaries can be seen in the staggering career alternatives his fellow Alsatian Karl Brandt (1904–48) contemplated at the beginning of the 1930s: Hitler's future personal physician had considered either following Schweitzer's example and going into the jungle or entering the SS. He chose the latter.[174]

8

How Beautiful! The Last Years (1957–1965)

In May 1957, Helene left Lambarene for the last time. Her health had worsened, and she was accompanied by a Dutch nurse, Toni van Leer, who was on leave to visit her ill father. From Paris, Helene's daughter, Rhena, took her to a clinic in Zurich, but the doctors there were unable to save her life. Helene Schweitzer Bresslau died on 1 June 1957, aged 78 years. The autopsy her husband asked to be carried out revealed all too clearly the physical suffering her numerous severe illnesses had caused her for much of her life. She had had several small heart attacks shortly before her death. Four days later a funeral service took place in a crematorium in Zurich. According to Helene's own wishes, the song 'Are You with Me' from the *Notebook for Anna Magdalena Bach* was played, a song that expressed the intimacy she and Albert had felt together. Half a year later, her husband buried her ashes in Lambarene, together with some earth from their Alsatian home. Shortly afterwards, in August 1957, Schweitzer travelled to Europe to settle his wife's affairs and move her possessions to Gunsbach, as the house in Königsfeld was to be sold.

Decolonization and Criticism

Gabon gained political independence in 1960 and the following year became a presidential republic. Not long after his inauguration, the new President Léon M'ba asked Schweitzer whether he would represent the African states in the French delegation to the United Nations Commission on Human Rights. Schweitzer had a close relationship with M'ba, who addressed him in his letters as 'Cher Docteur et

Ami'.[1] But Schweitzer declined the offer, saying that he was needed at the hospital.[2] M'ba's political opponents expressed open hostility towards Schweitzer. In one incident two politicians from the opposition party arrived at Schweitzer's hospital and in front of all the patients and employees claimed that since the doctor had received his licence from the colonialists and as these had now been driven out of the country he was a collaborator and would also have to leave. The hospital inmates shouted down the two politicians, who then left the hospital. The situation settled down. A similar incident took place three years later. While the opposition was calling Schweitzer a symbol of white colonization and demanding his return to Europe, President M'ba awarded him Gabon's highest honours.[3] Although Schweitzer was critical of African independence, not everyone saw him as a paternalistic colonialist.

During the last year of his life, Schweitzer did not restrict his work to his hospital, but became active in world politics as an opponent of the Vietnam War. In March 1965, Linus Pauling once again appealed to Schweitzer, this time urging him to sign a petition that was to be given to Lyndon B. Johnson demanding an immediate ceasefire in Vietnam. In his reply of 11 April 1965, Schweitzer condemned the determination of the USA to remain in Vietnam, although he requested that his letter to Pauling not be published.[4] He signed the petition after it had been slightly altered by Pauling. It read:

> The war in Vietnam challenges the world's conscience. None of us can read reports about killing, mutilation, and burning day after day without demanding that an end be put to this inhumanity. It is our present intention not to assign blame to the different combatant groups. The one imperative necessity is that this crime against everything that humanity calls civilized should end. Peace is possible. [...] In the name of our common humanity, the undersigned Nobel Peace Prize recipients call on all governments and parties concerned to take immediate measures to achieve a ceasefire and a negotiated settlement of this tragic conflict.[5]

On 3 June 1965, Schweitzer spoke out for the last time on foreign affairs other than nuclear armament: he called on the United States to terminate all combat operations in Vietnam immediately and for the appointment of an international court of arbitration to resolve the conflict.[6]

Even in his last years, construction work in Lambarene taxed Schweitzer much more than international politics did. In 1963, he could look back over fifty years since Lambarene had been founded. Yet it was still necessary to add on to the hospital if it was to accommodate an ever-growing number of patients. In 1961 six doctors and thirty-five nurses looked after some 450 patients, and in 1964 the same number of hospital staff were responsible for 600 patients. In order to accommodate the visitors Schweitzer still encouraged to see the work being done at Lambarene, provisions had to be made to house them in neighbouring villages. As Schweitzer was no longer able to attend to each patient individually, the hospital gradually became less personal. It had also been gradually modernized and was now equipped with several refrigerators and freezers, as well as air conditioning in one building and a number of jeeps. To keep his animals safe from the traffic, Schweitzer put up road signs imposing speed limits of 10 kilometres per hour.[7]

All the while, Schweitzer succeeded in attracting more and more volunteer doctors and nurses to come to Lambarene, and he was thus able to continue expanding the hospital. But the infrastructure posed a considerable problem, as neither the water supply nor the sewage system could keep up with the increasing demands placed upon them. At times, he would quarrel with Rhena, who worked mainly in the pathology lab, over the running of the hospital. She questioned the wisdom of relying for water on the well that was her father's pride. Schweitzer would often be extremely irritated when criticized and would completely ignore suggestions for improvement. Only when the wells ran dry during the next drought did he take her advice to heart. Rhena, who as a child had longed to become a doctor, still felt the urge to go her own way. Initially, Schweitzer had opposed the idea of his daughter training as an assistant in the pathology lab, because he did not think it was a good idea for her to work for him. However, over time he changed his mind, not least for practical reasons. Even before the two-year training course was over, Schweitzer had transferred the sole responsibility for the pathology lab to his daughter. Yet Rhena was never able to tell how her father would react to change. Her feelings for him were ambivalent: love and admiration went hand in hand with detachment and irritability. If she started an argument with the words: 'But yesterday you said […]', he would respond: 'I'm not a book with a well-constructed plot. I'm a man, with all a man's contradictions.'[8]

Rhena was not only involved in Lambarene, where little by little she tried to put her own ideas into practice; she spent much of her time away from Lambarene travelling the world and collecting donations in her father's name to start up a number of humanitarian projects. Despite her involvement, Schweitzer did not prepare her to take over the hospital until shortly before his death.

Rhena wanted to change Lambarene. She thought that some things, such as running water, ought to be available throughout the hospital and that the staff deserved better than just a trough in which to wash themselves or a petrol lamp for reading and writing. Schweitzer considered such innovations to be unnecessary; he saw only his hospital, and it was well run and successful. Patients still flocked to it. Among experts, however, Lambarene was controversial. One leprosy specialist criticized the hospital for focusing on the surgical treatment of leprosy instead of its prevention. But another doctor who had been highly critical of the hospital changed his mind after he visited it, and he ended up praising it as a jewel of tropical medicine.[9] The hospital was, in any case, highly efficient. According to data collected by Schweitzer's successor, Walter Munz, the number of operations, births, and deaths in the jungle hospital rose from 500 in 1958 to 1,000 in 1963, five years later.

In 1965, the year of Schweitzer's death, the hospital was doing well in comparison to the late 1940s. It had over 478 hospital beds, and these were almost always occupied. The leprosy village, which had been founded in 1950 and was run by the Japanese doctor Isao Takahashi, accommodated 150 patients. Altogether, 5,998 African and 77 European patients were treated in Lambarene in 1965.[10] Schweitzer's medical work was, therefore, an unequivocal success— at least in terms of numbers. Between 1924 and 1966, 137,112 patients were treated in Lambarene, and 18,593 operations carried out. Since 1936 nearly 3,000 children had been born, and roughly 600 of the 861 people suffering from leprosy had been healed or could be transferred to other hospitals for further treatment.[11]

The Ninetieth Birthday

Albert Schweitzer celebrated his ninetieth birthday on 14 January 1965. Among the guests gathered in Lambarene was the President of Gabon, Léon M'ba. In Schweitzer's honour the main road in

Lambarene was christened *Boulevard Dr Albert Schweitzer*. To mark the occasion, he spoke to his employees:

> At this table, in this room, we are full of joy as we celebrate this birthday. However, what is most important for me, in my life, is my hospital. And now you are here. You, who work in the hospital, friends, and acquaintances, who are at the hospital and help continue its work. And as we are now gathered here together, I remember the beginning of this work. In my mind's eye I see those who were the first to work together with me under demanding and difficult circumstances. None of them is still alive. But I remember them, those who had the courage to join me in starting this endeavour. And then I think of those who are alive, who are here now, and of all those who have worked alongside me in earlier generations to make this hospital reality. For what I had in mind was an adventure, and I felt and feared it, and everything that I had felt and feared came to pass. But there was always progress, and I can no longer describe how we made our way to found and build this hospital. Together we found the right way to lead this hospital in the simplest way and to create a spirit that has borne it onwards.[12]

Schweitzer knew that he had very little time left. Numerous letters now went unanswered, and he had to be driven to visits in the leprosy village in the hospital jeep. The extent to which the media harried him for statements on his unrelenting fight against nuclear weapons was beginning to tell on his health. In the summer of 1964 Schweitzer built his own wooden coffin. He was uncertain whether the hospital would continue to exist after he died and, if it did, how. Schweitzer decided that Walter Munz, who had worked in Lambarene for several years, should be the medical director of the hospital following his death. Meanwhile, the question of who should take on its management remained unanswered for a long time—at least for its employees and the public. On 23 August 1965, Schweitzer announced in a letter to the International Schweitzer Association in Strasbourg that his daughter, Rhena Eckert-Schweitzer, was to take over direction of the hospital. From this moment on, Schweitzer's health began to deteriorate. He missed occasional meals, and he was seen in the hospital less often than usual. At breakfast on the morning of 28 August, the hospital staff saw how unwell he was. After the meal he excused himself and retired to his room, where he told his daughter that he was very tired. On 2 September, Schweitzer took his last tour of the hospital, accompanied by one of the nurses, Alida Silver, and Walter Munz. He remarked: 'And yet the hospital has its charm, don't you agree?'[13] Two days later he listened for the last time to the Andante from Beethoven's Fifth Symphony. His last words before losing consciousness were: 'How very beautiful.'[14]

On 4 September 1965, half an hour before midnight, *le grand docteur* died in his Lambarene at the age of 90. In his plain coffin were also placed a sack of rice, leaves of the wild vine that grew in front of his house in Gunsbach, the loden coat he had always worn on his journeys to Lambarene, and an old felt hat.[15] On the next day Schweitzer was buried alongside his wife in the cemetery in Lambarene. In the adjoining graves lie the bodies of the three women who devoted their lives to Lambarene: Emma Haussknecht, Mathilde Kottmann, and Alida Silver.

The cemetery in Lambarene provides further evidence of Schweitzer's religious tolerance. After both the Catholic and the Protestant Missions on the Ogowe River had refused to allow a group of Muslim merchants to bury their dead in their cemeteries, Schweitzer immediately gave the Muslims permission to do so in Lambarene. Today gravestones bearing the crescent moon remind visitors to Lambarene of his religious tolerance. He also did not build a chapel in Lambarene, as he preferred to hold services in the open.[16]

Even in the face of death Schweitzer wanted no special treatment: a plain wooden cross is all that marks his grave behind the hospital. Walter Munz officiated at the funeral service. He read Psalm 90, which Schweitzer had often recited himself at the grave when a patient died. The mourners then sang all the verses of Schweitzer's favourite song 'Abide, O Dearest Jesus'. Prayer, chorales, the ringing of bells—these were the rhythms of traditional piety, in Lambarene as elsewhere. To Schweitzer they expressed the feeling he had held his whole life that the Lutheran church was his spiritual home. Presumably it was precisely this form of lived piety that was the main reason—despite his critical stance towards religious dogma—he never turned his back on the Lutheran church.

After the song at the burial service, there were eulogies. The first to speak was the personal representative of the president of Gabon Léon M'ba. He was followed by the French ambassador to Gabon, and

Walter Munz concluded the ceremony with a prayer. A date palm that Schweitzer had grown from a seed was placed in his coffin. A date palm in Lambarene as a symbol of Schweitzer's life's work in Africa is a symbol that is both touching and saddening. Date palms do not naturally grow in Lambarene as they need the salt air of the West African coast, which does not penetrate into the tropical rainforest. Schweitzer was referring to this tree when he said to his niece Suzanne Oswald: 'I want to lie by it; it is a stranger to this country, as I am.'[17]

Schweitzer never really became an African. At most he was a 'big brother' to Africans, a brother who came from Europe and never really rid himself of his colonial pith helmet. At the same time, he was deeply admired and honoured for his life's work in Africa. Perhaps this date palm is then a fitting symbol of the life and work of Albert Schweitzer. Albert Schweitzer was a practical man. He was a deeply mystical, pious, and intellectually practical man, not an academic in an ivory tower. And he always remained a European, a European who engaged with Africa with all his heart and mind, but who remained an older brother in the land of his younger brother.

9

Conclusion

Myth and Reality

How does someone become a myth? Each age creates its own Albert Schweitzer, a person who comes to its shores unknown and without a name. But, if his life and work have an essential core, then perhaps it is authenticity, not only in his words, but also in his deeds. Albert Schweitzer was able to overcome the 'foul divide' between ethical theory and practice, between claim and reality, and in doing so he became a symbol of humanity. He became the myth of the selfless jungle doctor of Lambarene.

Following the devastating catastrophe that was the Second World War, many people were searching for new values and a feeling of wholeness. Schweitzer was the ideal person onto which these needs could be projected. In 1960, the German magazine *Der Spiegel* described him aptly as

> a place one longs to return to, as the author Robert Jungk put it, in which there is still a feeling for 'radiance, harmony, ideals, and warmth', but which cannot be reconciled with their existence in the hard, cold struggle for survival in the modern 'world of angst'. But Albert Schweitzer was able to keep the one without abandoning the other. Certainly, he could become the idol of an epoch only by escaping its problems and finding a place outside this world. He did not go into the desert as a hermit. Instead, he went into the jungle as redeemer and teacher. It was there and in this role that he was able credibly to restore the unity of morality and reality with the aid of another unity: the identity of life and teaching.[1]

Creating an identity of life and teaching is a very demanding goal for anyone to set themselves. It is not, however, the task of the biographer to find evidence for this identity; rather it is to show where his subject has failed to live up to this ideal. However, not everyone would agree. Norman Cousins, for example, after numerous meetings with Schweitzer where they discussed their shared commitment against nuclear weapons, wrote about the 'myth of Schweitzer':

> In the case of Schweitzer, later generations will not clutter their minds with petty reflections about his possible faults or inconsistencies. In his life and work will be found energy for moral imagination. This is all that will matter. [...] If Albert Schweitzer is a myth, the myth is more important than the reality. For mankind needs such an image in order to exist. [...] Long after the Hospital at Lambarene is forgotten, the symbol of Albert Schweitzer will be known and held high. It would simplify matters if Albert Schweitzer were totally without blemish [...] In the presence of renunciation and dedicated service such as few men are able to achieve, we can at least attempt responsible judgments and we can derive spiritual nourishment from the larger significance of his life as distinct from the fragmented reality.[2]

Cousins preferred to uphold the myth rather than portray the reality with all its shortcomings. Friedrich Wilhelm Katzenbach, a theologian from Strasbourg, attempted to explain Schweitzer's popularity by drawing comparisons with other intellectual giants of history:

> Albert Schweitzer is perhaps the most famous European of the twentieth century. American journalism has lavishly adorned him with the predicate 'the greatest man in the world'. Schweitzer has suffered from the consequences of his worldwide publicity and popularity. [...] Schweitzer's appearance is like a force of nature. Yet it must be acknowledged that a certain historical constellation was necessary so that others could grasp the timelessness of his humanity. It was no different with Frances of Assisi, Martin Luther, Blaise Pascal, or Søren Kierkegaard. [...] He never prided himself on his life and work. [...] Although Schweitzer's life may be described as modest, it is not as simple and uncomplicated as the uncritical portrayals written by countless of Schweitzer's enthusiastic admirers.[3]

But both Katzenbach and Cousins are simplifying things. Schweitzer was not modest; in fact, he was a master at staging himself. Helene Christaller's book *Albert Schweitzer: A Life for Others* gives a sense of how striking his presence could be. Recalling a meeting with him, she writes: 'As he entered the sickbay, a little stooped from the exhaustion of the long lecture trip, I felt something of what the ill must have felt as the Saviour stepped up to their beds.'[4]

In his autobiography *Out of my Life and Thought*, Schweitzer gives the impression that there was a direct and purposeful connection between his decision in 1896 to dedicate his life to the service of humanity after his thirtieth birthday and his decision to study medicine. A closer look, however, reveals that he underwent a long and at times painful path of self-discovery, which he shared with only one person, his 'faithful comrade' Helene Bresslau. The principle of Reverence for Life, which was supposedly revealed to Schweitzer during a boat trip on the Ogowe River in 1915, can already be found in lecture notes for the winter semester 1911–12 at the University of Strasbourg. But Schweitzer was not trying to bend the truth when he spoke of the great moments that affected the course of his life. However, as is often the case with autobiographies, he did smooth over the rough edges of his life, making the times when he changed his mind disappear. Another inconsistency was his change from being a vehement critic of colonialism when he left Europe with Helene for the first time to a somewhat overbearing 'older brother' figure towards Africans, to whom the independence movements sweeping Africa during the last years of his life meant little. And, for a man who held a reputation for being especially modest, he repeatedly sat for sketches, oil paintings, and busts.[5] While far from unusual, this form of self-promotion is disturbing, especially in Schweitzer. The magazine *Der Spiegel* voiced the suspicion that

Schweitzer preserves his own monument, and is perhaps the best at this task. Schweitzer's exterior habitus also strengthens this mistrust: his shabby frock coat and collar, and his Nietzschean moustache […] 'Is he really a shy, humble man or Garbo with a beard?' the *Sunday Express* asked. Certainly his sentimental manner of expressing himself is as real as his modesty concerning his material possessions and comforts; his style has remained unchanged since the turn of the century, and his frugality, which borders on miserliness, is accompanied by the will to live a simple life (and sit on hard surfaces). But it is equally certain that he has done nothing to curb the cult surrounding Schweitzer. He has let himself—with his full head of hair—be photographed from all angles and has given out autographs in the manner of a movie star. All this has its origin in human weakness: not in a small one such as vanity, but in the same 'high estimation of the self' that he once attributed to the historical Jesus in his psychiatric research. When they were in America, and his wife asked him to mind his health and not sign autographs for hours, his answer revealed his sense of himself as a saviour: 'I must not disappoint anyone who believes that I can help him—and if it is only by giving him an autograph. Perhaps in some dark hour he will receive encouragement from it.'[6]

That Schweitzer was more than a little vain and as a young man was concerned about his appearance can be seen in the many photographs from his youth and student days of him sporting a flat cap or a stand-up collar.[7] It is hardly far-fetched to conclude that his travelling third class in a threadbare jacket was part of a conscious attempt to promote a certain image of himself. Schweitzer must have been aware that he was a person of public interest—certainly after his 1949 visit to the United States—and he acted accordingly. When he heard that he had received the Nobel Peace Prize in 1952, he was reportedly surprised by the news. But the sources suggest otherwise: he was well aware that for some time he had been on a shortlist for the award. In any case, the tens of thousands of letters Schweitzer wrote show that he was neither modest nor politically naive. Indeed, though he lived in the middle of the jungle, he was a true citizen of the world.

The fascination Schweitzer holds is not only due to his apparent authenticity and integrity but also to his many-sided talents. His great strengths were his organizational skills combined with leadership qualities as well as the ability to think strategically and practically. Quite a few people have degrees in both theology and philosophy, but not many of them can raise the money for a hospital and then build it, all the while writing bestsellers and performing as a world-class organist. While it is this cultured breadth that fascinates Europeans, Americans tend to admire more Schweitzer's 'pioneering spirit' and the man who, it seemed, had abandoned a brilliant academic career in Europe to become a selfless doctor in Africa.

Schweitzer was doubtlessly a child of his time, a time when after the Second World War many people were searching for new values. But seeing him in this way does not wholly do him justice. For, if his principle of Reverence for Life is one thing above all else, it is timeless. This principle does not contain all the answers to life's questions, but instead demands from those who would practise it that they constantly make ethical decisions. And it may be for this reason that Reverence for Life is more relevant today than ever before. In a time of globalization, fragmented specialization, and individualization, in a time of global economic crises, unsustainable development, and environmental degradation, there is a need for people who can unite thought and action, who are able to think and live their convictions in a global context. Perhaps this is why Schweitzer is considered a 'great humanitarian' and is often named alongside such inspiring individuals as Mahatma Gandhi and Mother Theresa. A humanitarian is a person deeply interested in people, who is touched by them. It is a person who in turn, by his or her words and actions, touches others. Stirring people all over the world to take action—this is the most important achievement of his life's work at a small hospital in the middle of the jungle. He always thought of the hospital as an 'improvisation', as an attempt at a lived ethics.[8] Many Africans in Lambarene noted what might have been his greatest achievement. It may not have been building a hospital, but instead convincing a Galoan to carry a stretcher bearing a member of the enemy Fang tribe. The place Schweitzer chose for his life's work is aptly named. 'Lambarene' is derived from the Galoan *lembareni* and means 'we shall try'.[9] What Schweitzer tried to do was to live by the universal principle of Reverence for Life. And this was for him more important even than his hospital. His Reverence for Life inspires people to change their way of thinking and reflect on their actions in ethical terms. He gave this inspiration a face and this enthusiasm a place in Lambarene—and this is what makes Albert Schweitzer one of the great individuals of the twentieth century.

Notes

Introduction

1. L. von Ranke, *Sämtliche Werke*, xxxiii, 3rd edn (Leipzig, 1885), p. vii.
2. 'Albert Schweitzer: Mythos des 20. Jahrhunderts', *Der Spiegel*, 21 December 1960.
3. W. Quenzer, 'Zu Schweitzers autobiographischen Schriften', in H. W. Bähr (ed.), *Albert Schweitzer: Sein Denken und sein Weg* (Tübingen, 1962), 238.
4. S. Zweig, J. Feschotte, and R. Grabs, *Albert Schweitzer: Genie der Menschlichkeit* (Hamburg, 1955).
5. 'Reverence for Life', *Time Magazine*, 11 July 1949.
6. E. Gräßer, *Albert Schweitzer als Theologe* (Tübingen, 1979); M. Hauskeller (ed.), *Ethik des Lebens: Albert Schweitzer als Philosoph* (Zug, 2006); L. Simmank, *Der Arzt: Wie Albert Schweitzer Not linderte* (Berlin, 2008).
7. A. Schweitzer, 'Nochmals Falkenjägerei', *Atlantis* (March 1932); A. Schweitzer, *Afrikanische Geschichten* (Leipzig, 1938); A. Schweitzer and A. Wildikann, *Ein Pelikan erzählt aus seinem Leben* (Hamburg, 1950). Writing popular stories and essays was one of Schweitzer's most efficient means of collecting donations. He wrote about his pelicans in Lambarene to help Dr Anna Wildikann, a Jewish doctor from the Baltic region who had worked with him in Lambarene, to buy a car for her future work in Israel.
8. According to information from the Albert Schweitzer Central Archive Gunsbach. The letters, largely unpublished, are located mainly in the Albert Schweitzer Central Archive Gunsbach. These letters are sorted not by person, but by topic. Accordingly, Folder T contains the theological correspondence, Folder PH the philosophical, Folder AT the letters concerning the anti-nuclear movement, and Folder GO (Gouvernement) Schweitzer's letters to politicians. Letters addressed to Schweitzer are collected in the Folders Régnants 1926–1959 and Régnants 1960–1965.
9. 'Albert Schweitzer: Mythos des 20. Jahrhunderts', 61.

1. A Sense of Devotion

1. G. Jahn, 'Presentation Speech for the Nobel Peace Prize 1952', 29 June 2012 <www.nobelprize.org> (accessed 17 December 2008).
2. 'Albert Schweitzer: Mythos des 20. Jahrhunderts', *Der Spiegel*, 21 December 1960, 58.
3. H. Steffahn, *Albert Schweitzer*, 12th edn (Hamburg, 1996), 25.

4. F. W. Kantzenbach, *Albert Schweitzer: Wirklichkeit und Legende* (Göttingen, 1969), 22.
5. J. Bentley, *Albert Schweitzer: Eine Biographie* (Düsseldorf, 2001), 166.
6. A. Schweitzer, *Out of my Life and Thought*, trans. C. T. Campion (London, 1948), 78.
7. 'Albert Schweitzer: Mythos des 20. Jahrhunderts', 52.
8. A. Schweitzer, *Memoirs of Childhood and Youth*, trans. C. T. Campion. (New York, 1949), 9.
9. Schweitzer, *Childhood and Youth*, 11.
10. Schweitzer, *Childhood and Youth*, 28–9.
11. Schweitzer, *Childhood and Youth*, 40.
12. Schweitzer, *Childhood and Youth*, 40.
13. Schweitzer, *Childhood and Youth*, 41.
14. Schweitzer, *Life and Thought*, 15. Here Schweitzer refers to his first publication, in the year 1898: *Eugène Munch 1857–1898* (Mülhausen, 1898). The twenty-eight pages were published anonymously.
15. Schweitzer, *Childhood and Youth*, 24.
16. Schweitzer, *Childhood and Youth*, 14.
17. Schweitzer, *Childhood and Youth*, 43.
18. Schweitzer, *Childhood and Youth*, 38.
19. Schweitzer, *Childhood and Youth*, 23–4.
20. Kantzenbach, *Albert Schweitzer*, 102.
21. Schweitzer, *Life and Thought*, 12.
22. Schweitzer, *Childhood and Youth*, 11.
23. J. Brabazon, *Albert Schweitzer: A Biography*, 2nd edn (Syracuse, 2000), 24–5.
24. Schweitzer, *Childhood and Youth*, 8–9.
25. Schweitzer, *Childhood and Youth*, 11.
26. Schweitzer, *Childhood and Youth*, 23.
27. Schweitzer, *Childhood and Youth*, 32.
28. Schweitzer, *Life and Thought*, 15.
29. Schweitzer, *Childhood and Youth*, 38.
30. Schweitzer, *Childhood and Youth*, 39.
31. Schweitzer, *Childhood and Youth*, 57.
32. Schweitzer, *Childhood and Youth*, 56.
33. Schweitzer, *Childhood and Youth*, 46.
34. Brabazon, *Albert Schweitzer*, 22.
35. Brabazon, *Albert Schweitzer*, 22.
36. Schweitzer, *Life and Thought*, 102–3.
37. Brabazon, *Albert Schweitzer*, 37.
38. W. Munz, *Albert Schweitzer im Gedächtnis der Afrikaner und in meiner Erinnerung*. Albert-Schweitzer-Studien 3 (Bern, 1991), 270.
39. Personal interview with Gerald Götting, 29 October 2008, in Berlin-Köpenick.
40. Personal interview with Sonja Poteau, Director of the Albert Schweitzer Central Archive Gunsbach, 29 July 2008.

41. Schweitzer, *Life and Thought*, 121.
42. Schweitzer, *Life and Thought*, 120–1.
43. Schweitzer, *Life and Thought*, 16.
44. Schweitzer, *Life and Thought*, 17.
45. Schweitzer, *Life and Thought*, 20.
46. Schweitzer, *Life and Thought*, 21.
47. Schweitzer, *Life and Thought*, 24–5.
48. Kantzenbach, *Albert Schweitzer*, 26.
49. Cf. Schweitzer, *Life and Thought*, 31.
50. Schweitzer, *Life and Thought*, 31.
51. Steffahn, *Albert Schweitzer*, 62. In his positive evaluation of Schweitzer's doctoral thesis in philosophy, Harald Steffahn largely relies on H. Groos, *Albert Schweitzer: Größe und Grenzen* (Munich, 1974), 606–36.
52. *GW* i. 40–1; Steffahn, *Albert Schweitzer*, 62. According to H. J. Meyer, Schweitzer's conclusion was that Kant never completed the religious and philosophical scheme he proposed in *Critique of Pure Reason*. Schweitzer established that the philosophy of religion and its three postulates—God, freedom, and immortality—are not those he proposed in his *Critique of Pure Reason*. Instead, it consists of a compromise between the religious and philosophical scheme of transcendental dialectics and the original scheme of *The Critique of Practical Reason*. H. J. Meyer, 'Albert Schweitzers Doktorarbeit über Kant', in H. W. Bähr, *Albert Schweitzer: Sein Denken und sein Weg* (Tübingen, 1962), 69.
53. Meyer, 'Albert Schweitzers Doktorarbeit über Kant', 69–70.
54. Albert Schweitzer to Helene Bresslau, Strasbourg, 30 April 1904, in *AS–HB* 67.
55. Schweitzer, *Life and Thought*, 31.
56. Schweitzer, *Life and Thought*, 33.
57. Albert Schweitzer to Rudolf Grabs, Lambarene, 12 April 1951, in *TPB* 244.
58. Albert Schweitzer to Fritz Buri, Lambarene, 22 December 1950, in A. U. Sommer (ed.), *Albert Schweitzer–Fritz Buri: Existenzphilosophie und Christentum: Briefe 1935–1964* (Munich, 2000), 132–3.
59. A. Schweitzer, *The Philosophy of Civilisation*. i. *The Decay and Restoration of Civilisation*, trans. C. T. Campion (London, 1923), 10–11.
60. E. Gräßer, *Albert Schweitzer als Theologe* (Tübingen, 1979), 13. Theobald Ziegler (1846–1918) was considered one of the 'leading minds' of historicism und positivism. He was a proponent of a coupling of a theological and philosophical tradition in the spirit of the Tübinger Stift, where he was a lecturer. Theologically, he was influenced above all by David Friedrich Strauß. The Neo-Kantian Wilhelm Windelband (1848–1915) was a student of Hermann Lotzes, founder of the Southwest German School and paved the way for the 'philosophy of values', which was developed by his student Heinrich Rickert.
61. Schweitzer, *Life and Thought*, 31–6.

228   *Notes to pages 26–36*

62. Adolf von Harnack to the Prussian Academy of Sciences, Berlin, 7 March 1929, in *TPB* 294; emphasis in original.
63. Albert Schweitzer to Planck at the Prussian Academy of Sciences, Königsfeld, 11 July 1929, in Folder T (Correspondence with Adolf von Harnack), GA.
64. Albert Schweitzer to the Harnack family, Gunsbach, 19 July 1930, in H. W. Bähr (ed.), *Albert Schweitzer: Letters 1905–1965*, trans. Joachim Neugroschel (New York, 1992), 111.
65. Schweitzer, *Life and Thought*, 34.
66. Schweitzer, *Life and Thought*, 172–4.
67. Albert Schweitzer to Hans Walter Bähr, Lambarene, 2 January 1962, in *TPB* 38–9.
68. Schweitzer, *Life and Thought*, 176.
69. Schweitzer, *Life and Thought*, 176.
70. Brabazon, *Albert Schweitzer*, 78.
71. Personal interview with Rhena Schweitzer Miller, 7 May 2005, in Pacific Palisades, Los Angeles.
72. M. A. Rosanoff, 'Edison in his Laboratory', *Harper's Monthly*, September 1932.
73. J. Gollomb, *Albert Schweitzer: Genius in der Wildnis* (Stuttgart, 1957).
74. Brabazon, *Albert Schweitzer*, 78.
75. Schweitzer, *Life and Thought*, 42.
76. Schweitzer, *Life and Thought*, 39.
77. Personal interview with Sonja Poteau, Director of the Albert Schweitzer Central Archive Gunsbach, 29 July 2008.
78. Schweitzer, *Life and Thought*, 39.
79. Schweitzer, *Life and Thought*, 38.
80. 'Albert Schweitzer: Mythos des 20. Jahrhunderts', 54.
81. G. Sauter, *Einführung in die Eschatologie* (Darmstadt, 1995), 31.
82. J. Weiß, *Die Predigt Jesu vom Reiche Gottes* (Göttingen, 1892); Sauter, *Einführung in die Eschatologie*, 32.
83. Albert Schweitzer to Hugo Gerdes, Lambarene, 5 May 1953, in Folder T, GA.
84. Sauter, *Einführung in die Eschatologie*, 33.
85. Sauter, *Einführung in die Eschatologie*, 49–50.
86. A. Schweitzer, *The Quest of the Historical Jesus: A Critical Study of its Progress from Reimarus to Wrede*, trans. William Montgomery (London, 1910), 399.
87. *GW* iii. 886.
88. M. Lönnebo, *Das ethisch-religiöse Ideal Albert Schweitzers* (Stockholm, 1964), 331.
89. Groos, *Albert Schweitzer*, 464.
90. 'Albert Schweitzer: Mythos des 20. Jahrhunderts', 50–1.
91. Albert Schweitzer to Helene Bresslau, Strasbourg, 28 October 1906, in *AS–HB* 114.
92. Albert Schweitzer to Rudolf Grabs, Königsfeld, 19 March 1949, in *TPB* 239.
93. *Christian Register*, 126 (1947), 324.

94. G. Altner, 'Albert Schweitzer', in *Gestalten der Kirchengeschichte: Die neueste Zeit III*, ed. M. Greschat (Stuttgart, 1985), 271.

95. A. Schweitzer, *Das Abendmahl im Zusammenhang mit dem Leben Jesu und der Geschichte des Urchristentums* (Tübingen, 1901): first book [doctoral thesis 1900]: *Das Abendmahlsproblem auf Grund der wissenschaftlichen Forschungen des 19. Jahrhunderts und der historischen Berichte*; second book [habilitation thesis 1902]: *Das Messianitäts- und Leidensgeheimnis: Eine Skizze des Lebens Jesu.*

96. Groos, *Albert Schweitzer*, 81.

97. Schweitzer, *Life and Thought*, 48.

98. Albert Schweitzer to Rudolf Grabs, Königsfeld, 19 March 1949, in *TPB* 239.

99. H. Weinel, 'Neutestamentliche Rezensionen des Jahres 1902 von H. Weinel', *Theologische Rundschau*, 5 (1902), 244.

100. W. Wrede, *Das Messiasgeheimnis in den Evangelien: Zugleich ein Beitrag zum Verständnis des Markus-Evangeliums* (Göttingen, 1901).

101. H. J. Holtzmann, *Die synoptischen Evangelien: Ihr Ursprung und geschichtlicher Charakter* (Leipzig, 1863).

102. H. J. Holtzmann, 'Die Marcus-Kontroverse in ihrer heutigen Gestalt', *Archiv für Religionswissenschaft*, 10 (1907), 191.

103. Schweitzer, *Life and Thought*, 55.

104. Schweitzer, *Life and Thought*, 55–6.

105. Albert Schweitzer to Helene Bresslau, Strasbourg, 26 November 1903, in *AS–HB* 51.

106. Schweitzer, *Life and Thought*, 55.

107. A. Schweitzer, *Von Reimarus zu Wrede: Eine Geschichte der Leben Jesu-Forschung* (Tübingen, 1906).

108. For an exegetic and systematic state of the discussion around 1900, cf. J. H. Claußen, *Die Jesus-Deutung von Ernst Troeltsch im Kontext der liberalen Theologie* (Tübingen, 1997), 78 ff.

109. A. Schweitzer, *Kultur und Ethik* (Munich, 1990), 69–70.

110. Groos, *Albert Schweitzer*, 439.

111. A. Schweitzer, *Die Weltanschauung der Ehrfurcht vor dem Leben: Kulturphilosophie*, iii. *Dritter und vierter Teil*, ed. Claus Günzler and Johann Zürcher (Munich, 2000), 380.

112. *GW* iv. 25; A. Schweitzer, *The Mysticism of Paul the Apostle*, trans. William Montgomery (London, 1931), 1.

113. *GW* iv. 28; Schweitzer, *The Mysticism of Paul the Apostle*, 3.

114. *GW* iv. 20–1.

115. *GW* iv. 509–10; Schweitzer, *The Mysticism of Paul the Apostle*, 395–6.

116. Rudolf Bultmann to Albert Schweitzer, Marburg, 28 August 1930, in *TPB* 181–2.

117. Schweitzer, *Das Abendmahl.*

118. Weinel, 'Neutestamentliche Rezensionen des Jahres 1902', 245.

119. Weinel, 'Neutestamentliche Rezensionen des Jahres 1902', 244–5.

120. Albert Schweitzer to Helene Bresslau, Strasbourg, 20 May 1905, in *AS–HB* 93.

2. Saving the Whole

1. K. Eidam, *Das wahre Leben des Johann Sebastian Bach* (Munich, 1999), 13.
2. Adolf von Harnack to the Prussian Academy of Sciences, Berlin, 7 March 1929, in *TPB* 293.
3. A. Schweitzer, *Out of my Life and Thought*, trans. C. T. Campion (London, 1948), 82.
4. Schweitzer, *Life and Thought*, 82.
5. *HSB* 270; personal interview with Sonja Poteau, Director of the Albert Schweitzer Central Archive Gunsbach, 29 July 2008.
6. A. Schweitzer, *J. S. Bach*, trans. Ernest Newman, 2 vols (New York, 1967), i. 3–4.
7. Eidam, *Johann Sebastian Bach*, 1.
8. H. Keller, 'Das Bach-Buch Albert Schweitzers', in H. W. Bähr (ed.), *Albert Schweitzer: Sein Denken und sein Weg* (Tübingen, 1962), 294–8.
9. A. Schweitzer, *Jean-Sébastien Bach, le musicien-poète* (Leipzig, 1905).
10. A. Schweitzer, *Selbstdarstellung* (Leipzig, 1929), 1–2.
11. Schweitzer, *Life and Thought*, 87.
12. J. Müller-Blattau, 'Albert Schweitzers Weg zur Bach-Orgel und zu einer neuen Bach-Auffassung', in Bähr (ed.), *Albert Schweitzer*, 245–6.
13. Schweitzer, *Life and Thought*, 155–6; *J. S. Bach* (1967), 273–4.
14. Schweitzer, *Life and Thought*, 97.
15. Schweitzer, *Life and Thought*, 88.
16. A. Schweitzer, *Music in the Life of Albert Schweitzer*, ed. and trans. C. R. Joy (London, 1953), 188.
17. A. Schweitzer, 'Brief aus Lambarene', in W. Gurlitt (ed.), *Bericht über die Freiburger Tagung für Deutsche Orgelkunst vom 27. Juli bis 30. Juli 1926* (Augsburg, 1926), 10.
18. Schweitzer, *Music in the Life of Albert Schweitzer*, 165.
19. Schweitzer, *Music in the Life of Albert Schweitzer*, 189.
20. Schweitzer, *Life and Thought*, 93.
21. Schweitzer, *Life and Thought*, 93–4.
22. Schweitzer, *Life and Thought*, 96–7.
23. Schweitzer, *Life and Thought*, 97.
24. C. M. Widor and A. Schweitzer, 'Über die Wiedergabe der Präludien und Fugen für Orgel von J. S. Bach', *Die Orgel*, 10 (1910), 217–20, 245–9.
25. C. M. Widor, preface to A. Schweitzer, *J. S. Bach* (1967), i, p. vi.
26. Müller-Blattau, 'Albert Schweitzers Weg zur Bach-Orgel und zu einer neuen Bach-Auffassung', 256.
27. Widor, preface to Schweitzer, *J. S. Bach* (1967), i, p. vii; J. Brabazon, *Albert Schweitzer: A Biography*, 2nd edn (Syracuse, 2000), 164.
28. Schweitzer, *Life and Thought*, 76.
29. Schweitzer, *Life and Thought*, 76–7.
30. Schweitzer, *Life and Thought*, 81–2.
31. Schweitzer, *Life and Thought*, 77.

32. German foreword to A. Schweitzer, *J. S. Bach*, German edn (Leipzig, 1908), p. iv.
33. L. Schrade, 'Die Ästhetik Albert Schweitzers: Eine Interpretation J. S. Bachs', in Bähr (ed.), *Albert Schweitzer*, 264.
34. Schweitzer, *Life and Thought*, 82.
35. Keller, 'Das Bach-Buch Albert Schweitzers', 297.
36. Schrade, 'Die Ästhetik Albert Schweitzers: Eine Interpretation J. S. Bachs', 264.
37. *AS–HB* 47.
38. *AS–HB* 52.
39. *AS–HB* 73.
40. *AS–HB* 87.
41. E. R. Jacobi, *Albert Schweitzer und die Musik* (Wiesbaden: 1975), 21.
42. Schweitzer, *Life and Thought*, 81.
43. Schweitzer, *Life and Thought*, 80.
44. Schweitzer, *Life and Thought*, 78.
45. Schweitzer, *Life and Thought*, 78–9.
46. Schweitzer, *Life and Thought*, 81.
47. Schweitzer, *Life and Thought*, 84–5.
48. A. Schweitzer, 'My Recollections of Cosima Wagner', in *Music in the Life of Albert Schweitzer*, 54.
49. Schweitzer, *Life and Thought*, 23.
50. Schweitzer, *Life and Thought*, 213.
51. Quoted in E. R. Jacobi, *Albert Schweitzer und Richard Wagner: Eine Dokumentation* (Tribschen, 1977), 17.
52. Schweitzer, *J. S. Bach* (1967), ii. 25.
53. Schweitzer, *J. S. Bach* (1967), ii. 25.
54. A. Schweitzer, *Die Musik*, 5/1 (1905–6), 75–6, quoted in Jacobi, *Albert Schweitzer und die Musik*, 30–2.
55. Schweitzer, *Life and Thought*, 154–5.
56. G. Marshall and D. Poling, *Schweitzer: A Biography* (London, 1971), 32; Jacobi, *Albert Schweitzer und die Musik*, 26–7.
57. G. Bret, 'Bach, Schweitzer und die Pariser Bach-Gesellschaft', in Bähr (ed.), *Albert Schweitzer*, 289; Jacobi, *Albert Schweitzer und die Musik*, 11.
58. H. Schützeichel, *Die Konzerttätigkeit Albert Schweitzers* (Bern and Stuttgart, 1991); Schweitzer, *Life and Thought*, 120.
59. Schweitzer, *Life and Thought*, 131.
60. Schweitzer, *Life and Thought*, 102–3.
61. W. G. Kümmel and C.-H. Ratschow, *Albert Schweitzer als Theologe: Zwei akademische Reden* (Marburg, 1966), 33.
62. Albert Schweitzer to Gustav von Lüpke, Strasbourg, 10 June 1908, quoted in A. Schweitzer, *Das Albert Schweitzer Lesebuch*, ed. H. Steffahn, 4th edn (Munich, 2009), 119.
63. H. Steffahn, *Albert Schweitzer*, 12th edn (Hamburg, 1996), 65.
64. *AS–HB* 15.

65. B. M. Nossik, *Albert Schweitzer: Ein Leben für die Menschlichkeit* (Leipzig, 1978), 102.
66. E. Gräßer, *Albert Schweitzer als Theologe* (Tübingen, 1979), 19.
67. F. Meinecke. *Straßburg, Freiburg, Berlin. Erinnerungen 1901–1919* (Stuttgart, 1949), 25–6.
68. Schweitzer, *Life and Thought*, 120.
69. Schweitzer, *Life and Thought*, 76.
70. Schweitzer, *Life and Thought*, 114.
71. Schweitzer, *Life and Thought*, 102.
72. Schweitzer, *Life and Thought*, 106–7.
73. N. O. Oermann, *Mission, Church and State Relations in South West Africa under German Rule (1884–1915)* (Stuttgart, 1999); T. Altena, *'Ein Häuflein Christen mitten in der Heidenwelt des dunklen Erdteils': Zum Selbst- und Fremdverständnis protestantischer Missionare im kolonialen Afrika 1884–1918* (Munster, 2003); U. van der Heyden and H. Stoecker (eds), *Mission und Macht im Wandel politischer Orientierungen: Europäische Missionsgesellschaften in politischen Spannungsfeldern in Afrika und Asien zwischen 1800 und 1945* (Stuttgart, 2005).
74. Albert Schweitzer to Helene Bresslau, Strasbourg, 20 May 1905, in *AS–HB* 93.
75. Albert Schweitzer to Helene Bresslau, Strasbourg, 3 March 1903, in *AS–HB* 17.
76. Albert Schweitzer to Helene Bresslau, Strasbourg, 27 February 1906, in *AS–HB* 99.
77. Albert Schweitzer to Helene Bresslau, Strasbourg, 26 November 1903, in *AS–HB* 32–3.
78. Quoted in Steffahn, *Albert Schweitzer*, 70.
79. Schweitzer, *Life and Thought*, 102.
80. Interview with Sonja Poteau, Director of the Albert Schweitzer Central Archive Gunsbach, 29 July 2008.
81. Albert Schweitzer to Alfred Boegner, Strasbourg, 9 July 1905, in H. W. Bähr (ed.), *Albert Schweitzer: Letters 1905–1965*, trans. Joachim Neugroschel (New York, 1992), 4; Albert Schweitzer to the Director of the Paris Mission Society, Strasbourg, 9 July 1905. The handwritten original is printed in S. Poteau and G. Leser, *Albert Schweitzer: Homme de Gunsbach et citoyen du monde* (Mulhouse, 1994), 30–1.
82. Albert Schweitzer to Alfred Boegner, Strasbourg, 9 July 1905, in Bähr (ed.), *Albert Schweitzer: Letters 1905–1965*, 3.
83. Albert Schweitzer to Alfred Boegner, Strasbourg, 9 July 1905, in Bähr (ed.), *Albert Schweitzer: Letters 1905–1965*, 4.
84. Albert Schweitzer to Alfred Boegner, Strasbourg, 9 July 1905, in Bähr (ed.), *Albert Schweitzer: Letters 1905–1965*, 5.
85. Albert Schweitzer to Alfred Boegner, Strasbourg, 9 July 1905, in Poteau and Leser, *Albert Schweitzer*, 31.
86. Albert Schweitzer to Alfred Boegner, Strasbourg, 9 July 1905, in Poteau and Leser, *Albert Schweitzer*, 31.

87. Albert Schweitzer to Helene Bresslau, Strasbourg, 9 May 1905, in *AS–HB* 82–3.

88. Albert Schweitzer to Helene Bresslau, Paris, 12 October 1905, in *AS–HB* 91–2.

89. Steffahn, *Albert Schweitzer*, 71.

90. Schweitzer, *Life and Thought*, 119.

91. Schweitzer, *Life and Thought*, 128.

92. Schweitzer, *Life and Thought*, 126–7f.

93. Jacobi, *Albert Schweitzer und die Musik*, 20.

94. Albert Schweitzer to Helene Bresslau, Strasbourg, 18 April 1908, in *AS–HB* 202.

95. Albert Schweitzer to Helene Bresslau, Santa Margherita, 15 April 1908, in *AS–HB* 140.

96. Schweitzer, *Life and Thought*, 128.

97. W. Augustiny, *Albert Schweitzer und Du*, 4th edn (Witten, 1959), 83.

98. Schweitzer, *Life and Thought*, 131.

99. Brabazon, *Albert Schweitzer*, 201.

100. Albert Schweitzer to Theodor Heuss, Gunsbach, 23 September 1949, in Folder GO, GA.

101. Quoted in I. Kleberger, *Albert Schweitzer: Das Symbol und der Mensch* (Berlin, 1989), 63.

102. A. Schweitzer, *Straßburger Vorlesungen*, ed. Erich Gräßer and Johann Zürcher (Munich, 1998), 723.

103. A. Schweitzer, *The Psychiatric Study of Jesus*, trans. Charles R. Joy (Boston: 1948). The awarding of the doctoral degree in medicine is now often dated to February 1913, rather than December 1912. According to the CV that had to be handed into the Prussian Academy of Sciences, Schweitzer received his doctorate in December 1912. Compare Albert Schweitzer's handwritten CV in the estate of Adolf von Harnack, sent to Schweitzer by Axel von Harnack, Tübingen, 9 January 1960, in Folder T, GA.

104. Kleberger, *Albert Schweitzer*, 67.

105. G. de Loosten, *Jesus Christus vom Standpunkte des Psychiaters* (Bamberg, 1905); W. Hirsch, *Religion und Civilisation vom Standpunkte des Psychiaters* (Munich, 1910); E. Rasmussen, *Jesus: Eine vergleichende psychopathologische Studie* (Leipzig, 1905).

106. Schweitzer, *The Psychiatric Study of Jesus*, 27.

107. Schweitzer, *The Psychiatric Study of Jesus*, 27.

108. Brabazon, *Albert Schweitzer*, 219.

109. Brabazon, *Albert Schweitzer*, 219.

110. *AS–HB*; *HSB*.

111. Personal interview with Rhena Schweitzer Miller, 7 May 2005, in Pacific Palisades, Los Angeles.

112. *AS–HB* 20.

113. Compare with the CV that Helene Bresslau submitted for admission to the nursing examination at Frankfurt in 1910, in *AS–HB* 16.

114. *HSB* 29, 274.
115. *HSB* 43.
116. *HSB* 47.
117. Albert Schweitzer to Helene Bresslau, Santa Margherita, 15 April 1908, in *AS–HB* 1.
118. Quoted in *HSB* 49.
119. Albert Schweitzer to Helene Bresslau, Gunsbach, August 1906 [n.d.], in *AS–HB* 110–11.
120. *HSB* 52–3.
121. Albert Schweitzer to Helene Bresslau, Strasbourg, 3 November 1902, in *AS–HB* 11.
122. *HSB* 53.
123. *AS–HB* 66–7.
124. *HSB* 61.
125. M. Fleischhack, *Helene Schweitzer: Stationen ihres Lebens* (Berlin, 1969).
126. Albert Schweitzer to Helene Bresslau, Strasbourg, 4 July 1903, in *AS–HB* 21.
127. *HSB* 67.
128. *HSB* 69.
129. Albert Schweitzer to Helene Bresslau, Strasbourg, 31 October 1903, in *AS–HB* 29.
130. *HSB* 73.
131. Helene Bresslau to Albert Schweitzer, Berlin, 17 December 1903, in *AS–HB* 34.
132. Albert Schweitzer to Helene Bresslau, Strasbourg, 19 January 1904, in *AS–HB* 58.
133. *HSB* 80.
134. *HSB* 91.
135. *HSB* 108.
136. Fleischhack, *Helene Schweitzer*, 16.
137. *HSB* 117.
138. *HSB* 123.
139. S. Oswald, *Mein Onkel Bery: Erinnerungen an Albert Schweitzer*, 2nd edn (Zurich, 1972), 127.
140. *HSB* 125.
141. *HSB* 131.
142. Albert Schweitzer to Helene Bresslau, Strasbourg, 1 January 1912, in *AS–HB* 223.
143. Schweitzer, *Life and Thought*, 134–5.
144. Nossik, *Albert Schweitzer*, 92.
145. 'Albert Schweitzer: Mythos des 20. Jahrhunderts', *Der Spiegel*, 21 December 1960, 60.
146. Personal interview with Claus Jacobi, 16 October 2008, in Hamburg.
147. Quoted in F. W. Kantzenbach, *Albert Schweitzer: Wirklichkeit und Legende* (Göttingen, 1969), 11.

3. The Spiritual Adventurer

1. A. Schweitzer, *Das Albert Schweitzer Lesebuch*, ed. H. Steffahn, 4th edn (Munich, 2009), 125.

2. Minutes of the Société des Missions Evangéliques de Paris from 4 December 1911, quoted in *HSB* 139.

3. A. Schweitzer, *Out of my Life and Thought*, trans. C. T. Campion (New York, 1948), 136–7.

4. Schweitzer, *Das Albert Schweitzer Lesebuch*, 126.

5. S. Oswald, *Mein Onkel Bery: Erinnerungen an Albert Schweitzer*, 2nd edn (Zurich, 1972), 55.

6. G. Woytt, 'Albert Schweitzer scheidet aus dem Lehrkörper der Strassburger Universität aus', in R. Brüllmann (ed.), *Albert-Schweitzer-Studien 2* (Bern, 1991), 144–5.

7. Albert Schweitzer to Adolf von Harnack, Gunsbach, 5 May 1921, in *TPB* 276.

8. M. Fleischhack, *Helene Schweitzer: Stationen ihres Lebens* (Berlin, 1969), 31.

9. A. Schweitzer, *On the Edge of the Primeval Forest*, trans. C. T. Campion (London, 1924), 6.

10. Schweitzer, *Primeval Forest*, 16.

11. Quoted in Fleischhack, *Helene Schweitzer*, 34.

12. Schweitzer, *Primeval Forest*, 23.

13. A. Schweitzer, *Zwischen Wasser und Urwald: Erlebnisse und Beobachtungen eines Arztes im Urwalde Äquatorialafrikas* (Bern, 1921).

14. Schweitzer, *Primeval Forest*, 23.

15. Schweitzer, *Primeval Forest*, 25.

16. Schweitzer, *Primeval Forest*, 25.

17. A. Schweitzer, *Afrikanische Geschichten* (Leipzig, 1938), 11.

18. *HSB* 145.

19. Schweitzer, *Primeval Forest*, 32.

20. Schweitzer, *Primeval Forest*, 94–110.

21. *HSB* 160.

22. Helene Schweitzer to her parents, Lambarene, 29 April 1915, in *HSB* 171.

23. A. Schweitzer, *The Story of my Pelican*, trans. Martha Wardenburg (New York, 1965).

24. Schweitzer, *Primeval Forest*, 15–16.

25. C. R. Joy and M. Arnold, *The Africa of Albert Schweitzer* (London, 1949), 30.

26. *GW* i. 518.

27. J. Brabazon, *Albert Schweitzer: A Biography*, 2nd edn (Syracuse, 2000), 246.

28. Brabazon, *Albert Schweitzer*, 247.

29. *GW* i. 518.

30. *GW* i. 518–19.

31. Schweitzer, *Primeval Forest*, 35.

32. Schweitzer, *Primeval Forest*, 34.

33. B. M. Nossik, *Albert Schweitzer: Ein Leben für die Menschlichkeit* (Leipzig, 1978), 319.
34. Quoted in *HSB* 158.
35. *HSB* 163.
36. J. Bentley, *Albert Schweitzer: Eine Biographie* (Düsseldorf, 2001), 163.
37. Albert Schweitzer to Jean Bianquis, 30 October 1914, quoted in *HSB* 164.
38. Schweitzer, *Primeval Forest*, 145–6.
39. Bentley, *Albert Schweitzer*, 164.
40. Albert Schweitzer to Louis Schweitzer, [Lambarene], 15 August 1916, quoted in Oswald, *Mein Onkel Bery*, 89.
41. Schweitzer, *Life and Thought*, 193, and *GW* v. 183.
42. Handwritten note from Albert Schweitzer in Martin Niemöller's letter, Darmstadt, 21 May 1958: 'Later I found out that Niemöller commanded this submarine [U 151].' In his letter from 11 January 1961 Niemöller informs Schweitzer that the Protestant Church of Hessen-Nassau wanted to donate 10,000 German marks for his work in Lambarene in honour of Schweitzer's 85th birthday, in Folder T, GA.

4. It Is Good to Preserve Life

1. A. Schweitzer, *Out of my Life and Thought*, trans. C. T. Campion (New York, 1948), 184–6.
2. Schweitzer, *Life and Thought*, 190.
3. A. Schweitzer, *Straßburger Vorlesungen*, ed. Erich Gräßer and Johann Zürcher (Munich, 1998), 693; emphasis in original.
4. In *Wir Epigonen: Kultur und Kulturstaat*, ed. Ulrich Körtner and Johann Zürcher (Munich, 2005), Schweitzer frequently quotes the work of his philosophy teacher W. Windelband, *Geschichte der Philosophie*, 6th edn (Tübingen, 1916), and also F. Jodl, *Geschichte der Ethik als philosophischer Wissenschaft*, ii, 2nd edn (Stuttgart, 1912).
5. *HSB* 176.
6. A. Schweitzer, *Kulturphilosophie*. i. *Verfall und Wiederaufbau der Kultur*; ii. *Kultur und Ethik* (Munich, 2007). English edition: A. Schweitzer, *The Philosophy of Civilisation*. i. *The Decay and the Restoration of Civilisation*; ii. *Civilisation and Ethics*, trans. C. T. Campion (London, 1923). Reprinted as *The Philosophy of Civilization* (Amherst, NY, 1987).
7. Schweitzer, *Wir Epigonen*, 22–3.
8. H. Groos, *Albert Schweitzer: Größe und Grenzen* (Munich, 1974), 65.
9. A. Schweitzer, *Predigten 1898–1948*, ed. Richard Brüllmann and Erich Gräßer (Munich, 2001), 1269; A. Schweitzer, *Was sollen wir tun? 12 Predigten über ethische Probleme* (Heidelberg, 1974), 77–8, emphasis in original.
10. Schweitzer, *Was sollen wir tun?*, 113, emphasis in original.
11. Claus Günzler, Epilogue, in Schweitzer, *Kulturphilosophie*, 348.

12. A. Schweitzer, *Die Weltanschauung der Ehrfurcht vor dem Leben. Kulturphiloso-phie*, iii. *Erster und zweiter Teil*, ed. C. Günzler and J. Zürcher (Munich, 1999); *Dritter und vierter Teil*, ed. C. Günzler and J. Zürcher (Munich, 2000).
13. C. Günzler, *Albert Schweitzer: Einführung in sein Denken* (Munich, 1996), 28.
14. Schweitzer, *Die Weltanschauung der Ehrfurcht vor dem Leben. Kulturphilosophie*, iii. *Zweiter Teil*, 223.
15. J. Brabazon, *Albert Schweitzer: A Biography*, 2nd edn (Syracuse, 2000), 326.
16. Albert Schweitzer to Oswald Spengler, Lambarene, 28 November 1932, in Folder PH, GA.
17. A. Schweitzer, *Kultur und Ethik in den Weltreligionen*, ed. Ulrich Körtner and Johann Zürcher (Munich, 2001), 234.
18. Schweitzer, *Wir Epigonen*, 66–70.
19. Schweitzer, *Wir Epigonen*, 77.
20. Schweitzer, *Wir Epigonen*, 236.
21. Schweitzer, *Wir Epigonen*, 292, 305–6.
22. The publishers C. H. Beck has the complete original manuscript of *Wir Epigonen* in a copy from 1915–16. 'Civilized Nations and the Colonies' is the tenth and last chapter of the original manuscript.
23. Schweitzer, *Die Weltanschauung der Ehrfurcht vor dem Leben. Kulturphilosophie*, iii. *Dritter und vierter Teil*, 386.
24. Schweitzer, *Wir Epigonen*, 27.
25. A. Schweitzer, *On the Edge of the Primeval Forest*, trans. C. T. Campion (London, 1924), 112.
26. Günzler, *Albert Schweitzer*, 58.
27. A. Schweitzer, *Goethe: Vier Reden* (Munich, 1950). English edn: A. Schweitzer, *Goethe: Four Studies by Albert Schweitzer*, ed. C. R. Joy (Boston, 1949).
28. A. Schweitzer, 'The Goethe Prize Address. Delivered at the Goethe House, Frankfurt am Main, on receiving the Goethe Prize from the City of Frankfurt, August 28, 1928', in *Goethe: Four Studies*, 107.
29. J. W. Goethe, *Wilhelm Meisters Wanderjahre, Zweites Buch, 1. Kapitel*, 154–7, in *Goethe, Werke. Hamburger Ausgabe in 14 Bänden* (Hamburg ,1948 ff.), viii. Translation taken from J. W. Goethe, *Wilhelm Meister's Journeyman Years or The Renunciations*, trans. Krishna Winston, in *Goethe's Collected Works*, x, ed. J. K. Brown (New York, 1989), 203 ff.
30. Schweitzer, *Predigten 1898–1948*, 978, 1034.
31. *GW* v. 532–3.
32. J. W. Goethe, *Faust I*, 1237.
33. *GW* v. 537.
34. *GW* v. 173–5.
35. Schweitzer, *Wir Epigonen*, 153.
36. Schweitzer, *Wir Epigonen*, 153 n. 256.
37. Albert Schweitzer to Helene Bresslau, Strasbourg, 6 September 1903, in *AS–HB* 23–4.

38. Schweitzer, *Straßburger Vorlesungen*, 692–723 (at 704); emphasis in original.
39. T. Kleffmann, *Nietzsches Begriff des Lebens und die evangelische Theologie: Eine Interpretation Nietzsches und Untersuchungen zu seiner Rezeption bei Schweitzer, Tillich und Barth* (Tübingen, 2003), 337.
40. A. Schweitzer, 'The One Hundredth Anniversary Memorial Address. Delivered at the Centennial Celebration of Goethe's Death, in his Native City of Frankfurt am Main, March 22, 1932', in *Goethe: Four Studies*, 50.
41. *GW* v. 158.
42. G. Altner, 'Albert Schweitzer', in *Gestalten der Kirchengeschichte. Die neueste Zeit III*, ed. M. Greschat (Stuttgart, 1985), 282.
43. Schweitzer, *Life and Thought*, 186.
44. Schweitzer, *Life and Thought*, 186–7.
45. Schweitzer, *Life and Thought*, 187.
46. Schweitzer, *Life and Thought*, 187.
47. Schweitzer, *Life and Thought*, 187–8.
48. Schweitzer, *Life and Thought*, 189.
49. N. O. Oermann and J. Zachhuber, *Einigkeit und Recht und Werte: Der Verfassungsstreit um das Schulfach LER in der öffentlichen und wissenschaftlichen Diskussion* (Munster, 2001), 116–20.
50. F. Nietzsche, *Zur Genealogie der Moral I2*, in *Kritische Studienausgabe*, ed. G. Colli and M. Montinari, v, 2nd edn (Munich, 1999), 253, 7–12. English edition: F. Nietzsche, *On the Genealogy of Moral and Ecce Homo*, ed. and trans. Walter Kaufman (New York, 1969), 26.
51. Nietzsche, *Zur Genealogie der Moral I2*, v. 34.
52. Nietzsche, *Zur Genealogie der Moral I2*, v. 34.
53. F. Nietzsche, *Jenseits von Gut und Böse* (Leipzig, 1886). English edition: F Nietzsche, *Beyond Good and Evil*, trans. Helen Zimmern (New York, 1906/1997).
54. Schweitzer, *Die Weltanschauung der Ehrfurcht vor dem Leben. Kulturphilosophie*, iii. *Dritter und vierter Teil*, 120–1.
55. Schweitzer, *Life and Thought*, 176.
56. Schweitzer, *Die Weltanschauung der Ehrfurcht vor dem Leben. Kulturphilosophie*, iii. *Dritter und vierter Teil*, 388.
57. Schweitzer, *Die Weltanschauung der Ehrfurcht vor dem Leben. Kulturphilosophie*, iii. *Dritter und vierter Teil*, 376.
58. Albert Schweitzer to Oskar Kraus, Gunsbach, 2 January 1924, in *TPB* 431; G. Seaver, *Albert Schweitzer als Mensch und Denker*, 8th edn (Göttingen, 1956), 355–6; Kleffmann, *Nietzsches Begriff des Lebens*, 391.
59. Kleffmann, *Nietzsches Begriff des Lebens*, 391.
60. Quoted in Groos, *Albert Schweitzer*, 599.
61. Schweitzer, *Civilisation and Ethics*, 69.
62. 'Albert Schweitzer: Mythos des 20. Jahrhunderts', *Der Spiegel*, 21 December 1960, 60; A. Schweitzer, *Die Weltanschauung der indischen Denker: Mystik und Ethik* (Munich, 1935; 2nd edn, Munich, 1965); A. Schweitzer, *Geschichte des chinesischen Denkens*, ed. B. Kaempf and J. Zürcher (Munich, 2002).

63. M. Basse, '"Ehrfurcht vor dem Leben": Karl Barths Auseinandersetzung mit Albert Schweitzer in den 1920er Jahren', *Evangelische Theologie*, 65 (2005), 215.

64. K. Barth, *Einführung in die Evangelische Theologie*, 2nd edn (Zurich, 1977), 111.

65. Albert Schweitzer to Herbert Bahr, Lambarene, 1 June 1958, in Folder T, GA.

66. Schweitzer, *Die Weltanschauung der Ehrfurcht vor dem Leben. Kulturphilosophie*, iii. *Dritter und vierter Teil*, 386.

67. Schweitzer, *Die Weltanschauung der Ehrfurcht vor dem Leben. Kulturphilosophie*, iii. *Dritter und vierter Teil*, 387.

68. Schweitzer, *Civilisation and Ethics*, 177.

69. Schweitzer, *Life and Thought*, 188.

70. Helene Schweitzer to her parents, Lambarene, 29 April 1915, in *HSB* 171.

71. Schweitzer, *Civilisation and Ethics)*, 264.

72. *GW* v. 27–39.

73. *GW* i. 667.

74. A. Schweitzer, *On the Edge of the Primeval Forest*, trans. C. T. Campion (London, 1924), 143.

75. P. Ernst, *Ehrfurcht vor dem Leben: Versuch der Aufklärung einer aufgeklärten Kultur, Ethische Vernunft und christlicher Glaube im Werk Albert Schweitzers* (Frankfurt, 1991), 36.

76. A. Schweitzer, 'Nochmals Falkenjägerei', *Atlantis* (March 1932), 175, quoted in A. Schweitzer, *Ehrfurcht vor den Tieren*, ed. E. Gräßer (Munich, 2006), 108–12.

77. A. Schweitzer, *The Animal World of Albert Schweitzer: Jungle Insights into Reverence for Life*, trans. C. R. Joy (Boston, 1950), 177.

78. Schweitzer, *The Animal World of Albert Schweitzer*, 177.

79. Schweitzer, *Ehrfurcht vor den Tieren*, 112–13.

80. A. Schweitzer, Letter to the Editor in *Christ und Welt*, 4, 22 January 1965, in Schweitzer, *Ehrfurcht vor den Tieren*, 115–16.

5. The Iron Door Yields

1. A. Schweitzer, *Out of my Life and Thought*, trans. C. T. Campion (New York, 1948), 194–5.

2. J. Bentley, *Albert Schweitzer: Eine Biographie* (Düsseldorf, 2001), 171.

3. H. Steffahn, *Albert Schweitzer*, 12th edn (Hamburg, 1996), 57.

4. Schweitzer, *Life and Thought*, 200.

5. Schweitzer, *Life and Thought*, 205.

6. Schweitzer, *Life and Thought*, 205.

7. Personal interview with Rhena Schweitzer Miller, 2 April 2008, in Pacific Palisades, Los Angeles.

8. Albert Schweitzer's handwritten CV in the estate of Adolf von Harnack, sent to Schweitzer by Axel von Harnack, Tübingen, 9 January 1960, in Folder T, GA.
9. S. Oswald, *Mein Onkel Bery: Erinnerungen an Albert Schweitzer*, 2nd edn (Zurich, 1972), 98.
10. Schweitzer, *Life and Thought*, 212.
11. <http://www.zb.uzh.ch/sondersa/hands/nachlass/schweitzer/schweitzerteil2-sacs.pdf> (accessed 12 August 2008). In Sondersammlung Albert Schweitzer in the Archive of the University of Zurich.
12. Schweitzer, *Life and Thought*, 215.
13. Schweitzer, *Life and Thought*, 216.
14. A. Schweitzer, *Kultur und Ethik in den Weltreligionen*, ed. Ulrich Körtner and Johann Zürcher (Munich, 2001), 159; *GW* i. 195.
15. Nathan Söderblom to Albert Schweitzer, Uppsala, 5 December 1919, in *TPB* 627–8.
16. G. Marshall and D. Poling, *Schweitzer: A Biography* (London, 1971), 151.
17. Albert Schweitzer to Hans Walter Bähr, Lambarene, 2 January 1962 ('highly personal'), in *TPB* 39.
18. Quoted in *TPB* 626; *GW* i. 195–6.; *GW* v. 185–6. Schweitzer, *Life and Thought*, 217.
19. Albert Schweitzer to Nathan Söderblom, Gunsbach, 27 June 1921, in Folder T, GA. In this letter Schweitzer writes: 'I wonder whether you had your hand in this invitation [to Oxford]? Your goodness and your power balance each other.'
20. Albert Schweitzer to Anna Söderblom, Lambarene, 31 August 1931, in *TPB* 642.
21. Private letter Albert Schweitzer to Greta Lagerfelt, Lambarene, 17 August 1938, in private collection Schweitzer, GA. A short version of this letter was compiled by Sonja Poteau, Director of the Albert Schweitzer Central Archive Gunsbach; many thanks to her.
22. Schweitzer, *Life and Thought*, 219.
23. Schweitzer, *Life and Thought*, 219–20.
24. Dedication in the German original: A. Schweitzer, *Die Mystik des Apostels Paulus* (Tübingen, 1930), p. v.
25. Schweitzer, *Life and Thought*, 217.
26. Schweitzer, *Life and Thought*, 230.
27. A. Schweitzer, *Kulturphilosophie*. i. *Verfall und Wiederaufbau der Kultur;* ii. *Kultur und Ethik* (Munich, 2007). English edition: A. Schweitzer, *The Philosophy of Civilisation*. i. *The Decay and the Restoration of Civilisation;* ii. *Civilisation and Ethics*, trans. C. T. Campion (London, 1923). Reprinted in *The Philosophy of Civilization* (Amherst, NY, 1987).
28. A. Schweitzer, *Das Christentum und die Weltreligionen* (Munich, 1923). English edition: A. Schweitzer, *Christianity and the Religions of the World*, trans. Johanna Powers (London, 1939).

29. Schweitzer, *Life and Thought*, 237; A. Schweitzer, *Aus meiner Kindheit und Jugendzeit* (Bern, 1924). English edition: A. Schweitzer, *Memoirs of Childhood and Youth*, trans. C. T. Campion (New York, 1949).

30. Oskar Pfister to Albert Schweitzer, Biel, 8 May 1922, in *TPB* 568–9.

31. *TPB* 559–60, n. 4.

32. Schweitzer, *Life and Thought*, 237; Bentley, *Albert Schweitzer*, 15–16.

33. Personal interview with Rhena Schweitzer Miller, 2 April 2008, in Pacific Palisades, Los Angeles.

34. *HSB* 207.

35. Schweitzer, *Life and Thought*, 238.

36. K. Stoevesandt, 'Albert Schweitzer als Arzt und Helfer der Menschheit', *Evangelische Theologie*, 15 (1955), 102–3.

37. A. Schweitzer, *Mitteilungen aus Lambarene. Erstes Heft*, Spring 1924 to Autumn 1924 (Bern, 1925); *Zweites Heft*, Autumn 1924 to Autumn 1925 (Bern, 1926); *Drittes Heft*, Autumn 1925 to Autumn 1927 (Munich, 1928). *Mitteilungen aus Lambarene* were so successful that the publishers C. H. Beck reissued them under the title *Briefe aus Lambarene 1924–1927* (Munich, 1955); cf. *GW* i. 477–685.

38. *GW* i. 501–2.

39. *GW* i. 622.

40. *GW* v. 27–48.

41. Schweitzer, *Life and Thought*, 245–6.

42. G. Seaver, *Albert Schweitzer als Mensch und Denker*, 8th edn (Göttingen, 1956), 130.

43. Schweitzer, *Die Mystik des Apostels Paulus*; English edition: A. Schweitzer, *The Mysticism of Paul the Apostle*, trans. William Montgomery (London, 1931).

44. Schweitzer, *Life and Thought*, 247.

45. Schweitzer, *Life and Thought*, 252.

46. *HSB* 224.

47. Quoted in *HSB* 225.

48. Quoted in *TPB* 626; Schweitzer, *Life and Thought*, 217.

49. Schweitzer, *Life and Thought*, 131.

50. Unpublished letter to Margit Jacobi, quoted in Steffahn, *Albert Schweitzer*, 74.

51. Personal interview with Sonja Poteau, Director of the Albert Schweitzer Central Archive Gunsbach, 13 February 2009.

52. Personal interview with Sonja Poteau, Director of the Albert Schweitzer Central Archive Gunsbach, 13 February 2009.

53. Albert Schweitzer, 'Die Beziehungen zwischen den weißen und farbigen Rassen' [n.d., probably 1927], in A. Schweitzer, *Wir Epigonen: Kultur und Kulturstaat*, ed. Ulrich Körtner and Johann Zürcher (Munich, 2005), 335.

54. Albert Schweitzer, 'Die Beziehungen zwischen den weißen und farbigen Rassen' [n.d., probably 1927], in Schweitzer, *Wir Epigonen*, 335, 337.

55. A. Schweitzer, *On the Edge of the Primeval Forest*, trans. C. T. Campion (London, 1924), 112.

56. Albert Schweitzer to Helene Bresslau, Parsonage Rothau, 2 September 1905, in *AS-HB* 110.

57. Helene Bresslau to Albert Schweitzer, from England, 28 August 1905, in *AS-HB* 108.
58. Schweitzer, *Primeval Forest*, 112.
59. Schweitzer, *Primeval Forest*, 113.
60. Schweitzer, *Primeval Forest*, 117.
61. Schweitzer, *Primeval Forest*, 118–19.
62. Schweitzer, *Primeval Forest*, 122–3.
63. Personal interview with Sonja Poteau, Director of the Albert Schweitzer Central Archive Gunsbach, 13 February 2009.
64. Schweitzer, *Wir Epigonen*, 16–17, 308.
65. *GW* i. 610.
66. W. Picht, *Albert Schweitzer: Wesen und Bedeutung* (Hamburg, 1960), 159.
67. N. Cousins, *Dr Schweitzer of Lambaréné* (New York, 1960), 95.
68. 'Albert Schweitzer: Mythos des 20. Jahrhunderts', *Der Spiegel*, 21 December 1960, 50.
69. Schweitzer, *Primeval Forest*, 22–3.
70. Schweitzer, *Primeval Forest*, 130.
71. Schweitzer, *Primeval Forest*, 130–1.
72. Schweitzer, *Primeval Forest*, 135.
73. J. Gunther, *Inside Africa* (New York, 1955), 713; 'Albert Schweitzer: Mythos des 20. Jahrhunderts', 60.
74. 'Obituary: Albert Schweitzer (1875–1965)', *New York Times*, 5 September 1965.
75. Personal interview with Claus Jacobi, 16 October 2008, in Hamburg.
76. Schweitzer, *Primeval Forest*, 132–3.
77. J. Cameron, *Point of Departure* (London, 2006), 175.
78. Albert Schweitzer to Herbert Bahr, Lambarene, 3 May 1951, in Folder T, GA.
79. Quoted in Cameron, *Point of Departure*, 167.
80. Brabazon, *Albert Schweitzer*, 438.
81. Statistics about treated patients, numbers of births and deaths between 1924 and 1966 on the basis of the operation logbooks kept in Lambarene, may be found in J. Munz and W. Munz, *Mit dem Herzen einer Gazelle und der Haut eines Nilpferds: Albert Schweitzer in seinen letzten Lebensjahren und die Entwicklung seines Spitals bis zur Gegenwart* (Frauenfeld, 2005), 199.
82. A. Schweitzer, quoted in C. R. Joy and M. Arnold, *The Africa of Albert Schweitzer* (London, 1949), 156.
83. Albert Schweitzer, 'Die Beziehungen zwischen den weißen und farbigen Rassen' [n.d., probably 1927], in Schweitzer, *Wir Epigonen*, 338.

6. With Central African Greetings

1. *Goethe: Four Studies by Albert Schweitzer*, ed. C. R. Joy (Boston, 1949), 31–2, 56, 58.
2. *Goethe: Four Studies*, 59.

3. G. Seaver, *Albert Schweitzer als Mensch und Denker*, 8th edn (Göttingen, 1956), 165.

4. Quoted in *HSB* 222.

5. *HSB* 224.

6. *HSB* 227–8.

7. Quoted in *HSB* 228.

8. Quoted in *HSB* 229.

9. M. Born, *Mein Leben: Die Erinnerungen des Nobelpreisträgers* (Munich, 1975), 330.

10. Born, *Mein Leben: Die Erinnerungen des Nobelpreisträgers*, 330.

11. Albert Schweitzer to Margit and Eugen Jacobi, 16 September 1930, in *HSB* 231.

12. J. Munz and W. Munz, *Mit dem Herzen einer Gazelle und der Haut eines Nilpferds: Albert Schweitzer in seinen letzten Lebensjahren und die Entwicklung seines Spitals bis zur Gegenwart* (Frauenfeld, 2005), 199.

13. A. Schweitzer, *Das Albert Schweitzer Lesebuch*, ed. H. Steffahn, 4th edn (Munich, 2009), 334–5.

14. G. Marshall and D. Poling, *Schweitzer: A Biography* (London, 1971), 194; B. M. Nossik, *Albert Schweitzer: Ein Leben für die Menschlichkeit* (Leipzig, 1978), 273; Seaver, *Albert Schweitzer als Mensch und Denker*, 167.

15. Marshall and Poling, *Schweitzer: A Biography*, 197–8.

16. Börsenverein des Deutschen Buchhandels (ed.), *Friedenspreis des Deutschen Buchhandels: Reden und Würdigungen 1951–1960* (Frankfurt, 1961), 21.

17. Seaver, *Albert Schweitzer als Mensch und als Denker*, 171.

18. *HSB* 232.

19. Nossik, *Albert Schweitzer*, 283.

20. *GW* v. 60.

21. *HSB* 234.

22. Personal interview with Rhena Schweitzer Miller, 7 May 2005, in Pacific Palisades, Los Angeles.

23. *GW* v. 55.

24. Ladislas Goldschmid was active as a doctor in Lambarene from 2 April 1933 until 9 August 1935, from 1 July 1936 until July 1938, and from 22 December 1938 until 15 June 1947. Cf. *TPB* 665.

25. *GW* v. 55, 57. Anna Wildikann worked in Lambarene from 1935 until 1937 and from 1940 until 1945 and afterwards in Israel. Cf. *TPB* 145.

26. *HSB* 242.

27. Helene Schweitzer to Luise Bresslau-Hoff, 18 November 1940, in *HSB* 242.

28. Helene Schweitzer to Luise Bresslau-Hoff, 18 November 1940, in *HSB* 245.

29. *GW* v. 57; P. H. Freyer, *Albert Schweitzer: Ein Lebensbild*, 3rd edn (Berlin, 1982), 206.

30. Munz and Munz, *Mit dem Herzen*, 199.

31. *GW* v. 53.

32. *GW* v. 56.
33. *GW* v. 59.
34. J. Brabazon, *Albert Schweitzer: A Biography*, 2nd edn (Syracuse, 2000), 391.
35. Pierhal, *Albert Schweitzer*, 234.
36. Brabazon, *Albert Schweitzer*, 394.
37. Helene Schweitzer to Luise Bresslau-Hoff, 30 April 1945, in *HSB* 250.
38. Quoted in *GW* v. 72. Translation from Brabazon, *Albert Schweitzer*, 395.
39. *GW* v. 75.
40. Munz and Munz, *Mit dem Herzen*, 199.
41. E. R. Jacobi, *Albert Schweitzer und die Musik* (Wiesbaden, 1975), 15.

7. Exorcising the Ghost of the Nuclear War

1. G. Marshall and D. Poling, *Schweitzer: A Biography* (London, 1971), 217.
2. Marshall and Poling, *Schweitzer: A Biography*, 217–22.
3. Helene Schweitzer Bresslau to Luise Bresslau-Hoff, 2 August 1948, quoted in *HSB* 252.
4. Marshall and Poling, *Schweitzer: A Biography*, 293.
5. 'Albert Schweitzer: Jungle Philosopher', *Life Magazine*, 6 October 1947.
6. Albert Schweitzer to Albert Einstein, Lambarene, 30 April 1948, in H. W. Bähr (ed.), *Albert Schweitzer: Letters 1905–65*, trans. Joachim Neugroschel (New York, 1992), 197–8.
7. 'Reverence for Life', *Time Magazine*, 11 July 1949.
8. Quoted in *HSB* 254.
9. J. Bentley, *Albert Schweitzer: Eine Biographie* (Düsseldorf, 2001), 196.
10. J. Brabazon, *Albert Schweitzer: A Biography*, 2nd edn (Syracuse, 2000), 405.
11. E. R. Jacobi, *Albert Schweitzer und die Musik* (Wiesbaden, 1975), 5.
12. *HSB* 254; Bentley, *Albert Schweitzer*, 195.
13. A. Schweitzer, *Goethe: Five Studies*, trans. C. R. Joy (Boston, 1961), 65; *GW* v. 554.
14. Quoted in Brabazon, *Albert Schweitzer*, 409.
15. R. Schütz, *Anekdoten über Albert Schweitzer* (Munich, 1966), 57; P. H. Freyer, *Albert Schweitzer: Ein Lebensbild*, 3rd edn (Berlin, 1982), 216.
16. Schütz, *Anekdoten um Albert Schweitzer*, 57.
17. 'Albert Schweitzer: Mythos des 20. Jahrhunderts', *Der Spiegel*, 21 December 1960, 58.
18. 'Albert Schweitzer: He that Lives his Life shall Find it', *Time Magazine*, 11 July 1949.
19. 'Reverence for Life', *Time Magazine*, 11 July 1949.
20. In *Breakfast at Tiffany's* (1961) Holly Golightly, alias Audrey Hepburn, lists Albert Schweitzer, Nero, and Leonard Bernstein as her ideal candidates for marriage. In his bestseller *Fahrenheit 451* (1953), Ray Bradbury names Albert Schweitzer alongside Albert Einstein. See R. Bradbury, *Fahrenheit 451* (New York, 1987), 151.

21. S. Poteau and G. Leser, *Albert Schweitzer: Homme de Gunsbach et citoyen du monde* (Mülhausen, 1994), 282.
22. Brabazon, *Albert Schweitzer*, 423.
23. M. Tau, *Das Leben lieben: Max Tau in Briefen und Dokumenten 1945–1976*, ed. H. Däumling (Würzburg, 1988), 123.
24. Quoted in M. Tau, *Auf dem Weg zur Versöhnung* (Hamburg, 1968), 170.
25. Tau, *Das Leben lieben*, 125.
26. Tau, *Auf dem Weg zur Versöhnung*, 170–2.
27. Quoted in S. Oswald, *Mein Onkel Bery: Erinnerungen an Albert Schweitzer*, 2nd edn (Zurich, 1972), 125.
28. *HSB* 263.
29. Tau, *Das Leben lieben*, 130; Tau, *Auf dem Weg zur Versöhnung*, 176.
30. Quoted in Tau, *Auf dem Weg zur Versöhnung*, 173.
31. Quoted in Tau, *Auf dem Weg zur Versöhnung*, 175.
32. Jacobi, *Albert Schweitzer und die Musik*, 6–7.
33. *HSB* 260–1.
34. Brabazon, *Albert Schweitzer*, 446. Personal interview with Rhena Schweitzer Miller, 7 May 2005, in Pacific Palisades, Los Angeles.
35. Quoted in Oswald, *Mein Onkel Bery*, 124.
36. H.W. Bähr (ed.), *Albert Schweitzer: Letters 1905–1965*, trans. Joachim Neugroschedl (New York, 1992), 243.
37. 'Albert Schweitzer: Mythos des 20. Jahrhunderts', 58.
38. H. Bertlein, *Das Selbstverständnis der Jugend heute: Eine empirische Untersuchung über ihre geistigen Probleme, ihre Leitbilder und ihr Verhältnis zu den Erwachsenen*, 2nd edn (Hanover, 1964), 153, 177.
39. Bertlein, *Das Selbstverständnis der Jugend heute*, 178.
40. Bertlein, *Das Selbstverständnis der Jugend heute*, 177.
41. Bertlein, *Das Selbstverständnis der Jugend heute*, 178.
42. J. Pierhal, *Albert Schweitzer: Das Leben eines guten Menschen* (Munich, 1955).
43. *Revue*, 13 November 1954 (photographs by Erica Anderson).
44. Quoted in Brabazon, *Albert Schweitzer*, 432; J. Cameron, *Point of Departure* (London, 2006), 167.
45. Quoted in Brabazon, *Albert Schweitzer*, 433.
46. Cameron, *Point of Departure*, 174–5.
47. N. Cousins, *Dr Schweitzer of Lambaréné* (New York, 1960), 91–2.
48. Brabazon, *Albert Schweitzer*, 485–6.
49. 'Obituary: Albert Schweitzer (1875–1965)', *New York Times*, 5 September 1965.
50. 'Albert Schweitzer: An Anachronism', *Time Magazine*, 21 June 1963.
51. A. Audoynaud, *Le Docteur Schweitzer et son hôpital à Lambaréné: L'Envers d'un mythe* (Paris, 2005). It was evidently the goal of former Director of the Hôpital Administratif of Lambarene (1963–6), André Audoynaud, to push his former 'rival' from his pedestal, to demystify him. Audoynaud wanted to demonstrate that the Schweitzer legend was not supported by his life and work (p. 11). He denied the originality of Schweitzer's hospital

as essentially different from other hospitals of the time (p. 205) and pointed out that in Schweitzer's hospital, too, patients had to pay for treatment (p. 210). It is true that for those who were able, Schweitzer asked for payment in cash or in kind or with work. Audoynaud's fundamental criticism—which is supported by hardly any facts—culminated in the claim that the medical standards in Lambarene were hopelessly out dated as there had been no improvements between 1924 and 1965 (p. 85).

52. Oswald, *Mein Onkel Bery*, 152.
53. J. Gunther, *Inside Africa* (New York, 1955), 713.
54. Personal interview with Claus Jacobi, 16 October 2008, in Hamburg.
55. C. R. Joy and M. Arnold, *Bei Albert Schweitzer in Afrika* (Munich, 1948), 83.
56. N. Cousins, *Dr Schweitzer of Lambaréné* (New York, 1960), 93–4.
57. Cousins, *Dr Schweitzer of Lambaréné*, 94–5.
58. C. Scipio, 'Is Schweitzer Dead?', *Atlantic Monthly* (August 1966), 41–4; C. C. O'Brien, 'Africa's Answer to Schweitzer', *Atlantic Monthly* (March 1966), 68–71; M. M. Davenport, 'The Moral Paternalism of Albert Schweitzer', *Ethics*, 84 (1973–4), 116–27.
59. Poteau and Leser, *Albert Schweitzer*, 320.
60. O. Spear, *Albert Schweitzers Ethik: Ihre Grundlinien in seinem Denken und Leben* (Hamburg, 1978), 27.
61. A. Schweitzer, 'The Concept of the Kingdom of God in the Transformation of Eschatology', appendix to E. N. Mozley, *The Theology of Albert Schweitzer for Christian Enquirers* (London, 1950), 107.
62. *TPB*. 501; Brabazon, *Albert Schweitzer*, 443–4.
63. *TPB* 215.
64. Quoted in A. Herrmann, *Einstein: Der Weltweise und sein Jahrhundert: Eine Biographie* (Munich, 1994), 359.
65. Albert Schweitzer to Theodor Heuss, Lambarene, 17 May 1958, in *TPB* 337.
66. Albert Schweitzer to Theodor Heuss, Lambarene, 17 May 1958, in *TPB* 337–8.
67. Albert Schweitzer to Albert Einstein, Lambarene, 20 February 1955, in Bähr (ed.), *Albert Schweitzer: Letters 1905–1965*, 257.
68. R. Jungk, 'Der Menschenfreund gegen die Atomversuche', in J. Pierhal, *Albert Schweitzer* (Frankfurt, 1982), 253.
69. Quoted in Brabazon, *Albert Schweitzer*, 445.
70. A. Schweitzer, 'An den Daily Herald', 14 April 1954, in *Menschlichkeit und Friede: Kleine philosophisch-ethische Texte*, ed. G. Fischer (Berlin, 1991), 133. Translation from Brabazon, *Albert Schweitzer*, 444.
71. N. Cousins, *Dr Schweitzer of Lambaréné* (New York, 1960). 95.
72. H. Steffahn, *Albert Schweitzer*, 12th edn (Hamburg, 1996), 125.
73. Quoted in Brabazon, *Albert Schweitzer*, 445.
74. Quoted in Spear, *Albert Schweitzers Ethik: Ihre Grundlinien in seinem Denken und Leben*, 25.

75. *TPB* 626–8; M. Fröhlich, *Dag Hammarskjöld und die Vereinten Nationen: Die politische Ethik des UNO-Generalsekretärs* (Paderborn, 2002), 117.
76. Britt Engvall to Albert Schweitzer, Stockholm, 18 October 1961, in Régnants 1960–1965, GA.
77. A. Schweitzer, *Out of my Life and Thought*, trans. C. T. Campion (New York, 1948), 218; Nathan Söderblom to Albert Schweitzer, Uppsala, 5 December 1919, in *TPB* 628.
78. Brabazon, *Albert Schweitzer*, 441–2.
79. Fröhlich, *Dag Hammarskjöld und die Vereinten Nationen*, 180.
80. H. W. Kahn, *Der Kalte Krieg*, i. *Spaltung und Wahn der Stärke 1945–1955* (Cologne: 1986), 240–1.
81. Brabazon, *Albert Schweitzer*, 445; Kahn, *Der Kalte Krieg*, i. 263.
82. H. Steffahn dates this visit to late 1956. Steffahn, *Albert Schweitzer*, 128.
83. Cousins, *Dr Schweitzer of Lambaréné*, 52–3.
84. Cousins, *Dr Schweitzer of Lambaréné*, 115.
85. Cousins, *Dr Schweitzer of Lambaréné*, 95.
86. Dwight D. Eisenhower to Albert Schweitzer, Washington DC, 29 May 1957, in Régnants 1926–1959, GA.
87. Cousins, *Dr Schweitzer of Lambaréné*, 167.
88. Cousins, *Dr Schweitzer of Lambaréné*, 165.
89. Cousins, *Dr Schweitzer of Lambaréné*, 175–6.
90. Fritz Bopp, Max Born, Rudolf Fleischmann, Walther Gerlach, Otto Hahn, Otto Haxel, Werner Heisenberg, Hans Kopfermann, Max von Laue, Heinz Maier-Leibnitz, Josef Mattauch, Friedrich Adolf Paneth, Wolfgang Paul, Wolfgang Riezler, Fritz Straßmann, Wilhelm Walcher, Carl Friedrich von Weizsäcker, and Karl Wirtz.
91. Printed in K. Wagenbach (ed.), *Vaterland, Muttersprache: Deutsche Schriftsteller und ihr Staat seit 1945*, 3rd edn (Berlin, 2004), 139.
92. B. Stöver, *Der Kalte Krieg 1947–1991: Geschichte eines radikalen Zeitalters* (Munich, 2007), 221–2.
93. Albert Schweitzer to Konrad Adenauer, [no place], 15 June 1957, in Folder GO, GA.
94. Stöver, *Der Kalte Krieg 1947–1991*, 222–3.
95. *GW* v. 564–77; A. Schweitzer, *Friede oder Atomkrieg: Vier Schriften*, 2nd edn (Munich, 1982), 33–49.
96. Albert Schweitzer to Theodor Heuss, Lambarene, 17 May 1958, in *TPB* 338.
97. H. W. Kahn, *Der Kalte Krieg*, ii. *Alibi für das Rüstungsgeschäft 1955–1973* (Cologne, 1987), 82.
98. Pierhal, *Albert Schweitzer*, 258.
99. *GW* v. 565 ff., translation from <https://www.wagingpeace.org/a-declaration-of-conscience/> (accessed 4 June 2016).
100. Brabazon, *Albert Schweitzer*, 459.
101. Quoted in W. Gerlach and D. Hahn, *Otto Hahn: Ein Forscherleben unserer Zeit* (Stuttgart, 1984), 158.

102. Albert Schweitzer to Theodor Heuss, Lambarene, 17 May 1958, in *TPB* 338–9.
103. Albert Schweitzer to Theodor Heuss, Lambarene, 17 May 1958, in *TPB* 339, 501.
104. Albert Schweitzer to Martin Buber, Lambarene, 3 March 1958, in *TPB* 147.
105. *GW* v. 578–611; A. Schweitzer, *Peace or Atomic War?* (New York, 1958).
106. Tau, *Das Leben lieben*, 145–6.
107. *Neue Zürcher Zeitung*, 10 September 1958.
108. Letter unpublished to date, GA.
109. Dag Hammarskjöld to Albert Schweitzer, New York, 17 March 1961, in Régnants 1960–1965, GA.
110. Dag Hammarskjöld to Albert Schweitzer, New York, 17 March 1961, in Régnants 1960–1965, GA.
111. 'Profile: Dag Hammarskjöld', *Observer*, 5 April 1953.
112. Schweitzer, *Civilisation and Ethics*, 297.
113. Schweitzer, *Civilisation and Ethics*, 300.
114. A. Schweitzer, 'Friedensartikel für Dr Wilhelm Kayser', in *Menschlichkeit und Friede*, ed. Fischer, 176.
115. Albert Schweitzer to John F. Kennedy, Lambarene, 20 April 1962, in *TPB* 420.
116. Quoted in C. Wyss, 'Friede oder Atomkrieg: Albert Schweitzers Engagement gegen die Atombomben', in Schweizer Hilfsverein für das Albert-Schweitzer-Spital in Lambarene (ed.), *Berichte aus Lambarene* (April 2007), 14.
117. Albert Schweitzer to John F. Kennedy, Lambarene, 24 October 1962, in *TPB* 423–4.
118. Albert Schweitzer to John F. Kennedy, Lambarene, 23 November 1962, in *TPB* 426–7.
119. Quoted in Wyss, 'Friede oder Atomkrieg', 14.
120. *GW* v. 614.
121. Albert Schweitzer to John F. Kennedy, Lambarene, August 1963, in Bähr (ed.), *Albert Schweitzer: Letters 1905–1965*, 335.
122. C. Jacobi, 'Schweitzers Uhr geht anders', *Der Spiegel*, 21 December 1960, p. 63.
123. Gerald Götting to Albert Schweitzer, Berlin, 14 January 1955, in Régnants 1926–1959, GA.
124. Personal interview with Gerald Götting, 29 October 2008, in Berlin-Köpenick.
125. BArch/ FA O.2242; Zulassungsprotokolle DEFA; AU II.8–040159/ 08Z.
126. G. Götting, *Begegnung mit Albert Schweitzer* (Berlin, 1961).
127. Gerald Götting confirmed in the interview on 26 October 2008 in Berlin-Köpenick that the visit from the Peace Council was undertaken with the explicit goal of gaining Schweitzer's support for the GDR and its policies.

128. Götting, *Begegnung mit Albert Schweitzer*, 10.
129. Personal interview with Gerald Götting, 29 October 2008, in Berlin-Köpenick.
130. BArch /FA O. 2242; Zulassungsprotokoll No. 0171/60 from 9 April 1960.
131. BStU, 'Ministry of State Security employee "Fidelio" zu Gerald Götting, general secretary, in the Ministry of State Security, AP 11730/92 Gerald Götting, p. 133.
132. BStU, Leutnant Busch, 'Information from Hauptabteilung V/3, Berlin, den 17 December 1959', in the Ministry of State Security, AP 11730/92 Gerald Götting, p. 133.
133. BStU, Leutnant Busch, 'Information from Hauptabteilung V/3, Berlin, den 17 December 1959', in the Ministry of State Security, AP 11730/92 Gerald Götting, p. 133, and AP 13722/92 Gerald Götting, p. 41.
134. B. M. Nossik, *Albert Schweitzer: Ein Leben für die Menschlichkeit* (Leipzig, 1978), 347.
135. Robert Havemann to Albert Schweitzer, Lambarene, January 1960, in Folder C, GA, printed in G. Götting and S.-H. Günther, *Was heißt Ehrfurcht vor dem Leben? Begegnung mit Albert Schweitzer* (Berlin, 2005), 124–5.
136. Albert Schweitzer to Robert Havemann, Lambarene, 9 August 1961, in Folder C, GA.
137. Robert Havemann to Albert Schweitzer, Berlin, 6 April 1964, in Folder C, GA.
138. BStU, Albert Schweitzer to Robert Havemann, Lambarene, 22 April 1964, in Ministry for State Security, AOP 54689/89, vol. 4, p. 351.
139. BStU, Deputy Minister, AG Auswertung, Berlin, 1 April 1964, in Ministry for State Security, AOP 54689/89, vol. 4, p. 199.
140. Gerald Götting to Albert Schweitzer, Berlin, 5 May 1964, in Folder GO, GA.
141. Gerald Götting to Nils Ole Oermann, Berlin, 26 February 2009, in Oermann's private archive.
142. Walter Ulbricht to Albert Schweitzer, Berlin, 20 July 1961, in Régnants 1960–1965, GA.
143. Albert Schweitzer to Walter Ulbricht, Lambarene, 9 August 1961, in Folder GO (originally Kottmann estate), GA.
144. Willy Brandt to Albert Schweitzer, Berlin, 19 May 1959, in Régnants 1926–1959, GA.
145. Quoted in Cousins, *Albert Schweitzer und sein Lambarene*, 98.
146. Brabazon, *Albert Schweitzer*, 479.
147. Gerald Götting to Albert Schweitzer, Berlin, 21 August 1961, in Régnants 1960–1965, GA.
148. Albert Schweitzer to Gerald Götting, Lambarene, 25 March 1962, in Régnants 1960–1965, GA; Gerald Götting to Albert Schweitzer, Berlin, 10 July 1962, in Régnants 1960–1965, GA.
149. Gerald Götting to Albert Schweitzer, Berlin, 16 October 1962, in Régnants 1960–1965, GA.

150. Gerald Götting to Albert Schweitzer, Berlin, 25 February 1964, in Régnants 1960–1965, GA.
151. Gerald Götting to Albert Schweitzer, Berlin, 25 February 1964, in Régnants 1960–1965, GA.
152. Walter Ulbricht to Albert Schweitzer, Berlin, 14 January 1965, in Régnants 1960–1965, GA.
153. A. Schweitzer, *Kultur und Ethik in den Weltreligionen*, ed. Ulrich Körtner and Johann Zürcher (Munich, 2001), 234.
154. Walter Ulbricht to Albert Schweitzer, Berlin, 28 March 1962, in Régnants 1960–1965, GA.
155. Nossik, *Albert Schweitzer*, 351.
156. Albert Schweitzer to the minister for post and telecommunications, Lambarene, 12 November 1964, in 'Erinnerungsblatt Albert Schweitzer zu Ehren herausgegeben aus Anlaß der Vollendung seines 90. Lebensjahres', copy No. 1497, Oermann's private archive.
157. Brabazon, *Albert Schweitzer*, 447–8.
158. Personal interview with Walter Munz, 4 April 2009, in Lambarene.
159. Willy Brandt to Albert Schweitzer, Berlin, 10 March 1965, in Régnants 1960–1965, GA.
160. F. Walter, 'Geheimnis der Machtmenschen: Warum Politiker nicht die Klügsten sind', *Spiegel-Online*, 22 February 2009, with reference to: F. Walter, *Charismatiker und Effizienzen: Porträts aus 60 Jahren Bundesrepublik* (Frankfurt, 2009).
161. Börsenverein des Deutschen Buchhandels (ed.), *Friedenspreis des Deutschen Buchhandels: Reden und Würdigungen 1951–1960* (Stuttgart, 1961), 20.
162. A. Schweitzer, *Memoirs of Childhood and Youth*, trans. C. T. Campion (New York, 1949), 35.
163. Schweitzer, *Childhood and Youth*, 35–6.
164. F. W. Kantzenbach, *Albert Schweitzer: Wirklichkeit und Legende* (Göttingen, 1969), 100.
165. Albert Schweitzer to Gerald Götting, Lambarene, 3 May 1963, in Régnants 1960–1965, GA.
166. 'Albert Schweitzer: Mythos des 20. Jahrhunderts', 57.
167. Senator Helmut Schmidt to Albert Schweitzer, Hamburg, 4 April 1962, in Régnants 1960–1965, GA.
168. The context is the Morocco crisis in 1911; cf. K. Hildebrand, *Das vergangene Reich: Deutsche Außenpolitik von Bismarck bis Hitler* (Stuttgart: 1995), 303–13.
169. Helene Bresslau to Albert Schweitzer, Schwartau, 26 August 1911 in *AS–HB* 213–14; emphasis in original.
170. Albert Schweitzer to Helene Bresslau, 28 August 1911 on a train to Colmar, in *AS–HB* 214–15.
171. Albert Schweitzer to Helene Bresslau, 28 August 1911 on a train to Colmar, in *AS–HB* 214–15.

172. J. Munz and W. Munz, *Mit dem Herzen einer Gazelle und der Haut eines Nilpferds: Albert Schweitzer in seinen letzten Lebensjahren und die Entwicklung seines Spitals bis zur Gegenwart* (Frauenfeld, 2005), 159.
173. H. W. Bähr (ed.), *A. Schweitzer: Leben, Werk und Denken 1905–1965: Mitgeteilt in seinen Briefen* (Heidelberg: 1987), 322, quoted in E. Gräßer, 'Das Prinzip "Ehrfurcht vor dem Leben"', in Albert Schweitzers Ethik für unsere Zeit', in R. Brüllmann (ed.), *Albert-Schweitzer-Studien 2* (Bern, 1989), 43.
174. U. Schmidt, *Hitlers Arzt Karl Brandt: Medizin und Macht im Dritten Reich*, 2nd edn (Berlin, 2009), 76–82.

8. How Beautiful! The Last Years (1957–1965)

1. Léon M'ba to Albert Schweitzer, Libreville, 26 December 1961, in Régnants 1960–1965, GA.
2. J. Brabazon, *Albert Schweitzer: A Biography*, 2nd edn (Syracuse, 2000), 477.
3. B. M. Nossik, *Albert Schweitzer: Ein Leben für die Menschlichkeit* (Leipzig, 1978), 357–8.
4. Albert Schweitzer to Linus Pauling, Lambarene, 11 April 1965, in *TPB* 557.
5. *TPB* 558.
6. F. W. Kantzenbach, *Albert Schweitzer: Wirklichkeit und Legende* (Göttingen, 1969), 100.
7. Brabazon, *Albert Schweitzer*, 492.
8. Quoted in Brabazon, *Albert Schweitzer*, 492–3.
9. Quoted in Brabazon, *Albert Schweitzer*, 487–8.
10. J. Munz and W. Munz, *Mit dem Herzen einer Gazelle und der Haut eines Nilpferds: Albert Schweitzer in seinen letzten Lebensjahren und die Entwicklung seines Spitals bis zur Gegenwart* (Frauenfeld, 2005), 199.
11. Munz and Munz, *Mit dem Herzen*, 199–200.
12. A. Schweitzer, *Das Albert Schweitzer Lesebuch*, ed. H. Steffahn, 4th edn (Munich, 2009), 394–5.
13. Personal interview with Walter Munz, 4 April 2009, in Lambarene.
14. *HSB* 270; personal interview with Sonja Poteau, Director of the Albert Schweitzer Central Archive Gunsbach, 29 July 2008.
15. Kantzenbach, *Albert Schweitzer*, 101.
16. Two personal interviews with Christoph Wyss and Roland Wolf, 3 April 2009, in Lambarene.
17. S. Oswald, *Mein Onkel Bery: Erinnerungen an Albert Schweitzer*, 2nd edn (Zurich, 1972), 196.

9. Conclusion

1. 'Albert Schweitzer: Mythos des 20. Jahrhunderts', *Der Spiegel*, 21 December 1960, 52.
2. N. Cousins, *Dr Schweitzer of Lambaréné* (New York, 1960), 219.

3. F. W. Kantzenbach, *Albert Schweitzer: Wirklichkeit und Legende* (Göttingen, 1969), 7–9.

4. H. Christaller, *Albert Schweitzer: Ein Leben für andere* (Stuttgart, 1954), 6–7.

5. E. Bauermann, *Das Menschenbild Albert Schweitzers* (Aachen, 1984), 13–14.

6. 'Albert Schweitzer: Mythos des 20. Jahrhunderts', 61.

7. S. Poteau, D. Mougin, and C. Wyss, *Albert Schweitzer: Von Gunsbach nach Lambarene* (Gunsbach, 2008), 26, 28, 50, 248, 300.

8. Personal interview with Christiane Engel, grand-daughter to Albert Schweitzer, 7 April 2009, in Lambarene.

9. W. Munz, *Albert Schweitzer im Gedächtnis der Afrikaner und in meiner Erinnerung*. Albert-Schweitzer-Studien 3 (Bern, 1991), 211.

Bibliography

1. Documents from Archives

Albert Schweitzer Central Archive Gunsbach
Folder AT
Folder GO
Folder PH
Folder T
Régnants 1926–1959
Régnants 1960–1965

Bundesarchiv Berlin-Lichterfelde
Zulassungsprotokolle DEFA, FA O. 2242
AU II.8–040159/08Z

Archive of the Federal Commissioner for the Records of the State Security Service of the former German Democratic Republic
MfS AP 11730/92 Gerald Götting
MfS AP 13722/92 Gerald Götting
MfS AOP 54689/89

Archive of the University of Zurich
Special Collection Albert Schweitzer <http://www.zb.uzh.ch/sondersa/hands/nachlass/schweitzer/schweitzerteil2-sacs.pdf> (12 August 2008)

2. Personal interviews

Christiane Engel, 7 April 2009, in Lambarene
Gerald Götting, 29 October 2008, in Berlin-Köpenick
Claus Jacobi, 16 October 2008, in Hamburg
Walter Munz, 4 April 2009, in Lambarene
Sonja Poteau, 29 July 2008 and 13 February 2009, in Gunsbach
Rhena Schweitzer Miller, 7 May 2005 and 2 April 2008, in Pacific Palisades, Los Angeles
Roland Wolf, 3 April 2009, in Lambarene
Christoph Wyss, 3 April 2009, in Lambarene

3. Internet Sources

www.nobelprize.org (accessed 17 December 2008)

4. Publications by Albert Schweitzer

Eugène Munch 1857–1898 (Mülhausen, 1898).

Die Religionsphilosophie Kants von der Kritik der reinen Vernunft bis zur Religion innerhalb der Grenzen der bloßen Vernunft (Tübingen, 1899).

Das Abendmahl im Zusammenhang mit dem Leben Jesu und der Geschichte des Urchristentums; i. *Das Abendmahlsproblem auf Grund der wissenschaftlichen Forschungen des 19. Jahrhunderts und der historischen Berichte* (Tübingen, 1901).

Das Abendmahl im Zusammenhang mit dem Leben Jesu und der Geschichte des Urchristentums; ii. *Das Messianitäts- und Leidensgeheimnis, Eine Skizze des Lebens Jesu* (Tübingen, 1901).

Jean-Sébastien Bach, le musicien-poète (Leipzig, 1905).

Deutsche und französische Orgelbaukunst und Orgelkunst (Leipzig, 1906).

Von Reimarus zu Wrede: Eine Geschichte der Leben-Jesu-Forschung (Tübingen, 1906; reissued in 1913 under the title *Geschichte der Leben-Jesu-Forschung*).

J. S. Bach, German edn (Leipzig, 1908).

Geschichte der Paulinischen Forschung von der Reformation bis auf die Gegenwart (Tübingen, 1911).

Geschichte der Leben-Jesu-Forschung (Tübingen, 1913).

Die psychiatrische Beurteilung Jesu: Darstellung und Kritik (Tübingen, 1913).

Zwischen Wasser und Urwald: Erlebnisse eines Arztes im Urwalde Äquatorialafrikas (Bern, 1921).

Das Christentum und die Weltreligionen (Munich, 1923).

Kulturphilosophie. i. *Verfall und Wiederaufbau der Kultur* (Munich, 1923).

Kulturphilosophie. ii. *Kultur und Ethik* (Munich, 1923).

Aus meiner Kindheit und Jugendzeit (Bern, 1924).

Selbstdarstellung (Leipzig, 1929).

Die Mystik des Apostels Paulus (Tübingen, 1930).

Aus meinem Leben und Denken (Bern, 1931).

Die Weltanschauung der indischen Denker: Mystik und Ethik (Munich, 1935).

Afrikanische Geschichten (Leipzig, 1938).

Das Spital im Urwald (Munich, 1948).

Goethe: Vier Reden (Munich, 1950).

Ein Pelikan erzählt aus seinem Leben, with A. Wildikann (Hamburg, 1950).

Das Problem des Friedens in der heutigen Welt (Munich, 1954).

Briefe aus Lambarene 1924–1927 (Munich, 1955); first published as *Mitteilungen aus Lambarene in drei Heften* (Bern, 1925–8).

Friede oder Atomkrieg (Munich, 1958).

Was sollen wir tun? 12 Predigten über ethische Probleme (Heidelberg, 1974).

'Einführung in das Schaffen Bachs'(1929), in A. Schweitzer, *Aufsätze zur Musik*, ed. S. Hanheide (Kassel, 1988), 85–98.

'Erinnerungen an Cosima und Siegfried Wagner' (1955), in A. Schweitzer, *Aufsätze zur Musik*, ed. S. Hanheide (Kassel, 1988), 204–15.

'An den Daily Herald', 14 April 1954, in *Menschlichkeit und Friede: Kleine philosophisch-ethische Texte*, ed. G. Fischer (Berlin, 1991), 133–4.

'Friedensartikel für Dr Wilhelm Kayser' (1962), in *Menschlichkeit und Friede: Kleine philosophisch-ethische Texte*, ed. G. Fischer (Berlin, 1991), 175–6.

5. English Translations of Schweitzer's Works

The Quest of the Historical Jesus: A Critical Study of its Progress from Reimarus to Wrede, trans. William Montgomery (London, 1910).

The Philosophy of Civilisation. i. *The Decay and Restoration of Civilisation*; ii. *Civilisation and Ethics*, trans. C. T. Campion (London, 1923). Reprinted as *The Philosophy of Civilization* (Amherst, NY, 1987).

On the Edge of the Primeval Forest, trans. C. T. Campion (London, 1924).

The Mysticism of Paul the Apostle, trans. William Montgomery (London, 1931).

Christianity and the Religions of the World, trans. Johanna Powers (London, 1939).

Out of my Life and Thought, trans. C. T. Campion (London, 1948).

The Psychiatric Study of Jesus, trans. Charles R. Joy (Boston, 1948).

Memoirs of Childhood and Youth, trans. C. T. Campion (New York, 1949).

Goethe: Four Studies by Albert Schweitzer, ed. C. R. Joy (Boston, 1949).

The Animal World of Albert Schweitzer: Jungle Insights into Reverence for Life, trans. C. R. Joy (Boston, 1950).

Music in the Life of Albert Schweitzer, ed. and trans. C. R. Joy (London, 1953).

Peace or Atomic War? (New York, 1958).

The Story of my Pelican, trans. Martha Wardenburg (New York, 1965).

J. S. Bach, trans. Ernest Newman, 2 vols (New York, 1967).

6. Albert Schweitzer's Complete Works

Albert Schweitzer Complete Works (in Japanese), 19 vols (Tokyo, 1956–61). First edition of complete works worldwide.

Albert Schweitzer, *Gesammelte Werke in fünf Bänden*, ed. Rudolf Grabs (Munich, 1974). i. *Aus meinem Leben und Denken; Aus meiner Kindheit und Jugendzeit; Zwischen Wasser und Urwald; Briefe aus Lambarene 1924–1927*; ii. *Verfall und Wiederaufbau der Kultur; Kultur und Ethik; Die Weltanschauung der indischen Dichter; Das Christentum und die Weltreligionen*; iii. *Geschichte der Leben-Jesu-Forschung*; iv. *Die Mystik des Apostels Paulus; Reich Gottes und Christentum*; v. *Aus Afrika; Kulturphilosophie und Ethik; Religion und Theologie; Deutsche und französische Orgelbaukunst und Orgelkunst; Goethe. Vier Reden; Ethik und Völkerfrieden*.

7. Works from the Literary Estate

Reich Gottes und Christentum, ed. Ulrich Luz, Ulrich Neuenschwander, and Johann Zürcher (Munich, 1995).

Straßburger Vorlesungen, ed. Erich Gräßer and Johann Zürcher (Munich, 1998).
Die Weltanschauung der Ehrfurcht vor dem Leben. Kulturphilosophie, iii. *Erster und zweiter Teil*, ed. Claus Günzler and Johann Zürcher (Munich, 1999).
Die Weltanschauung der Ehrfurcht vor dem Leben. Kulturphilosophie, iii. *Dritter und vierter Teil*, ed. Claus Günzler and Johann Zürcher (Munich, 2000).
Predigten 1898–1948, ed. Richard Brüllmann and Erich Gräßer (Munich, 2001).
Kultur und Ethik in den Weltreligionen, ed. Ulrich Körtner and Johann Zürcher (Munich, 2001).
Geschichte des chinesischen Denkens, with an epilogue by Heiner Roetz, ed. Bernard Kaempf and Johann Zürcher (Munich, 2002).
Vorträge, Vorlesungen, Aufsätze, ed. Claus Günzler, Ulrich Luz, and Johann Zürcher (Munich, 2003).
Wir Epigonen: Kultur und Kulturstaat, ed. Ulrich Körtner and Johann Zürcher (Munich, 2005).
Theologischer und philosophischer Briefwechsel 1900–1965, ed. Werner Zager in association with Erich Gräßer, assisted by Markus Aellig, Clemens Frey, Roland Wolf, and Dorothea Zager (Munich, 2006).

8. Individual Publications of Albert Schweitzer's Correspondence

Bähr, H. W. (ed.), *Albert Schweitzer: Leben, Werk und Denken 1905–1965: Mitgeteilt in seinen Briefen* (Heidelberg, 1987).
Bähr, H. W. (ed.), *Albert Schweitzer: Letters 1905–1965*, trans. Joachim Neugroschel (New York, 1992).
Schweitzer Miller, R., and Woytt, G. (eds), *Albert Schweitzer–Helene Bresslau: Die Jahre vor Lambarene, Briefe 1902–1912* (Munich, 1992).
Schweitzer-Miller, R., and Woytt, G. (eds), *The Albert Schweitzer–Helene Bresslau Letters 1902–1912* (New York, 2003).
Sommer, A. U. (ed.), *Albert Schweitzer–Fritz Buri: Existenzphilosophie und Christentum, Briefe 1935–1964* (Munich, 2000).
Spiegelberg, H. (ed.), 'The Correspondence between Bertrand Russell and Albert Schweitzer', *International Studies in Philosophy*, 12 (1980), 1–45.

9. Works by Albert Schweitzer in the Beck Series

Aus meiner Kindheit und Jugendzeit, 2nd edn (Munich, 2006).
Briefe aus Lambarene (Munich, 2009).
Das Albert Schweitzer Lesebuch, ed. H. Steffahn, 4th edn (Munich, 2009).
Das Christentum und die Weltreligionen: 2 Aufsätze zur Religionsphilosophie, with an introduction by U. Neuenschwander, 4th edn (Munich, 2001).
Die Ehrfurcht vor dem Leben: Grundtexte aus fünf Jahrzehnten, 9th edn (Munich, 2009).
Ehrfurcht vor den Tieren, ed. Erich Gräßer (Munich, 2006).

Friede oder Atomkrieg: Vier Schriften, 2nd edn (Munich, 1982).
Friede oder Atomkrieg: Vier Schriften, with a preface by E. Eppler, 2nd edn (Munich, 1982).
Gespräche über das Neue Testament, ed. W. Döbertin, 2nd edn (Munich, 1994).
Kultur und Ethik (Munich, 1990).
Kulturphilosophie. i. *Verfall und Wiederaufbau der Kultur*; ii. *Kultur und Ethik* (Munich, 2007).
Straßburger Predigten, ed. U. Neuenschwander, 3rd edn (Munich, 1993).
Zwischen Wasser und Urwald, 2nd edn (Munich, 2008).

10. Further Literature (a Selection)

Altena, T., *'Ein Häuflein Christen mitten in der Heidenwelt des dunklen Erdteils': Zum Selbst- und Fremdverständnis protestantischer Missionare im kolonialen Afrika 1884–1918* (Munster, 2003).
Altner, G., 'Albert Schweitzer', in *Gestalten der Kirchengeschichte. Die neueste Zeit III*, ed. M. Greschat (Stuttgart, 1985), 271–86.
Audoynaud, A., *Le Docteur Schweitzer et son hôpital à Lambaréné: L'Envers d'un mythe* (Paris, 2005).
Augustiny, W., *Albert Schweitzer und Du*, 4th edn (Witten, 1959).
Bähr, H. W., and Minder, R. (eds), *Begegnung mit Albert Schweitzer* (Munich, 1965).
Barth, K., *Einführung in die Evangelische Theologie*, 2nd edn (Zurich, 1977).
Basse, M., '"Ehrfurcht vor dem Leben": Karl Barths Auseinandersetzung mit Albert Schweitzer in den 1920er Jahren', *Evangelische Theologie*, 65 (2005), 211–25.
Bauermann, E., *Das Menschenbild Albert Schweitzers* (Aachen, 1984).
Bentley, J., *Albert Schweitzer: Eine Biographie* (Düsseldorf, 2001).
Bertlein, H., *Das Selbstverständnis der Jugend heute: Eine empirische Untersuchung über ihre geistigen Probleme, ihre Leitbilder und ihr Verhältnis zu den Erwachsenen*, 2nd edn (Hanover, 1964).
Blume, F., *J. S. Bach im Wandel der Geschichte* (Kassel, 1947).
Born, M., *Mein Leben: Die Erinnerungen des Nobelpreisträgers* (Munich, 1975).
Börsenverein des Deutschen Buchhandels (ed.), *Friedenspreis des Deutschen Buchhandels: Reden und Würdigungen 1951–1960* (Frankfurt, 1961).
Brabazon, J., *Albert Schweitzer: A Biography*, 2nd edn (Syracuse, 2000).
Bradbury, R., *Fahrenheit 451* (New York, 1987).
Bret, G., 'Bach, Schweitzer und die Pariser Bach-Gesellschaft', in H. W. Bähr (ed.), *Albert Schweitzer: Sein Denken und sein Weg* (Tübingen, 1962), 287–93.
Brüllmann, R. (ed.), *Albert-Schweitzer-Studien 2* (Bern, 1991).
Cameron, J., *Point of Departure* (London, 2006).
Cesbron, G., *Albert Schweitzer: Begegnungen* (Berlin, 1957).
Christaller, H., *Albert Schweitzer: Ein Leben für andere* (Stuttgart, 1954).
Claußen, J. H., *Die Jesus-Deutung von Ernst Troeltsch im Kontext der liberalen Theologie* (Tübingen, 1997).

Cousins, N., *Dr Schweitzer of Lambaréné* (New York, 1960).

Cullmann, O., 'Albert Schweitzers Auffassung der urchristlichen Reichsgotteshoffnung im Lichte der heutigen neutestamentlichen Forschung', *Evangelische Theologie*, 25 (1965), 643–56.

Davenport, M. M., 'The Moral Paternalism of Albert Schweitzer', *Ethics*, 84 (1973–4), 116–27.

Eidam, K., *Das wahre Leben des Johann Sebastian Bach* (Munich, 1999).

Ernst, P., *Ehrfurcht vor dem Leben: Versuch der Aufklärung einer aufgeklärten Kultur. Ethische Vernunft und christlicher Glaube im Werk Albert Schweitzers* (Frankfurt, 1991).

Fleischhack, M., *Helene Schweitzer: Stationen ihres Lebens* (Berlin, 1969).

Freyer, P. H., *Albert Schweitzer: Ein Lebensbild*, 3rd edn (Berlin, 1982).

Fröhlich, M., *Dag Hammarskjöld und die Vereinten Nationen: Die politische Ethik des UNO-Generalsekretärs* (Paderborn, 2002).

Götting, G., *Begegnung mit Albert Schweitzer* (Berlin, 1961).

Götting, G., and Günther, S.-H., *Was heißt Ehrfurcht vor dem Leben? Begegnung mit Albert Schweitzer* (Berlin, 2005).

Gollomb, J., *Albert Schweitzer: Genius in der Wildnis* (Stuttgart, 1957).

Gräßer, E., *Albert Schweitzer als Theologe* (Tübingen, 1979).

Groos, H., *Albert Schweitzer: Größe und Grenzen* (Munich, 1974).

Gunther, J., *Inside Africa* (New York, 1955).

Günzler, C., *Albert Schweitzer: Einführung in sein Denken* (Munich, 1996).

Gurlitt, W. (ed.), *Bericht über die Freiburger Tagung für Deutsche Orgelkunst vom 27. Juli bis 30. Juli 1926* (Kassel, 1926).

Hauskeller, M. (ed.), *Ethik des Lebens: Albert Schweitzer als Philosoph* (Zug, 2006).

Heyden, U. van der, and Stoecker, H. (eds), *Mission und Macht im Wandel politischer Orientierungen: Europäische Missionsgesellschaften in politischen Spannungsfeldern in Afrika und Asien zwischen 1800 und 1945* (Stuttgart, 2005).

Hildebrand, K., *Das vergangene Reich: Deutsche Außenpolitik von Bismarck bis Hitler* (Stuttgart, 1995).

Hirsch, W., *Religion und Civilisation vom Standpunkte des Psychiaters* (Munich, 1910).

Holtzmann, H. J., 'Die Marcus-Kontroverse in ihrer heutigen Gestalt', *Archiv für Religionswissenschaft*, 10 (1907), 18–40, 161–200.

Hygen, J. B., *Albert Schweitzers Kulturkritik* (Göttingen, 1955).

Jacobi, C., 'Schweitzers Uhr geht anders', *Der Spiegel*, 21 December 1960, 62–7.

Jacobi, E. R., *Albert Schweitzer und die Musik* (Wiesbaden, 1975).

Jacobi, E. R., *Albert Schweitzer und Richard Wagner: Eine Dokumentation* (Tribschen, 1977).

Jodl, F., *Geschichte der Ethik als philosophischer Wissenschaft*, ii, 2nd edn (Stuttgart, 1912).

Joy, C. R., and Arnold, M., *Bei Albert Schweitzer in Afrika* (Munich, 1948).

Joy, C. R., and Arnold, M., *The Africa of Albert Schweitzer* (London, 1949).

Jungk, R., 'Der Menschenfreund gegen die Atomversuche', in J. Pierhal, *Albert Schweitzer* (Frankfurt, 1982), 252–60.

Kahn, H. W., *Der Kalte Krieg*. i. *Spaltung und Wahn der Stärke 1945–1955* (Cologne, 1986); ii. *Alibi für das Rüstungsgeschäft 1955–1973* (Cologne, 1987).

Kantzenbach, F. W., *Albert Schweitzer: Wirklichkeit und Legende* (Göttingen, 1969).

Keller, H., 'Das Bach-Buch Albert Schweitzers', in H. W. Bähr (ed.), *Albert Schweitzer: Sein Denken und sein Weg* (Tübingen, 1962), 294–8.

Kleberger, I., *Albert Schweitzer: Das Symbol und der Mensch* (Berlin, 1989).

Kleffmann, T., *Nietzsches Begriff des Lebens und die evangelische Theologie: Eine Interpretation Nietzsches und Untersuchungen zu seiner Rezeption bei Schweitzer, Tillich und Barth* (Tübingen, 2003).

Kümmel, W. G., and Ratschow, C.-H., *Albert Schweitzer als Theologe: Zwei akademische Reden* (Marburg, 1966).

Lönnebo, M., *Das ethisch-religiöse Ideal Albert Schweitzers* (Stockholm, 1964).

Loosten, G. de, *Jesus Christus vom Standpunkte des Psychiaters* (Bamberg, 1905).

Marshall, G., and Poling, D., *Schweitzer: A Biography* (London, 1971).

Meyer, H. J., 'Albert Schweitzers Doktorarbeit über Kant', in H. W. Bähr (ed.), *Albert Schweitzer: Sein Denken und sein Weg* (Tübingen, 1962), 66–74.

Monestier, M., *Der grosse weisse Doktor Albert Schweitzer*, 5th edn (Bern, 1954).

Mühlstein, V., *Helene Schweitzer Bresslau: Ein Leben für Lambarene* (Munich, 1998).

Müller-Blattau, J., 'Albert Schweitzers Weg zur Bach-Orgel und zu einer neuen Bach-Auffassung', in H. W. Bähr (ed.), *Albert Schweitzer: Sein Denken und sein Weg* (Tübingen, 1962), 243–61.

Munz, J., and Munz, W., *Mit dem Herzen einer Gazelle und der Haut eines Nilpferds: Albert Schweitzer in seinen letzten Lebensjahren und die Entwicklung seines Spitals bis zur Gegenwart* (Frauenfeld, 2005).

Munz, W., *Albert Schweitzer im Gedächtnis der Afrikaner und in meiner Erinnerung*. Albert-Schweitzer-Studien 3 (Bern, 1991).

Nietzsche, F., *Jenseits von Gut und Böse* (Leipzig, 1886).

Nietzsche, F., *Zur Genealogie der Moral I 2*, in *Kritische Studienausgabe*, ed. G. Colli and M. Montinari, v, 2nd edn (Munich, 1999).

Nossik, B. M., *Albert Schweitzer: Ein Leben für die Menschlichkeit* (Leipzig, 1978).

O'Brien, C. C., 'Africa's Answer to Schweitzer', *Atlantic Monthly* (March 1966), 68–71.

Oermann, N. O., *Mission, Church and State Relations in South West Africa under German Rule (1884–1915)* (Stuttgart, 1999).

Oswald, S., *Mein Onkel Bary: Erinnerungen an Albert Schweitzer*, 2nd edn (Zurich, 1972).

Picht, W., *Albert Schweitzer: Wesen und Bedeutung* (Hamburg, 1960).

Pierhal, J., *Albert Schweitzer: Das Leben eines guten Menschen* (Munich, 1955).

Pierhal, J., *Albert Schweitzer* (Frankfurt, 1982).

Poteau, S., and Leser, G., *Albert Schweitzer: Homme de Gunsbach et citoyen du monde* (Mülhausen, 1994).

Poteau, S., Mougin, D., and Wyss, C., *Albert Schweitzer: Von Gunsbach nach Lambarene* (Gunsbach, 2008).

Quenzer, W., 'Zu Schweitzers autobiographischen Schriften', in H. W. Bähr (ed.), *Albert Schweitzer: Sein Denken und sein Weg* (Tübingen, 1962), 236–9.

Rasmussen, E., *Jesus: Eine vergleichende psychopathologische Studie* (Leipzig, 1905).

Sauter, G., *Einführung in die Eschatologie* (Darmstadt, 1995).

Schorlemmer, F., *Genie der Menschlichkeit: Albert Schweitzer* (Berlin, 2009).

Schrade, L., 'Die Ästhetik Albert Schweitzers: Eine Interpretation J. S. Bachs', in H. W. Bähr (ed.), *Albert Schweitzer: Sein Denken und sein Weg* (Tübingen, 1962), 262–80.

Schütz, R., *Anekdoten um Albert Schweitzer* (Munich, 1966).

Schützeichel, H., *Die Konzerttätigkeit Albert Schweitzers* (Bern and Stuttgart, 1991).

Scipio, C., 'Is Schweitzer Dead?' *Atlantic Monthly* (August 1966), 41–4.

Seaver, G., *Albert Schweitzer als Mensch und Denker*, 8th edn (Göttingen, 1956).

Simmank, L., *Der Arzt: Wie Albert Schweitzer Not linderte* (Berlin, 2008).

Spear, O., *Albert Schweitzers Ethik: Ihre Grundlinien in seinem Denken und Leben* (Hamburg, 1978).

Steffahn, H., *Albert Schweitzer*, 12th edn (Hamburg, 1996).

Stoevesandt, K., 'Albert Schweitzer als Arzt und Helfer der Menschheit', *Evangelische Theologie*, 15 (1955), 97–114.

Stöver, B., *Der Kalte Krieg 1947–1991: Geschichte eines radikalen Zeitalters* (Munich, 2007).

Suermann, T., *Albert Schweitzer als 'homo politicus': Eine biographische Studie zum politischen Denken und Handeln des Friedensnobelpreisträgers* (Berlin, 2012).

Tau, M., *Auf dem Weg zur Versöhnung* (Hamburg, 1968).

Tau, M., *Das Leben lieben: Max Tau in Briefen und Dokumenten 1945–1976*, ed. H. Däumling (Würzburg, 1988).

Thomas, M. Z., *Unser grosser Freund Albert Schweitzer* (Munich, 1960).

Wagenbach, K. (ed.), *Vaterland, Muttersprache: Deutsche Schriftsteller und ihr Staat von 1945*, 3rd edn (Berlin, 2004).

Walter, F., *Charismatiker und Effizienzen: Porträts aus 60 Jahren Bundesrepublik* (Frankfurt, 2009).

Weiß, J., *Die Predigt Jesu vom Reiche Gottes* (Göttingen, 1892).

Weinel, H., 'Neutestamentliche Rezensionen des Jahres 1902', *Theologische Rundschau*, 5 (1902), 231–45.

Werner, M., *Die Entstehung des christlichen Dogmas problemgeschichtlich dargestellt* (Bern, 1941).

Windelband, W., *Geschichte der Philosophie*, 6th edn (Tübingen, 1916).

Winnubst, B., *Das Friedensdenken Albert Schweitzers* (Amsterdam, 1974).

Wrede, W., *Das Messiasgeheimnis in den Evangelien: Zugleich ein Beitrag zum Verständnis des Markus-Evangeliums* (Göttingen, 1901).

Wyss, C., 'Friede oder Atomkrieg: Albert Schweitzers Engagement gegen die Atombomben', in Schweizer Hilfsverein für das Albert-Schweitzer-Spital in Lambarene (ed.), *Berichte aus Lambarene* (April 2007), 11–20.

Zweig, S., Feschotte, J., and Grabs, R., *Albert Schweitzer: Genie der Menschlichkeit* (Hamburg, 1955).

Index